Socially Just Pedagogies

Also Available from Bloomsbury

The Subject of Rosi Braidotti, Bolette Blaagaard and Iris van der Tuin
Posthuman Glossary, edited by Rosi Braidotti and Maria Hlavajova
Conflicting Humanities, edited by Rosi Braidotti and Paul Gilroy
On the Feminist Philosophy of Gillian Howie,
edited by Daniel Whistler and Victoria Browne
Ecosophical Aesthetics, edited by Patricia MacCormack
and Colin Gardner

Socially Just Pedagogies

Posthumanist, Feminist and Materialist Perspectives in Higher Education

Edited by
Vivienne Bozalek, Rosi Braidotti,
Tamara Shefer and Michalinos Zembylas

BLOOMSBURY ACADEMIC
LONDON • NEW YORK • OXFORD • NEW DELHI • SYDNEY

BLOOMSBURY ACADEMIC
Bloomsbury Publishing Plc
50 Bedford Square, London, WC1B 3DP, UK

BLOOMSBURY, BLOOMSBURY ACADEMIC and the Diana logo are trademarks
of Bloomsbury Publishing Plc

First published in Great Britain 2018

Cover design: Irene Martinez-Costa
Cover image © Nike Romano

A catalogue record for this book is available from the British Library.

A catalog record for this book is available from the Library of Congress.

ISBN: HB: 978-1-3500-3289-7
        ePDF: 978-1-3500-3288-0
        eBook: 978-1-3500-3290-3

Typeset by RefineCatch Limited, Bungay, Suffolk

To find out more about our authors and books visit www.bloomsbury.com
and sign up for our newsletters.

Table of Contents

Acknowledgements

This edited collection came to fruition through a research project which focused on socially just pedagogies in higher education. We are grateful to the South African National Research Foundation(NRF)[1] for providing funding for the project members to meet with each other and for providing support for people to pursue PhD studies, some of whom have co-written chapters in this book. This grant made it possible for project members to meet in the beautiful surrounds of Mont Fleur, in Stellenbosch, Cape Town, where the idea and plans for the book took shape.

We would also like to thank the reviewers of the chapters for their generous gesture of carefully providing blind peer reviews of the contributions for the volume.

Thanks also to those who are living with us for their patience when our attention has been diverted for long periods in preparing this manuscript.

---

[1] NRF Grant No. 105851

Notes on Contributors

Abdullah Bayat is a Senior Lecturer in the School of Business and Finance at the University of the Western Cape. His interests are in teaching and learning, social justice, ethics, leadership and subjectivity.

Vivienne Bozalek is a Professor of Social Work and the Director of Teaching and Learning at the University of the Western Cape. She holds a PhD from Utrecht University. Her research interests and publications include the political ethics of care and social justice, posthumanism and feminist new materialisms, innovative pedagogical practices in higher education. Recent publications include the following co-edited books – *Discerning Hope in Educational Practices* and *Theorising Learning to Teach in Higher Education.*

Rosi Braidotti is Distinguished University Professor and founding Director of the Centre for the Humanities at Utrecht University (2007–16). Her latest books are: *Nomadic Subjects* and *Nomadic Theory: The Portable Rosi Braidotti* (both Columbia UP 2011), and *The Posthuman* (Polity Press 2013). In 2016 she co-edited with Paul Gilroy *Conflicting Humanities*, Bloomsbury Academic. Forthcoming in is *The Posthuman Glossary* (Bloomsbury 2018). For more information and updates, please visit www.rosibraidotti.com.

Rosemarie Buikema is Professor of Art, Culture and Diversity at Utrecht University. She chairs the UU Graduate Gender Programme and is the scientific director of the Netherlands Research School of Gender Studies (NOG). She coordinates the UU share in the Erasmus Mundus Master's Degree in Gender Studies (GEMMA) and is the UU PI for EU Horizon 2020 Marie Curie (ITN GRACE). Her latest publications include *Doing Gender in Media, Art and Culture* (Routledge 2017) and *Revoltes in de Cultuurkritiek* (Amsterdam UP 2017).

Delphi Carstens is a Lecturer in Humanities 100/Extended Curriculum Programme at the University of the Western Cape. He holds a PhD from Stellenbosch University. His research interests and publications include the

Anthropocene, Deleuzoguattarian theory, environmental justice pedagogies, science fiction and new materialisms. Recent publications include chapters in edited volumes by Palgrave (Indigenous Creatures, Native Knowledges, and the Arts) and Sternberg (Fiction as Method: Counterfactuals and Effective Virtualities in Art and Culture) as well as articles in South African education journals.

Rebecca C. Christ, Ph.D. currently adjuncts for the University of Missouri (MU) in Columbia, Missouri, from where she obtained her doctorate in Social Studies Education with a graduate certificate in Qualitative Research. Her research interests include genocide education, global and multicultural education, and (post)qualitative research method(ologies). She is also interested in incorporating critical, postcolonial, poststructural, and posthuman theoretical concepts into qualitative research and pedagogical practice. Her scholarship has been published in *Qualitative Inquiry* and in several edited books.

Daniela Gachago is a Senior Lecturer in the Centre for Innovative Educational Technology at the Cape Peninsula University of Technology. Her research interests lie in the potential of emerging technologies to transform teaching and learning in higher education. Current research projects focus on the ethics of blended and open learning in contexts of inequality and multimodal pedagogies such as digital storytelling as decolonial classroom practices.

Chantelle Gray van Heerden is a Senior Researcher at the Institute for Gender Studies at the University of South Africa. Her research centres on the philosophical collaboration between Gilles Deleuze and Félix Guattari, particularly its relevance for the production of new subjectivities. She is a member of the editorial team for the journal *Gender Questions*, and she has written on a number of topics, including socially just and anarchist pedagogies, gender, the non-human, and masochism. She is currently working on an edited volume, *Deleuze and Anarchism*, for the Deleuze Connections series.

Candace R. Kuby is an Associate Professor of Early Childhood Education at the University of Missouri. Her research interests are the ethico-onto-epistemologies of literacy desiring(s) when young children work with materials to create multimodal texts. In addition, she inquiries into qualitative methodologies drawing upon poststructural and posthumanist theories. Candace is the co-author of *Go Be a Writer!: Expanding the Curricular Boundaries of Literacy*

Learning (Teachers College Press 2016); author of *Critical Literacy in the Early Childhood Classroom: Unpacking Histories, Unlearning Privilege* (Teachers College Press 2016); and co-editor of *Disrupting Qualitative Inquiry: Possibilities and Tensions in Educational Research* (Peter Lang 2014). Journals in which her scholarship appears include *Qualitative Inquiry*; *International Journal of Qualitative Studies in Education*; *Journal of Early Childhood Literacy*; *Education, Citizenship, and Social Justice*; and *Language Arts*.

Erin Manning is Professor and Research Chair in Relational Art and Philosophy in the Faculty of Fine Arts at Concordia University, where she also directs SenseLab. Recent artwork includes *The Colour of Time*, Tunis Art-Rue 2017; *Threadways*, Gent Museum of Fine Arts 2016, 2017; *The Smell of Red*, Glasshouse New York 2014, Vancouver Art Museum 2015; and *Stitching Time* (Moscow Biennale 2013, Sydney Biennale 2012). Recent books include *The Minor Gesture* (Duke UP 2016), *Always More Than One* (Duke UP 2013) and, with Brian Massumi, *Thought in the Act* (Minnesota UP 2014).

Veronica Mitchell is a PhD candidate at the University of the Western Cape and a facilitator in the Department of Obstetrics and Gynaecology at the University of Cape Town, South Africa. Her physiotherapy background and her experiences in human rights education led to her interest in exploring the medical curriculum and the force it has on students' becoming. Her publications include a research blog at http://phd4veronica.blogspot.co.za, authored websites, and journal papers.

Siddique Motala is a Senior Lecturer at the Cape Peninsula University of Technology in Cape Town, South Africa. He lectures Geographic Information Systems (GIS) and surveying. He is currently a PhD candidate in education at the University of the Western Cape. His areas of research include engineering education, posthumanism, historical mapping and participatory GIS. He is a Research Fellow at the Centre for the Humanities at Utrecht University.

Kathryn Muller grew up and was schooled in Windhoek, Namibia. She completed the PGCE (Foundation Phase) course at the University of Cape Town (UCT) in 2015. Prior to that she graduated with a BA in Fine Arts from the Michaelis School of Fine Art (UCT) where she majored in sculpture and developed a sense of thing-power. She is currently living and teaching in northern KwaZulu-Natal, South Africa.

Karin Murris is Professor of Pedagogy and Philosophy at the School of Education, University of Cape Town (UCT). Her current research interests are: childhood studies, posthumanism in education, postqualitative research. Books include: *The Posthuman Child: Educational Transformation through Philosophy with Picturebooks* (2016), *Teaching Philosophy with Picture Books* (1992) and, with Joanna Haynes, *Picturebooks, Pedagogy and Philosophy* (2012). She is co-editor of the Routledge *International Handbook on Philosophy for Children*.

Denise Newfield is a Professor and Associate Researcher at the University of the Witwatersrand, South Africa, where she taught for many years. She is director of ZAPP (South African Poetry Project) and leads a research study in educational transformation through indigenisation. Her publications – in the fields of English education, multimodality and posthumanist pedagogies – include *Multimodal Approaches to Research and Pedagogy* and *Mobilising and Modalising Poetry in a Soweto Classroom*.

Nike Romano is a visual artist who lectures history of art and design at the Cape Peninsula University of Technology. Her PhD research interrogates how the entanglements between arts-based practices and posthumanist pedagogies can generate students' visibility, agency and voice within South African higher education institutions.

Tamara Shefer is Professor of Women's and Gender Studies, Faculty of Arts, University of the Western Cape. Her scholarship focuses on gendered, intersectional power relations among young people, including research on HIV/AIDS, gender-based violence, sexualities education, critical masculinities, memory and apartheid, gender and care, gender and dis/ability, and social justice and feminist pedagogies. Her most recent book publications include *Engaging Youth in Activist Research and Pedagogical Praxis: Transnational and Intersectional Perspectives on Gender, Sex, and Race* (co-edited with Hearn, Ratele and Boonzaier, in press for 2018, Routledge) and *Care in Context: Transnational Gender Perspective* (co-edited with Reddy, Meyer and Meyiwe (2014) HSRC Press).

Carol A. Taylor is Professor of Gender and Higher Education in the Sheffield Institute of Education at Sheffield Hallam University, UK. Carol's research has been published widely and focuses on the use of feminist, neo-materialist, and posthumanist methodologies to explore gendered inequalities, spatial practices, and higher education participation. She is co-editor of the international journal *Gender and Education*, and her recent books include: Taylor and Ivinson (Routledge 2016) (Eds.) *Material Feminisms: New Directions for Education* and Taylor and Hughes (2016), (Eds.) *Posthuman Research Practices in Education* (Palgrave Macmillan, 2016).

Kathrin Thiele is Associate Professor in Gender Studies at Utrecht University, NL. She has published widely in the fields of continental philosophy, feminist and queer theories of difference and posthuman(ist) studies. Her most recent book publications are *Symptoms of the Planetary Condition: A Critical Vocabulary* (Meson 2017, co-edited with M. Bunz and B.M. Kaiser) *Doing Gender in Medien-, Kunst- und Kulturwissenschaften* (co-edited with R. Buikema LitVerlag (2017)) and *Doing Gender in Media, Art and Culture* (co-edited with R. Buikema and L. Plate Routledge, (2017)). She is also co-founder of the Humanities initiative *Terra Critica: Interdisciplinary Network for the Critical Humanities.*

Michalinos Zembylas is Professor of Educational Theory and Curriculum Studies at the Open University of Cyprus. He is Visiting Professor and Research Fellow at the Institute for Reconciliation and Social Justice, University of the Free State, South Africa, and Research Associate at the Centre for Critical Studies in Higher Education Transformation at Nelson Mandela University. He has written extensively on emotion and affect in relation to social justice pedagogies, intercultural and peace education, human rights education and citizenship education.

Foreword

Rosi Braidotti

'Liberating education consists in acts of cognition, not in transferals of information'

Paulo Freire: *Pedagogy of the Oppressed (1970)*

Interest in pedagogy, both from the methodological and the conceptual angles, has been increasing in contemporary posthuman scholarship, as this volume brilliantly shows. My working definition of the posthuman is a convergence phenomenon unfolding at the intersection between post-humanism on the one hand and post-anthropocentrism on the other. The former criticises the idea of 'Man' as the allegedly universal standard-bearer for the human, whereas the latter objects to species hierarchy. Although they are often discussed together, they refer to distinct philosophical genealogies and produce divergent political stances as well as different world-historical events. It has also become quite feasible, following Edward Said (2003), to criticise Humanism in the name of Humanism, while leaving anthropocentrism firmly in place. Theoretical and philosophical critiques of Humanism have been carried out in European philosophy ever since Nietzsche. More recently, the critique has been advanced by movements of thought such as post-structuralism (Foucault 1970; Deleuze and Guattari 1987), neo-materialism, the radical strands of punk and cyber-feminism, the science-fiction movement and a range of trans-humanist and extropian schools. The critique of anthropocentrism, on the other hand, is strong in Science and Technology Studies, vegetarian and vegan movements, animal rights, deep ecology and green politics. The convergence of these two lines of critique in what I call the posthuman predicament is producing a chain of theoretical, social and political effects that is more than the sum of its parts. It points to a qualitative leap in new conceptual directions (Braidotti 2013): posthuman scholarship.

It is not surprising that the posthuman turn is producing some unexpected and, in my assessment, internally contradictory reactions. For instance, a very dominant stance in posthuman scholarship is the combination of analytic posthumanism with normative neo-humanism. The most striking example of this approach is the Oxford Institute for the Future of Humanity, based on trans-humanist principles of human enhancement, implemented through a research program called 'super-intelligence'. Directed by Nick Bostrom (2014), it combines brain research with robotics and computational sciences, plus clinical psychology and analytic philosophy, to define the posthuman as a super-human meta-rationalist entity. It combines a twenty-first century diagnosis about technological mediation, with a reiteration of the eighteenth-century humanist ideal of the progress of 'Man'-kind through an unquestioned ideal of scientific rationality.

I find this internally contradictory stance unsatisfactory on several accounts: first because it glosses over the conceptual challenges of combining a transversal project of human/non-human neural techno-enhancement, with a belief in a definition of reason that owes more to Cartesian dualism than to the notion of matter at work in contemporary neural and Life sciences. Instead of foregrounding a self-organising, dynamic fabric transversally connecting all entities which, in the case of humans, produces distributed and technologically mediated consciousness, trans-humanism reduces human intelligence back to the very binaries contemporary science claims to have left behind. These convulsive contradictions can only cause a massive case of theoretical and moral jet-lag. But the challenge of the posthuman condition is that we have to account for the complexity of the present; we need to be worthy of our times.

Second, the combination of post-anthropocentric and neo-humanist elements is unsatisfactory because it silences the socio-political implications of this project, namely the issue of entitlement and access. One shudders at the thought of the selection criteria that might be deployed to allow certain individuals or classes to qualify for enhancement. To present this socio-biological intervention as an evolutionary step that will emancipate our species as a whole amounts to adding insult to injury.

In reaction to these contemporary contradictions, I want to argue that a socially just pedagogy in posthuman times needs to fulfil two basic requirements. First, it has to be consistently posthuman, at both the analytic and the normative levels. This raises, in turn, the need for a posthuman ontology and a new ethics. Second, it has to foreground the socio-political aspects of the posthuman predicament, including the specific forms of de-humanisation and discrimination, the inhumane and necro-political aspects that define our era. Let me expand briefly on each of these pre-conditions and in the conclusion explore their implications for pedagogical practice.

A posthuman ontology

In order to avoid the contradictions highlighted above, I have proposed philosophical neo-materialism and nomadic becoming (Braidotti, 2011a; 2011b), inspired by neo-Spinozist vital ontologies (Deleuze, 1988; 1990) and feminist theory, as the ontological grounding for the posthuman predicament. This materialist posthuman approach, does not restrict subjectivity to bound individuals, but rather repositions it as the effect of a cooperative trans-species effort (Margulis and Sagan, 1995). Subject-formation takes place transversally, in between nature/technology; male/female; black/white; local/global; present/past – in assemblages that flow across and displace binary oppositions.

Neo-materialism emphasises immanence and marks the rejection of transcendental universalism and mind–body dualism. All matter or substance being one and immanent to itself, it is intelligent and self-organising in both human and non-human organisms: we are all part of a common matter (Lloyd 1994, 1996; Protevi 2013). Vital matter is driven by the ontological desire for the expression of its innermost freedom (*conatus*) to persevere in its existence and endure. This understanding of matter animates the composition of posthuman subjects of knowledge – embedded, embodied and yet flowing in a web of mediated relations with human and non-human others. Vital neo-materialism also provides the ontological grounding for critical posthuman scholarship as a transversal field of knowledge.

By extension, critical thinkers situate themselves in, and as part of, the world, defending an idea of knowledge production as embedded, embodied, affective and relational. The specific focus of my philosophical work is on what kind of knowing subjects we are in the process of becoming and what discourses underscore this process. The subjects of this exchange compose a relational community, defined as a nomadic, transversal 'assemblage' (Deleuze and Guattari 1987; Braidotti 1994) that involves non-human actors and technology. Material, mediated posthuman subjects constitute a community, 'people', bonded by affirmative ethics. That goes for academics as for any other constituency.

To operationalise this vital materialist position, I rely on the cartographic method. A cartography is a theoretically based and politically informed account of the present that aims at tracking the power relations operational in and immanent to the production and circulation of both knowledge and subjectivity (Braidotti 1994; 2011a; 2011b). The point is to expose these processes of power/knowledge as both entrapment (*potestas*) and as empowerment (*potentia*), while avoiding any polarisation of the two terms. Another crucial conceptual element of my cartographic approach is the feminist politics of locations (Rich, 1987), also known as situated knowledges (Harding 1986; 1991; Haraway 1988), which I take as the original manifestation of embodied and embedded carnal empiricism. This method accounts for one's position in terms both of space (geo-political or ecological dimension) and time (historical memory or genealogical dimension), thereby grounding politically and epistemically the production of alternative knowledges.

The cartographic approach does justice to the complexity of posthuman subjectivity. These transversal re-compositions of subject assemblages not only defy the logic of excluded middle by including non-human entities and components, but they also establish ontological relationality as the key force in the process of subject formation. The ontological importance of the relation (Glissant 1997) foregrounds the generative, affirmative character of binding – that is to say joyful – passions, values and encounters (Braidotti 2011b). Negative passions, on the other hand, have an arresting effect on one's ability to open up to others.

Relationality means the capacity and desire to move nomadically in the world, with and across a multitude of others. In order to cultivate it as affirmative ethics, however, we need to shift our self-understanding. That is to say, we need to learn to think differently about what we are in the process of becoming. Spinoza taught us, a few centuries back, that ethics begins with the enduring effort to reach an adequate understanding of what a body (as embrained and embodied, material and relational entity) can do. My contemporary neo-Spinozist approach, inspired by Gilles Deleuze, asserts that devising an immanent account of what embrained bodies and embodied brains (Marks, 1998) are allowed to do and are capable of doing, is the core of vital, neo-materialist ethics. This approach assumes a post-Foucauldian understanding of power as both restrictive (*potestas*) and productive (*potentia*). Entrapment and empowerment work in tandem in producing subject positions that are necessarily trans-individual, collective and hybrid: nomadic subjects indeed (Braidotti 1994; 2011b).

I have developed this insight further, arguing that, as a result of the great technological advances, any lingering notion of human nature is replaced by a 'naturecultures' continuum (Haraway 1997, 2003). This also brings to an end the categorical distinction between life as *bios,* the prerogative of *Anthropos,* as distinct from the life of animals and non-humans, or *zoe* (Braidotti 2006). What comes to the fore instead is new human-non-human linkages, new 'zoontologies' and 'posthumanities' (De Fontaney 1998; Wolfe 2003), and also complex media-technological interfaces and media ecologies (Fuller 2005) in the context of the Anthropocene.

These great technological developments – which are often celebrated as 'the fourth industrial revolution' – do not occur in a vacuum, but rather in the context of the specific political economy of knowledge production of advanced capitalism. This is a system that profits from the new scientific understanding of the codes – bio-genetic as well as algorithmic – of all that lives. The capital today is data, life-codes, vital information – this is the politics of Life itself (Rose 2001), or 'Life as surplus' (Cooper 2008), which under the spin of the global economy, often tips over into 'bio-piracy' (Shiva 1997), 'necro-politics' (Mbembe 2003) and 'systemic dispossession' (Sassen 2014).

The saturation of the transformative potential of the present by profit-driven motives, freezes and delays the actualisation of alternatives aimed at the common good. Where negativity dominates the social sphere, it brings about the violent erasure, or passive-aggressive blockage, of our collective desire for affirmative relational ethics. It instils a tyrannical sort of bleakness in our souls, blocking our ability to express and materialise virtual potentials. This reactive political economy also affects both subject-formation and knowledge practices. As a result, these negative setbacks also impact on the contemporary university, the scientific community and the art world.

In a system where knowledge-production is co-extensive with the entire social fabric, also known as 'cognitive capitalism' (Moulier-Boutang, 2012), the fundamental question is how to tell the difference between affirmative and instrumental or opportunistic modes of knowing. Because power, in my scheme of thought, is a multi-layered and dynamic entity, and further because, as embedded and embodied, relational and affective subjects, we are immanent to the very conditions we are trying to change, we need to make careful ethical distinctions. The ethical principle of affirmation is the main criterion of selection: it allows us to make qualitative distinctions between different speeds of knowledge production – for instance between the non-profit practices as opposed to the margins of institutional capitalisation.

To return to the fast-moving proliferation of posthuman scholarship, what prevents it from being integrated into cognitive capitalism, as just another form of epistemic accelerationism[1]? The answer is affirmative ethics, with the corollary of a political praxis of collective counter- actualisation of virtual alternatives. That is to say, to make this distinction we need an increased dose of collectively driven creativity. The barrier against the negative, entropic frenzy of capitalist axiomatic is provided by the politics that ensue from the ethic of affirmation. This, in turn, starts with the composition of transversal subject assemblages that actualise the unrealised or virtual potential of what Deleuze calls 'a missing people'. In the old language: de-accelerate and contribute to the collective construction of social horizons of hope.

This neo-materialist vital position is consistently posthuman, at both the normative and analytic levels. It offers a robust rebuttal of the nihilist accelerationism and profit-minded knowledge practices of bio-mediated, cognitive capitalism. It takes 'Living matter' as *zoe*-geo/techno-centred process that interacts in complex ways with the techno-social, psychic and natural environments and resists the over-coding by the capitalist profit principle – and the structural inequalities it entails. We thus end up on an affirmative plane of composition of transversal subjectivities, which can then be re-defined as expanded selves, or distributed consciousness (i.e. non-Cartesian). Their relational capacity is not confined within the human species, but includes non-anthropomorphic elements. *Zoe*, the non-human, vital force of Life is the transversal entity that allows us to think across previously segregated species, categories and domains. *Zoe*-centred egalitarianism is, for me, the core of a posthuman thought that might inspire, work with or subtend informational and scientific practices and resist the trans-species commodification of Life by advanced capitalism (Braidotti 2006).

This affirmative vision calls for a re-tuning of the scholar, as the prototype of the scientific subject of knowledge. Far from being a sovereign transcendental consciousness, it must be relocated as a complex singularity, an affective assemblage, and a relational vital entity. The *zoe*-driven, eco-sophical, geo-centered and techno-mediated turn that sustains critical posthuman scholarship, therefore, not only takes the form of a quantitative proliferation of non-human objects of study, but it also calls for qualitative and methodological shifts. In a world haunted by brutal regressions of all kinds, critical posthuman scholarship actualises an immanent politics that avoids the jet-lag of normative neo-humanism on the one hand, and the rhetorical generalisations about a pan-humanity bonded by the fear of extinction on the other. It offers a differential materialist approach to address the situated and complex singularity of heterogeneous contemporary subjects of knowledge.

This ontological frame affects also the epistemological concepts and their pedagogical applications. More specifically, the combination of supra-disciplinary energy, with the force of vital *zoe*/geo/techno-perspectives, renews an established tool of radical pedagogy, namely the task of de-familiarising our habits of thought. We are encouraged to expand from the postcolonial injunction of 'unlearning our privilege as our loss' (Spivak, 1990: 9) to a qualitative assessment of our relational deficits and injuries, notably towards non-human others. The frame of reference for the thinking subject becomes the world, in all its open-ended, inter-relational, transnational, multi-sexed, and trans-species flows of becoming: a binding vital force (Braidotti 2006; 2013). These are the building blocks of qualitative shifts towards critical posthuman knowledge.

The socio-political dimension

The second pre-condition for a socially just posthuman pedagogy is social justice. It would be inappropriate to take the posthuman as an intrinsically subversive category, narrowing our options down to the binary: extinction (i.e: liberation *from* the human) as opposed to enhanced evolution (liberation *of* the human). We need to check both reactions and resist with equal firmness this double fallacy. I want to insist that the 'posthuman' is normatively neutral and it does not automatically point to the end of the species, let alone to the end of gender/sexuality/class/race/ age, etc. power relations between members of the species. The posthuman rather offers a spectrum through which we can capture the complexity of ongoing processes of subject-formation. As such, it enables subtler and more complex analyses of powers and discourses, which start by questioning who might 'we' be, whose anxiety takes centre-stage in debates about the posthuman condition. My point is that the posthuman – a figuration carried by a specific cartographic reading of present material and discursive conditions – can define our relational ethics and give us a political praxis. It can be put to the collective task of constructing new subjects of knowledge, through immanent assemblages or transversal alliances between multiple actors. It is up to 'us' to make it possible, i.e: to actualise it.

To accomplish this, we need to move beyond the tendency to either mourn (apocalyptic variant) or celebrate (euphoric variant) the cause of a new pan-humanity, united in and by the Anthropocene, as both a vulnerable and insurgent category: 'we are in this together!' The reinvention of a pan-human is explicit in the conservative discourse of the Catholic Church, in corporate pan-humanism, military interventionism and UN humanitarianism. It is more oblique but equally strong in the progressive Left, where the legacy of Socialist humanism provides the tools to re-work anxiety into political rage. In all cases, we see the emergence of a category – the endangered human – both as evanescent and foundational.

Politically, it is difficult not to read this appeal to a vulnerable pan-humanity as a knee-jerk reaction by the centre – the dominant subject – which Deleuze and Guattari define (1987) as sharply as any feminist as: male/white/heterosexual/ owning wives and children/urbanised/speaking a standard language, i.e: 'Man', or rather by now – 'ex-Man'. Insofar as the Anthropocenic risks of climate change threaten the entire planet, however, one should avoid any cynicism. It is quite obvious that radical epistemologies like feminism and postcolonial theory are just as affected by the demise of Man/Anthropos (Chakrabarty, 2009), as the disciplinary and the universalist discourses.

A posthuman pedagogy of the oppressed, however, needs to foreground the missing people. Because of its highly specialised character, critical posthuman scholarship is currently framing multiple planes of re-organisation of knowledge. This raises the inevitable risk of re-segregating the critical discourses emerging within the posthuman landscape. It is significant to note for instance that, while the Environmental and the Digital Humanities – both of them eminently posthuman in premises, objects of study and methods – have become prominent in most highly ranked research universities, so few institutions have volunteered to launch new 'Feminist/Queer/Migrant/Poor/De-colonial/Diasporic/Diseased' Humanities. Clearly, the speed and intensity of the de-territorialisations of knowledge induced by cognitive capitalism differ dramatically and some people are, quite simply, missing (Braidotti 2016).

In what way can they be said to be 'missing' to begin with? First, at the empirical level, of course. Whether we look at indigenous knowledge systems, at feminists, queers, otherwise enabled, non-humans or technologically mediated existences, these are real-life subjects whose knowledge never made it into any of the official cartographies. They get constituted as political subjects of knowledge through transversal alliances. But the other missing people are the virtual ones. I argued before that, within a neo-materialist frame, the political is driven by the actualisation of the virtual and the ethics of affirmation. This entails the overthrowing of negativity through the formation of a collective assemblage ('we'). This transversal alliance today involves non-human agents, technologically mediated elements, Earth-others (land, waters, plants, animals) and non-human inorganic agents (plastic, wires, information highways, algorithms, etc.). A posthuman ethical praxis involves the formation of a new alliance, a new people, as a complex singularity. In this respect, the missing people is an emerging category, always in the process of becoming, as are their knowledges. It is the actualisation of a virtuality, travelling at different speed from capitalist acceleration.

The emerging categories are already at work in posthuman scholarship and the rhizomatic energy of the field is already acting productively. The strength of these minoritarian subjects (Feminist/Queer/Migrant/Poor/Decolonial/Diasporic/Diseased etc.) consists in their capacity to carry out alternative modes of knowing and becoming. Their ability to set up transversal relations breaks up segregational patterns and establishes border crossings that aim to actualise their knowledge and visions.

For instance, following on from Rob Nixon's (2011) seminal work on slow violence and the environmentalism of the poor, new connections are currently being made between postcolonial theories, the by now classical Environmental Humanities and indigenous epistemologies, resulting in more resonances and interaction between them. This results in more attention being paid to transnational environmental justice, Land Rights and the assessment of the environmental damage caused by warfare. It also produces new areas of studies, such as the Postcolonial Environmental Humanities, Transnational Environmental Literary Studies and the cross-over between Native American Studies and other Indigenous studies areas and Environmental studies (Povinelli 2016; Bignall, Hemming and Rigney 2016).

Similar developments are happening within the equally established Digital Humanities. The pioneering work of Lisa Nakamura (2002), followed up by Ponzanesi and Leurs (2014) is working towards the convergence field of Postcolonial Digital Humanities.[2] In my terms, these new trans-disciplinary assemblages propel 'classical' postcolonial studies into and across the re-territorialised Digital Humanities. Also in the context of Mignolo's decolonial theory (2011), new alliances are being forged between Environmentalists and Legal specialists, Indigenous and non-western epistemologies, First Nation peoples, new media activists, IT engineers and anti-globalisation forces, which constitute a significant example of new political assemblages.[3] They have produced the Decolonial Digital Humanities, for example the Hastac Scholars Forum.[4]

These new developments constitute another step forward into the complexity of posthuman discourses. In both cases, attention to the earth is combined with enduring care for the people who live closest to the earth – indigenous populations – thus raising the ethical and political stakes. The critique of Western imperialism and racism is therefore enhanced by an extra layer of dis-identification from anthropocentrism. This extra qualitative shift positions posthuman critical thinkers closer to the dispossessed and the disempowered, on the assumption that many of those are not necessarily human. These new transversal discourses – alternative collective assemblages – reconstitute not only the missing links – between post-humanism and post-anthropocentrism – in academic practices, but actualise also and especially the missing people.

The point of this actualisation is to provide an *adequate* expression of what bodies – as both embodied and embrained – can do, think and enact. Adequate to what? Adequate to what the missing peoples – those embodied, embrained, relational, affective transversal assemblages – can do. How much intensity they can sustain, how much negativity they can process in order to produce affirmation. The ethical task consists in turning the painful experience of inexistence into generative relational encounters and knowledge production. This is liberation through the understanding of our bondage, as Spinoza teaches us: it extracts knowledge from pain by re-working and transforming the negative affect, experience or relation. The politics of immanence compose planes of becoming for a missing people that was never fully part of 'Man' and barely qualified as 'Anthropos', let alone be preoccupied by its alleged crisis today.

This politics of radical immanence – to actualise the emergence of a missing people – also exposes the weakness of the reactive re-composition of pan-humanity, united as a threatened category. Instead of taking a flight into an abstract idea of a 'new' pan-human, bonded in negative passions like fear of extinction, in a world risk society (Beck, 1999), I want to plea for monistic affirmative politics grounded on immanent inter-connections and generative differences: a transversal composition of multiple assemblages of active minoritarian subjects, of many 'people' who are no longer missing.

Conclusion

Let me sum up some of the defining features of posthuman scholarship in order to assess its pedagogical implications. First, it is materially embodied and embedded in a radical and non-reductive form of vital empiricism. It is embedded in the world, environmentally, socially and affectively. It is a supra-disciplinary, rhizomic field of contemporary knowledge production that is contiguous with, but not identical to, the epistemic accelerationism of cognitive capitalism. It functions at different speeds, moves on different time-lines and is fuelled by radically different ethical affects.

Second, it builds on a post-Foucauldian vision of power as multi-layered (*potestas and potentia*) and of time as multi-directional (*Chronos & Aion*, the actual & the virtual). With cognitive capitalism being tuned into bio-genetics and informational codes, the task of critical thinkers is, more than ever, the praxis of speaking truth to power – in all its complexity – and working towards the composition of planes of immanence for missing peoples. Instead of new generalisations about an engendered pan-humanity, we need sharper focus on the complex singularities that constitute our respective locations.

Third, posthuman scholarship requires de-familiarisation, or the move toward anti-Oedipal pedagogy. The anti-Oedipal method argues productively against the anxiety of influence and for a culture of trust and inter-generational justice. A system of knowledge production that rests on affirmative ethics stresses the necessity of pursuing the actualisation of intensities and forces. The point, therefore, is to practice un-dutifulness, conceptual disobedience, or creative unfaithfulness as affirmative politics, in a sustainable and productive manner. De-familiarisation is a sobering process by which the knowing subject evolves from the normative vision of the self he or she had become accustomed to.

Since the 1970s many radical pedagogies have posited the method of dis-identifications from the dominant vision of the subject, along the axes of becoming-woman (sexualisation) and becoming-other (racialisation) and hence within the confines of anthropomorphism. A more radical shift is needed therefore today to develop post-anthropocentric forms of identification (ecologisation). Posthuman theory's vital geo/techno/centrism – the love of *zoe* – is an effort in the same direction. Becoming-world/earth or becoming-imperceptible introduce a radically immanent planetary dimension.

On the methodological front, de-Oedipalising the pedagogical relationship to the non-human other is a form of radical pacifism that sets strong ethical requirements upon the philosophical subject. It requires a form of dis-identification from a century-old habit of anthropocentric thought and humanist arrogance, which is likely to test the ability and willingness of the Humanities to question what exactly is 'human' about them. The frame of reference becomes the open-ended, inter-relational, multi-sexed, and trans-species flows of becoming by interaction with multiple others.

Last, but not least, comes the collaborative, not competitive character of posthuman knowledge production. One of the great innovations of vital materialist philosophy is the rigorous brand of methodological non-aggression that animates it. The monistic ontology that asserts we are all part of the same matter, which Deleuze adapts from Spinoza, plus a good dose of Bergsonian time-continuum, situates the researcher – be it the philosopher, the scientist, or the artist – in a situation of great intimacy with the world. There is no violent rupture or separation between the subjects and the objects of their inquiry, no predatory gaze of the cold clinician (Braidotti 2011a) intent upon unveiling the secrets of nature (Jordanova 1993). An elemental ontological unity structures the connections. This non-essentialist vitalist position calls for a collaborative re-definition of the scholar as subject of knowledge, as well as the process of scientific inquiry and its methodology.

The challenge today is how to transform, or deterritorialise, the human-non-human interaction in pedagogical practice, so as to intervene in, but not be over-coded or assimilated by, the fast-moving flows of data-mining by cognitive capitalism. How to bypass the dialectics of otherness, secularising the concept of human nature and the life that animates it, while embracing neo-naturalism in a *zoe*/geo/techno-perspective. I would speak of a generic becoming-minoritarian/ animal/world/earth/cosmos as a figuration for the humanoid hybrid subjects of posthuman knowledge we are in the process of becoming. It is clear that our science – bio-genetics and informatics – can deal with this post-anthropocentric shift, but can philosophy and the Humanities rise to the occasion?

The answer can only be ethical. The displacement of anthropocentrism and the recognition of trans-species solidarity are based on the awareness of 'our' being in this together; that is to say: environmentally-based, embodied, and embedded and in symbiosis with each other. The *zoe*-centered embodied subject is shot through with relational linkages of the symbiotic, contaminating/viral kind that interconnect it to a variety of others, starting from the environmental or eco-others. This non-essentialist brand of vitalism reduces the hubris of rational consciousness, which far from being an act of vertical transcendence, is rather recast as radical immanence, a grounding force. It is an act of unfolding of the self onto the world and the enfolding within of the world.

'We' – the dwellers of this planet at this point in time are inter-connected, but also internally fractured. The field of posthuman scholarship is not aiming at anything like a consensus about a new 'Humanity', but it gives us a frame for the actualisation of the many different ways of becoming posthuman. It actualises multiple missing people, whose marginalised knowledge is the breeding ground for possible futures. Of course, such a praxis is demanding, in terms of rigour, labour and imagination, but the advantages are plentiful. For one thing, the neo-materialist ethics of affirmation that sustains the complex re-composition of subjectivity through posthuman knowledge, is giving us an adequate measure of what we are actually in the process of becoming. The rest is a life's work.

Notes

1   With thanks to Sarah Nuttall.

2   See also the Postcolonial Digital Humanities blog and website at #dhpoco.tumbir. com.

3 See for instance the land/media/indigenous project based in British Columbia: Bleck, Dodds and Williams (2013).

4 Co-ordinated by Micha Cardenas, Noha F. Beydon and Alainya Kavaloski; see the website: www.hastac.org/initiatives/hastac-scholars/scholars-forums/decolonising-digital.

References

Beck, Ulrich. 1999. *World Risk Society.* Cambridge: Polity Press.

Bignall, S., S. Hemming and D. Rigney. 'The Ecosophies for the Anthropocene: Environmental Governance, Continental Posthumanism and Indigenous Expressivism.' *Deleuze Studies* 10.4 (2016): 455–78.

Bleck, Nancy, Dodds, Katherine and Chief Williams, Bill. 2013. *Picturing Transformations.* Vancouver: Figure 1 Publishing.

Bonta, Mark and John Protevi. 2004. *Deleuze and Geophilosophy. A Guide and Glossary.* Edinburgh: Edinburgh University Press.

Bostrom, Nick. 2014. *Superintelligence. Paths, Dangers, Strategies.* Oxford: Oxford University Press.

Braidotti, Rosi. 1994. *Nomadic Subjects: Embodiment and Sexual Difference in Contemporary Feminist Theory*, 1st edn, New York: Columbia University Press.

Braidotti, Rosi. 2006. *Transpositions: On Nomadic Ethics.* Cambridge: Polity Press.

Braidotti, Rosi. 2011a. *Nomadic Subjects: Embodiment and Sexual Difference in Contemporary Feminist Theory.* New York: Columbia University Press.

Braidotti, Rosi. 2011b. *Nomadic Theory. The Portable Rosi Braidotti.* New York: Columbia University Press.

Braidotti, Rosi. 2013. *The Posthuman.* Cambridge: Polity Press.

Braidotti, Rosi. 2016. 'The Contested Posthumanities', in Rosi Braidotti and Paul Gilroy (eds), 2016. *Contesting Humanities.* London and New York: Bloomsbury Academic.

Chakrabarty, Dipesh. 2009. 'The Climate of History: Four Theses'. *Critical Enquiry* 35: 197–222.

Cooper, Melinda. 2008. *Life as Surplus. Biotecnology & Capitalism in the Neoliberal Era.* Seattle: University of Washington Press.

Deleuze, G. and F. Guattari. 1994. *What is Philosophy?* New York: Columbia University Press.

Deleuze, Gilles and Felix Guattari. 1987. *A Thousand Plateaus: Capitalism and Schizophrenia.* Minneapolis: University of Minnesota Press.

Deleuze, Gilles. 1990. *Expressionism in Philosophy: Spinoza.* New York: Zone Books.

Deleuze, Gilles. 1988. *Spinoza: Practical Philosophy.* San Francisco: City Lights Books.

Fontenay, de Elizabeth. 1998. *Le silence des bêtes.* Paris: Fayard.

Foucault, Michel. 1970. *The Order of Things: An Archaeology of Human Sciences.* New York: Pantheon Books.

Freire, Paolo. 1970. *Pedagogy of the Oppressed*. New York: Herder and Herder.

Fuller, Matthew. 2005. *Media Ecologies: Materialist Energies in Art and Technoculture*. Cambridge, Mass and London: MIT Press.

Glissant, Edouard. 1997. *Poetics of Relation*. Ann Arbor: University of Michigan Press.

Haraway, Donna. 1988. 'Situated Knowledges. The Science Question in Feminism as a Site of Discourse on the Privilege of Partial Perspective'. *Feminist Studies*, 14(3): 575–99.

Haraway, Donna. 1997. *Modest_Witness@Second_Millennium. FemaleMan©_Meets_Oncomouse™*. London and New York: Routledge.

Haraway, Donna. 2003. *The Companion Species Manifesto. Dogs, People and Significant Otherness*. Chicago: Prickly Paradigm Press.

Harding, Sandra. 1986. *The Science Question in Feminism*. Ithaca: Cornell University Press.

Harding, Sandra. 1991. *Whose Science? Whose Knowledge?* Ithaca: Cornell University Press.

Jordanova, Ludmilla. 1989. *Sexual Visions: Images of Women in Medicine and Science*. Milwaukee, University of Wisconsin Press.

Lloyd, Genevieve. 1994. *Part of Nature: Self-knowledge in Spinoza's Ethic*. Ithaca/London: Cornell University Press.

Lloyd, Genevieve. 1996. *Spinoza and the Ethics*. London and New York: Routledge.

Margulis, Lynn and Sagan, Dorion 1995. *What Is Life?* Berkley and Los Angeles: University of California Press.

Marks, John. 1998.

Mbembe, Achille. 2003. 'Necropolitics'. *Public Culture*, 15(1): 11–40.

Mignolo, Walter. 2011. *The Darker Side of Western Modernity: Global Futures, Decolonial Options*. Durham: Duke University Press.

Moulier Boutang, Yann. 2012. *Cognitive Capitalism*. Cambridge: Polity Press.

Nakamura, Lisa. 2002. *Cybertypes. Race, Ethnicity and Identity on the Internet*. London and New York: Routledge.

Nixon, Rob. 2011. *Slow Violence and the Environmentalism of the Poor*. Cambridge, Mass.: Harvard University Press.

Ponzanesi, Sandra, and Koen Leurs. 2014. 'Introduction to the Special Issue: On Digital Crossings in Europe'. *Crossings, Journal of Migration and Culture* 4(1): 3–22.

Povinelli, Elizabeth. 2016. *Geontologies. A Requiem to Late Liberalism*. Durham: Duke University Press.

Protevi, John. 2013. *Life War Earth*. Minneapolis: University of Minnesota Press.

Rich, Adrienne. 1987. *Blood, Bread and Poetry*. London: Virago Press.

Rose, Nicholas. 2007. *The Politics of Life Itself: Biomedicine, Power and Subjectivity in the Twenty-First Century*. Princeton University Press.

Rosendhal Thomsen, Mads 2013. *The New Human in Literature: Posthuman Visions of Change in Body, Mind and Society after 1900*. London: Bloomsbury Academic.

Said, Edward 2003. *Orientalism*. London: Penguin Modern Classics.

Sassen, Saskia. 2014. *Expulsions – Brutality and Complexity in the Global Economy.* Cambridge Mass: Harvard University Press.

Shiva, Vandana 1997. *Biopiracy. The Plunder of Nature and Knowledge.* Boston: South End Press.

Spivak, Gayatri C. 1990. 'Criticism, Feminism and the Institution' in: *The Postcolonial Critic.* New York and London: Routledge.

Wolfe, Cary, (ed.), 2003. *Zoontologies. The Question of the Animal.* Minneapolis, University of Minnesota Press.

Introduction

Vivienne Bozalek, Tamara Shefer and Michalinos Zembylas

Internationally, neoliberalism and the political swing to the right in the United States, the United Kingdom, and some European contexts have profound effects on the higher education sector and more specifically on how pedagogies are enacted in this sector. Contemporary global contexts of inequality and injustice in higher education provide an important backdrop for the present book project. By way of example, there has been a great deal of concern about the current crisis in higher education in South Africa and its implications for future citizenship and social participation. These concerns are exemplified by calls to decolonise the university (as evidenced in the #Rhodesmustfall student protest movement started in 2015 at the University of Cape Town, an historically advantaged and white higher education institution) and demands for universal access to higher education (articulated by the #feesmustfall student movement spreading to other South African universities in 2015 and 2016). Such calls resonate across the globe, and are starting to provide an impetus for change in contexts other than South Africa, such as the movement of identifying racism in US higher education and the 'Rhodes must fall' movement at Oxford University in the United Kingdom, amongst others. These events indicate that there is an impetus for finding imaginative ways of engaging with the current dissatisfactions with higher education. A key purpose, then, for putting together this edited collection is the urgency to rethink social justice in higher education in ways that speak to current global contexts and draw on cutting edge ethico-onto-epistemological developments.

One way of engaging with the current crisis is to consider new theories which may open up new possibilities and provocations for the body of work in higher education. This book provides such a space by engaging with theories which call into question commonplace humanist assumptions, so prevalent in the imaginings of socially just higher education pedagogies. As an edited collection, the contributions in this volume consider how social justice from posthuman, affective and new feminist materialist perspectives might be put to work in higher education institutions and pedagogies. The chapters in this edited volume provide fresh ways of thinking about and enacting *socially just pedagogies* with ideas from the affective turn, critical posthumanism, and new feminist materialisms. While several chapters foreground southern contexts, particularly South Africa, the book is of international relevance, raising transnational areas of concern for the higher education sector.

A number of writers and researchers have considered critical posthumanism, new materialisms and the affective turn for other educational sectors, such as early childhood development (see for example Childers 2013, 2014; Davies 2014a and b, Hultman and Lenz Taguchi 2010; Lenz Taguchi 2010, 2012, 2013; Lenz Taguchi and Palmer 2013; Myers 2014; Ringrose and Rawlings 2015; Sellers 2013; Taylor 2013); however few texts have dealt specifically with higher education (Jackson and Mazzei 2012; Semetsky and Masny 2013; Snaza and Weaver, 2015; Taylor, 2017; Zabrodska et al. 2011), with even less visibility in the area of socially just pedagogies from these perspectives with a few exceptions (see for example Goodley 2007; Goodley and Roets 2008; Madriaga and Goodley 2010 which deal more with disabilities and higher education).

Critical posthumanism, new feminist materialisms and the affective turn have a great deal in common with each other, and can be seen as similar perspectives with slightly different emphases in each framework, all focusing on: relational ontologies; a critique of dualisms; and engagements with matter and the non-human/more-than-human. Feminist thinkers such as Rosi Braidotti, Donna Haraway, Karen Barad, Vinciane Despret, Isabelle Stengers, Elizabeth Grosz, Jane Bennet, Nancy Tuana, Vicky Kirby, and Stacey Alaimo, amongst others, have been identified both as critical posthumanists and new/feminist materialists, and have also contributed to ideas about the affective turn. Many of these scholars have been influenced by the work of Deleuze and Guattari and their notions of monism and vitalism, and have moved beyond the centrality of discourse and Cartesian dualisms to incorporate a vision of human/nonhuman, body/mind, subject/object, nature/culture, matter/meaning, continuity/discontinuity, beginning/returning and creation/renewal, continuity/discontinuity (Barad 2007) in their work.

Posthumanism builds on the epistemological and political foundations of anti-humanism, postcolonialism, post-anthropocentrism, anti-racism and material feminisms (Alaimo and Hekman 2008; Blagaard and van der Tuin 2014; Coole and Frost 2010; Dolphijn and van der Tuin 2012; Nayar 2014; Wolfe 2014). Critical posthumanism, in particular, embraces a critical view of a disembedded liberal humanism, with its assumptions of a society with equally placed autonomous agents and rational scientific control over others (Adams 2014; Donovan and Adams 2007).

Material feminisms have built on the linguistic turn which focused exclusively on discursive practices at the expense of the material world, developing an 'embedded and embodied' (Braidotti 2002, p. 2) material-discursive philosophy of difference and being in the world. Prominent theorists who have developed and written about new feminist materialisms are philosopher Rosi Braidotti (2002; 2006; 2011; 2013) and natural scientists and feminist theorists Karen Barad (2007; 2010; 2011; 2012; 2014) and Donna Haraway (1988; 1997; 2003; 2008). New feminist materialists have moved beyond a critical deconstruction and critique to alternative enactments of becoming, where power is not only seen as limiting but also as affirmative (Braidotti 2013). New/feminist materialisms have expanded Haraway's ideas on situated knowledges, critiquing universalist disembodied 'God's eye' views of the world, paving the way for ethical accountability in local and grounded knowledges. Rather than seeing epistemology, ontology and ethics as separate, new materialisms consider them as co-imbricated and entangled – Barad (2007) refers to her notion of agential realism as an ethico-onto-epistemological framework. Difference is celebrated as productive rather than seen as the abject other. Matter is seen as vital and vibrant, having agency and as being 'mutually constituted' with the discursive (Bennett 2010; Lenz Taguchi 2013; Phillips and Larson 2013).

The 'affective turn' (Clough 2007) in the humanities and social sciences has developed some of the most innovative and productive theoretical ideas in recent years, bringing together psychoanalytically informed theories of subjectivity and subjection, theories of the body and embodiment, Deleuzian and political theories and critical analysis (Massumi 2015). The affective turn marks 'critical theory's turn to affect' (2007, p. 2), as Patricia Clough writes, 'at a time when critical theory is facing the analytic challenges of ongoing war, trauma, torture, massacre, and counter/terrorism' (ibid.). Although there are clearly different approaches in the affective turn that range from psychoanalysis, post-Deleuzian perspectives, theories of the body and embodiment to affective politics, there is a substantial turn to the intersections of the social, cultural and political with the psychic and the pre/conscious. The affective turn, then, marks a shift in thought in critical theory through an exploration of the complex interrelations of discursive practices, the human body, social and cultural forces, and individually experienced, but historically situated emotions and affects.

This edited volume provides a space to re-imagine socially just pedagogies in higher education from different theoretical perspectives that question taken-for-granted humanist assumptions, such as representational thought, interpretivism and assumed localisation of agency and emotions as existing within and being possessed by humans. Such a reading opens up new possibilities and responsibilities as well as bringing potential challenges, dangers and new questions. Thus, this edited collection brings together a compendium of chapters that engages the reader with important questions such as the following:

- How do we enact 'socially just pedagogies' in higher education in light of the above theoretical developments and how would a socially just pedagogy work from these perspectives?
- What new avenues of exploration do these theoretical approaches provide for doing, and thinking, differently about socially just higher education pedagogies?
- What potentialities for re-imagining research methodologies and practices for socially just pedagogies are afforded by critical posthumanism, new materialisms and the affective turn?
- How does breaking binaries and dualisms such as between research and teaching allow questions to be asked about current forms and open up ways of being and doing differently in socially just pedagogies?
- How do ethical, ontological, epistemological, and affective configurations in these theoretical perspectives impact on socially just pedagogies?

Structure of the book

The book is divided into three parts: (a) Part One (Chapters 1–4) provides theoretical work from various perspectives and considers how these ideas might advance socially just educational praxes; and (b) Part Two (Chapters 5–8) highlights the ethical dimensions in higher education pedagogical practices, particularly, but not exclusively, that of response-ability, and (c) Part Three (Chapters 9–12) focuses on documenting and intra-acting with critical and innovative pedagogical practices, both within and outside the tertiary educational classroom.

Part One consists of four chapters. In Chapter 1, Chantelle Gray van Heerden discusses the current situation in South African Higher Education, focusing in particular at the recent Fallist Movement–#Rhodesmustfall #feesmustfall #itmustallfall–and what it has brought to light about education fees, neoliberal policies, and the legacies of Apartheid and colonialism. She uses Deleuze and

Guattari's work to examine the structural violence of racism and argues for a posthuman practice that can map new subjective potentialities and enact pedagogically the Fallist Movement. Gray van Heerden suggests that in seeking to address the social injustices of the past through Higher Education, educators need to engage with a pedagogy for a people to come in other words, a political and radicalised socially just pedagogy.

In Chapter 2, Rosemarie Buikema and Kathrin Thiele take on a major concern of twenty-first-century feminist activism and pedagogies, namely, that the achievements of the movement are in danger of becoming disconnected from their initial manifestations of equality for all as a result of neoliberalism. Buikema and Thiele contextualise this problem by focusing on feminist studies and their task of furthering social justice discourses in higher education today. Their particular aim is to create spaces within the university as a public institution and the institutionalised spaces of Gender Studies to counteract neoliberal trends and therefore enable different prospects for social justice struggles. To do so, they approach the issue from a feminist (new) materialist/critical posthuman(ist) perspective, arguing for its potential to continually allow for such speculative practical curricular spaces in which students and educators are trained 'to imagine otherwise' in order to enact solidarity and social justice.

In Chapter 3, Vivienne Bozalek and Michalinos Zembylas argue that diffractive methodologies have been largely developed in response to dissatisfaction with practices of reflexivity, which are seen to be grounded in the representational paradigm from the work of feminist natural scientists Donna Haraway and Karen Barad. While work on 'reflexivity' and 'critical reflection' has over the years become predominant in critical education and socially just pedagogies, Bozalek and Zembylas emphasise that there is still important conceptual work to be done putting into conversation these two practices – reflection and diffraction – and exploring their continuities and breaks as well as examining how they differ from each other and/or intersect and what consequences such understandings might have for research methodologies in socially just pedagogies in higher education. Their chapter raises important questions and prospects regarding the methodological implications of diffractive methodologies for socially just pedagogies in higher education.

In Chapter 4, Delphi Carstens critically examines negative anti-human, as well as more affirmative posthuman and new materialist gestures that help to explode the anthropocentric conceit that the world or cosmos is as it is for us only. Carstens argues that a sensory pedagogy and politics of animality utilises such moves to generate aesthetic corridors of 'disorientating affects' that enable 'new conditions for thought and action'. In addition, Carstens suggests that scientific narratives of extinction, cosmological and evolutionary deep-time scenarios, Deleuzo-Guattarian trickster cartographies, vibrant materialisms, sonic fictions and speculative fabulations (both visual and textual) provide potentially useful affect-laden classroom tools, for crafting an 'anti-speciesist pedagogy' appropriate to the new conditions of the Anthropocene.

Part Two comprises four chapters focusing on different but complementary ways of using posthuman ethics to think about higher education and the pedagogical practices associated with it. In Chapter 5, Carol Taylor elaborates on the ethical dimension of higher education pedagogy from a relational orientation. She holds that practices (what she refers to as actual/material practice-ings) that matter in pedagogy, derive from an enlarged sense of interconnections, which include the more-than-human. Her chapter provides a useful summary of humanist Enlightenment approaches to ethics which assume a white Western heterosexual rational economic man as a normative subject and position those who deviate from this position as other. She proposes a posthuman, new materialist ethics using the work of Barad, Braidotti and Haraway, which she posits provide relational orientations for ethical being, doing and thinking in higher education pedagogic practice. These orientations are affirmative in respecting and valuing all bodies, propose a logic of entanglement, are powered by affective politics, activate an ethic of concern and insist that intra-action matters.

Chapter 6, a co-authored chapter by Vivienne Bozalek, Abdullah Bayat, Daniela Gachago, Siddique Motala and Veronica Mitchell, focuses on how a response-able pedagogy in higher education might be configured by diffracting Joan Tronto's ideas of the political ethics of care through those of Karen Barad's and Donna Haraway's to generate inventive superpositions. More particularly, it focuses on these theorists' views of relational ontology and flourishing and in more depth on the moral elements of attentiveness and responsibility which all three theorists see as central to an ethics of response-ability. The chapter considers how an attentive pedagogy and then how a responsible pedagogy might be enacted, and what these pedagogies might look like in a South African context. The chapter makes use of a series of interviews conducted by the authors of the chapter on each other about their own higher education pedagogical practices in relation to social justice.

In Chapter 7, Erin Manning asks what undercommon currents of creative dissonance and asymmetrical experience cannot be accommodated, heard or listened to in higher education institutions undergirded by neoliberalism. She considers how conditions for neurodiversity can be created in, across or beyond the university through becoming attentive and attuning to the ways that the production of neurotypical knowledge has been resisted, queered and threatened by non-docile bodies, in contexts where neurotypical forms of knowledge are rarely addressed or defined as such. Through an exploration of diagrams of power/knowledge in the context of the university, this chapter moves with the urgency of undercommon modes of learning to ask how else learning can happen and what the stakes are in retaining the university as we know it as the paradigm for education.

In Chapter 8, Candace Kuby and Rebecca Christ use an ethico-onto-epistemological stance to explore the process of planning and teaching an introductory qualitative research course. This course could be considered a disruptive and enlarged space in that it provided students with the opportunities to go beyond formulaic practices and experience new possibilities of knowing, being and doing qualitative research intra-actively. Their challenge to educators who align themselves with critical posthumanism, new feminist materialisms and the affective turn is to consider how theoretical concepts entangle with and produce socially just pedagogies.

Part Three documents four different case studies in a particular geopolitical context that speak to social justice and decolonial pedagogical practices inspired by feminist, posthumanist and new materialist thinking and that open up new imaginaries for scholarly practice and ways of being and becoming. In Chapter 9, Karin Murris and Kathryn Muller present a posthuman approach to a compulsory year-long childhood studies course within foundation phase teacher education in South Africa. The chapter is concerned with elaborating how posthumanism has shaped the praxis and ethics of a teacher education programme that is directed at decolonising the curriculum. The authors argue that a decolonisation project requires what they term 'ongoing intra-generational work' that is never complete, but always in process. The authors describe the use of varied pedagogical innovations such as diffractive journals, creative art installations, field trips and innovative assessments in the curriculum geared at flagging intra-actions between humans and others living on the planet and queering binarisms endemic to colonialist and patriarchal pedagogies that are endemic in the academy.

Chapter 10, as with a number of others in this section and elsewhere in the book, draws on some of the rich narratives, both discursive and material, generated by current contexts of student activism in South African higher education. Author Tamara Shefer applies a feminist materialist lens to explore a number of recent occasions of activism, art and performance directed at gender and sexual justice spotlighting current examples of embodied activism and art, including: the performance of the ascendance of the Zimbabwe Bird while the Cecil John Rhodes statue at the University of Cape Town was taken down; the performative embodied protests of transgender activists in response to an exhibition which marginalised their experience and contributions; and the deployment of naked embodiment by women in sexual violence activism. The author argues the importance of engaging materiality in the larger project of disrupting the colonial, patriarchal and humanist heritages of injustice in and through higher education.

In Chapter 11, similarly located in current contexts of South African student activism, Nike Romano explores an art history pedagogical project that is directed at calls for a decolonised and African epistemological curriculum. Structured around the teaching and learning of Ancient Greek vase painting, the chapter explores pedagogical strategies that are centred around students' narratives and voice, through their embodied encounters with artefacts. Applying a Baradian diffractive methodology and Ettinger's work on the ontological possibilities of art to explore the intra-action between western art history through students' lived experience, the chapter illustrates how socially just pedagogies that foreground personal narratives can challenge Eurocentric dominance through recognising student experience and knowledges.

Finally, in Chapter 12, Denise Newfield draws on a South African poetry project to reflect on the contributions of multimodal and posthumanist approaches to social justice pedagogies. Drawing on 'Thebuwa' (which means 'To speak') which was founded in 1994, the year that South Africa became a democracy. The project was directed at a group of school-going students from a severely disadvantaged community within the racial capitalist apartheid system of categorisation. The chapter explores the diffraction of the two theoretical waves drawn on towards understandings of this poetry project within social justice pedagogical imperatives. The author shows how the multimodal reading centres students as agents of meaning and culture, while the posthumanist reading allows for an appreciation of relationality, thus deepening the reading of the value of the course.

Conclusion

The contributions towards the pursuit and exploration of socially just pedagogies in higher education in this volume point to new theoretical, ethical and methodological perspectives raised in re-conceptualising the meaning(s) and most importantly the enactment(s) of 'socially just pedagogies'. *Socially just pedagogies* are usually understood as the educators' efforts to enact pedagogical practices that improve the learning and life opportunities of all students, but particularly those regarded as underserved by higher education (Ladson-Billings, 1994), while equipping and empowering all students to work for a more socially just society themselves (Kincheloe and Steinberg 1998; King 2005). Together, the chapters in this volume demonstrate that fresh theoretical and empirical tools are necessary in an effort to envision and enact socially just pedagogies in various contexts, as a response to neoliberal developments.

References

Adams, C. J. (2014), 'The War on Compassion,' in P. MacCormack (ed) *The Animal Catalyst: Towards Ahuman Theory*. London: Bloomsbury, 15–25.

Alaimo, S. and S. Hekman (eds), (2008), *Material Feminisms*. Bloomington & Indianapolis: Indiana University Press.

Barad, K. (2007), *Meeting the Universe Halfway: Quantum Physics and the Entanglement of Matter and Meaning*. Durham NC & London: Duke University Press.

Barad, K. (2010), 'Quantum Entanglements and Hauntological Relations of Inheritance: Dis/continuities, SpaceTime Enfoldings, and Justice-to-Come.' *Derrida Today* 3(2):240–68.

Barad, K. (2011), 'Erasers and Erasures: Pinch's Unfortunate "Uncertainty Principle."' *Social Studies of Science* 41(3): 443–54.

Barad, K. (2012), 'On Touching – The Inhuman That Therefore I Am.' *D I F F E R E N c E S: A Journal of Feminist Cultural Studies* 23(3): 206–23.

Barad, K. (2014), 'Diffracting Diffraction: Cutting Together-Apart.' *Parallax*, 20(3): 168–187. doi:10.1080/13534645.2014.927623.

Bennett, J. (2010), *Vibrant Matter: A Political Ecology of Things*. Durham, NC: Duke University Press.

Blagaard, B. and I. van der Tuin (eds), (2014), *The Subject of Rosi Braidotti: Politics and Concepts*. London: Bloomsbury.

Braidotti, R. (2002), *Metamorphoses: Towards a Materialist Theory of Becoming*. Cambridge: Polity Press.

Braiddotti, R. (2006), *Transpositions: On Nomadic Ethics*. Cambridge: Polity Press.

Braiddotti, R. (2011), *Nomadic Theory: The Portable Rosi Braidotti*. New York: Columbia University Press.

Braiddotti, R. (2013), *The Posthuman*. Cambridge: Polity Press.

Childers, S. M. (2013), 'The Materiality of Fieldwork: An Ontology of Feminist Becoming.' *International Journal of Qualitative Studies in Education: QSE* 26(5): 599–609.

Childers, S. M. (2014), 'Promiscuous Analysis in Qualitative Research.' *Qualitative Inquiry: QI* 20(6): 819–26.

Clough, P. (ed.), (2007), *The Affective Turn: Theorising the Social*. Durham NC and London: Duke University Press.

Coole, D. and S. Frost (eds), (2010), *New Materialisms: Ontology, Agency, and Politics*. Durham NC & London: Duke University Press.

Davies, B. (2014a) *Listening to Children: Being and Becoming*. London and New York: Routledge.

Davies, B. (2014b), 'Reading Anger in Early Childhood Intra-Actions: A Diffractive Analysis.' *Qualitative Inquiry: QI* 20(6): 734–41.

Dolphijn, R. and I. van der Tuin (2012), *New Materialism: Interviews & Cartographies*. University of Michigan Library: Open Humanities Press.

Donovan, J. and Ca. J. Adams (eds), (2007), *The Feminist Care Tradition in Animal Ethics: A Reader*. New York: Columbia University Press.

Goodley, D. (2007), 'Towards Socially Just Pedagogies: Deleuzoguattarian Critical Disability Studies.' *International Journal of Inclusive Education* 11(3): 317–34.

Goodley, D. and G. Roets (2008), 'The (Be)Comings and Goings of "Developmental Disabilities": The Cultural Politics of "Impairment."' *Discourse: Studies in the Cultural Politics of Education* 29(2): 239–55.

Haraway, D. (1988), 'Situated Knowledges: *The Science Question in Feminism* and the Privilege of Partial Perspective.' *Feminist Studies* 14(3): 575–99.

Haraway, D. (1997), *Modest_Witness@Second_Millenium. FemaleMan(C)_Meets Onco-MouseTM*. London and New York: Routledge.

Haraway, D. (2003), *The Companion Species Manifesto: Dogs, People, and Significant Others*. Chicago: Prickly Paradigm Press.

Haraway, D. (2008), *When Species Meet*. Minneapolis: University of Minnesota Press.

Hultman, K. and H. Lenz Taguchi (2010), 'Challenging Anthropocentric Analysis of Visual Data: A Relational Materialist Methodological Approach to Educational Research.' *International Journal of Qualitative Studies in Education: QSE* 23(5): 525–42.

Jackson, A. Y. and L. A. Mazzei (eds) (2012), *Thinking with Theory in Qualitative Research: Viewing Data Across Multiple Perspectives*. London: Routledge.

Kincheloe, J. L. and S. R. Steinberg (1998), 'Addressing the Crisis of Whiteness: Reconfiguring White Identity in a Pedagogy of Whiteness', in J.L. Kincheloe, S. R. Steinberg, N.M. Rodriguez and R.E. Chennault (eds), *White Reign: Deploying Whiteness in America*, New York: St. Martin's Press, 3–29.

King, J. E. (2005), *Black Education: A Transformative Research and Action Agenda for the New Century*. Mahwah, NJ: Erlbaum.

Ladson-Billings, G. (1994), *Dreamkeepers: Successful Teachers of African American Children*. San Francisco: Jossey-Bass.

Lenz Taguchi, H. (2010), *Going Beyond the Theory/Practice Divide in Early Childhood Education: Introducing an Intra-active Pedagogy*. London and New York: Routledge.

Lenz Taguchi, H. (2012), 'A Diffractive and Deleuzian Approach to Analysing Interview Data.' *Feminist Theory*, 13(3): 265–281

Lenz Taguchi, H. (2013), 'Images of Thinking in Feminist Materialisms: Ontological Divergences and the Production of Researcher Subjectivities.' *International Journal of Qualitative Studies in Education: QSE* 26(6): 706–16.

Lenz Taguchi, H. and A. Palmer (2013), 'A More "Livable" School? A Diffractive Analysis of the Performative Enactments of Girls' Ill-/Well-Being With(in) School Environments.' *Gender and Education* 25(6): 671–87.

Madriaga, M. and D. Goodley (2010), 'Moving Beyond the Minimum: Socially Just Pedagogies and Asperger's Syndrome in UK Higher Education.' *International Journal of Inclusive Education* 14(2): 115–31.

Massumi, B. (2015), *Politics of Affect*. Cambridge: Polity Press.

Nayar P. K. (2014), *Posthumanism*. Cambridge: Polity Press.

Phillips, D. K. and M. L. Larson (2013), 'The Teacher–Student Writing Conference Reimaged: Entangled Becoming-Writing Conferencing.' *Gender and Education* 25(6): 722–37.

Sellers, M. (2013), *Young Children Becoming Curriculum: Deleuze, Te Whariki and Curricula Understandings*. London and New York: Routledge.

Semetsky, I. and D. Masny (eds), (2013), *Deleuze and Education*. Edinburgh: Edinburgh University Press.

Snaza, N. and J. A. Weaver (eds), (2015), *Posthumanism and Educational Research*. New York and London: Routledge.

Taylor, A. (2013), *Reconfiguring the Natures of Childhood*. London and New York: Routledge.

Taylor, C. (2017), 'Is a Posthumanist Bildung Possible? Reclaiming the Promise of Bildung for Contemporary Higher Education', *Higher Education*, 74:419–435.

Wolfe, C. (2010), *What is Posthumanism?* Minneapolis and London: University of Minnesota Press.

Zabrodska, K., S. Lnell, C. Laws, and B. Davies (2011), 'Bullying as Intra-Active Process in Neoliberal Universities.' *Qualitative Inquiry: QI* 17(8): 709–19.

Part One

Theoretical Perspectives

1

#Itmustallfall, or, Pedagogy for a People to Come

Chantelle Gray van Heerden

#Rhodesmustfall #Feesmustfall #Itmustallfall

On 9 March 2015, Chumani Maxwele covered a bronze statue of colonialist Cecil John Rhodes, located on the main campus of the most prestigious university in South Africa – the University of Cape Town (UCT) – with human faeces obtained from a portable flush toilet in Khayelitsha, a large 'township' (or district) outside of Cape Town. Shortly after this event, a group of students and staff called for the removal of the statue which, for them, represented the continuing institutional racism on campus. The statue was removed exactly a month later, with thousands of supporters observing. The student movement, initially directed at the removal of the statue and institutional racism, soon developed into more comprehensive discussions about decolonisation and white supremacy. This led to the eruption of a number of other, but related, protests on campuses throughout South Africa. In mid-October of the same year, another notable round of student-led protests, inspired by the #Rhodesmustfall movement, was initiated. These protests became known as #feesmustfall and were a response to an increase in fees at South African universities – a direct result of the significant underfunding of Higher Education institutions by the government, as well as neoliberal policies which contribute to the reproduction of inequality in society. While public opinion has been divided on the student movement, it has led to a number of significant outcomes: the removal of the Rhodes statue, as well as ongoing debates about racism, white supremacy, decolonisation, language policy, gender inequalities and so on. Importantly, there was also a suspension in university fee increases in 2016.

In September 2016, there was a resurgence of the #feesmustfall movement, though this time it was marked by violence, both from and against students. This, in turn, led to a pervasive polarisation in the academy, echoed also in the broader society. 'Whole universities are pitted against one another', writes David Everatt (2016). 'Some academics are accused of being blindly supportive of "the innocent students" and parading their colours as the immaculate left; while others are seen as blindly securocrat, unreconstructed racists, or terminally bewildered.' Facebook and other social media reflected and disseminated this diversity of opinions. The Arab Spring refrain, 'The revolution will be tweeted', is apropos, though the ugly face of racism has been equally well represented. But racism is not solely a South African problem, not solely an *African* problem. A recent article in *The Washington Post* with the heading, 'Slurs, blackface, and gorilla mask: The academic year opened with racial ugliness', reflects similar issues abroad (Svrluga, 2016). It is clear from reports and recurring student protests around the world that racism continues to be a structural problem in Higher Education institutions. This is arguably one of the main reasons for the violent outbursts of the recent #feesmustfall demonstrations. As the violence escalated, the exhortation, 'Burn to be heard', started circulating. The message was not a metaphor. 'Buildings and vehicles at several universities have been burned' (Duncan, 2016), we read, and there has been 'an arson attack on the law library of the University of Natal' (Dlamini and Shikwambane, 2016). We read also of a bus that was 'set alight by protesting Wits University students' (Ngcobo, Manyanthela and Bateman, 2016) and about fires at Rhodes University (Petersen, 2016). Jay Naidoo (2016), the founding General Secretary of Cosatu (the Congress of South African Trade Unions), describes the burning universities as a reflection of the entire country's protocol, where violence 'has *de facto* become the language of engagement'. Why is it, we have to wonder, that violence has become the only legitimate tactic for students? What does this reflect about the education system, marked by social injustices stemming from the apartheid era which historically positioned educational institutions in such a way that they privileged the white population? If the student movement has shown anything, it is that many of these discrepancies continue to exist, even though South Africa is now a democracy. And, despite the fact that there are many disparate opinions about the recent #feesmustfall movement and the violent strategies employed, there are a number of aspects pertaining to Higher Education that we can agree on, as Everatt (2016) states in his article. First, universities are severely underfunded and the resulting fee increases have primarily burdened African and coloured (mixed-race) students. Second, many students experience universities as disaffecting, Eurocentric spaces. Third, decolonisation is a daunting task with which 'virtually no university or further education college has genuinely grappled' and, finally, the commodification of knowledge and application of neoliberal principles and practices have rendered universities and colleges uniform, capitalist enterprises, marked by structural violence, binary organisation and the bottom line.

In France, the events now known as 'May '68', greatly influenced the collaborative philosophy of Gilles Deleuze and Félix Guattari so that they became increasingly sensitive to the political dimension of socio-cultural stratification and the effects and affects these produce. (It should be noted, however, that they were already politicised before the civil unrest of May '68. I am merely pointing towards the parallels between what they experienced during that time and the recent demonstrations in South Africa.) Accordingly, their philosophy offers a particularly apt lens for considering the recent South African student protests, collectively known as the Fallist Movement. In particular, I explore the student movement in terms of what Deleuze and Guattari term *faciality* – an ascription process which sets the trajectory conditions for people and which also affects the education system (so that pedagogy can be said to be facialised). The notion of faciality is expounded in the seventh chapter of *A Thousand Plateaus* (1987) in which Deleuze and Guattari explain how the face is located at the intersection between signifiance and subjectification. In other words, faciality describes the processes by which the face – and specifically the white, male, cisgender, ablest face – is imposed on all peoples universally, thus overcoding identities and over-determining ensuing subjectivities. Facialisation, however, 'is not necessarily about actual faces'; rather it is 'about the appropriation of expression by the signifying regime' (Beckman, 2013, p.157). Facialisation can thus be said to affect both subjectivity in Higher Education through racism, as well as education itself, in terms of the European modernism and binary humanist thought that continue to pervade curricula. Here, in particular, we see how contributions from new materialist and posthumanist praxis can be employed to combat facialisation. As Simone Bignall, Steve Hemming and Daryle Rigney (2016, p. 456) argue:

> Influenced strongly by Nietzschean antihumanism, and inspired in no small measure by the work of Deleuze and Guattari, the emerging paradigm of 'posthumanism' is [an effort] by contemporary Continental philosophers to challenge the conceptual foundations upon which modern Western philosophy rests.

In a similar vein, Victoria Pitts-Taylor (2016, p. 1) argues that 'Attention to matter, and mattering – matter's ongoing processes of self-generation – is transforming feminist thought'. This, she argues, is the result of dualisms being challenged in scientific thought, the attendance to power structures and the recognition that these are material-discursive, and a continuing inclusion of the body in feminist praxis. New materialists are thus 'interested in exposing the movement, vitality, morphogenesis, and becoming of the material world, [and] its dynamic processes' instead of the 'discovery of immutable truths' (Pitts-Taylor, 2016, p. 4), all of which are directly related to the Deleuze-Guattarian process framework. With this in mind, and as a tactic against faciality, I want to think here about becoming; the rupturing capacities of becoming, the materiality of becoming, and the disidentification processes of probe-heads as corporeal, posthuman praxes *par excellence* for confronting the effects and affects of faciality, particularly in our education system. Finally, I consider what we might learn from the Fallist Movement towards effectuating socially just pedagogies in South African Higher Education and what it might look like in the classroom by referring to my own Gender Theory course.

Black Skin, White Masks, a.k.a. The White Wall/Black Hole System

At the intersection of two very different semiotic systems, namely signifiance (the relations and effects/affects of signs, discursive practices and interpretation) and subjectification (forms of subjectivity), Deleuze and Guattari (1987, p. 167) tell us that we will find 'a very special mechanism' – the face. The face, they go on to argue, can be thought of as the *white wall/black hole* system. It is a system because it functions to overcode or conform symbolic codes, norms and values according to a centralised structure of social production and meaning-making, but it 'cannot be assumed to come ready-made' (Deleuze and Guattari, 1987, p. 168). *How does it work?* Distil the face. Think of a mask, Matisse's masks, for example. There he stands, in front of it: the blank canvas, the white wall. Now mark on this white wall the holes of the eyes. Mark the holes of the nose and the mouth. Mark them in black. (Do you see the face taking shape?) Black holes on a white wall. *It cannot be assumed to come ready-made.* And it cannot be just any face. A very specific face is required; one that will be defined by resonance and redundancy; one that defines a signifier– constructs it – on the white wall so that all ensuing signifiers bounce off it, reinforcing its dominant reality, its molar aggregates, by rejecting all that is *other than this*. Resonance and redundancy. 'Newspapers, news, proceed by redundancy, in that they tell us what we "must" think, retain, expect, etc.' (Deleuze and Guattari 1987, p. 79). In the same way, this one face – the Christ face – tells us what we must think, retain, expect. In other words, the distilled Christ face can be said to be redundant because it has been repeated and spread through the entire social field and thus has no original referent anymore (that is, the referent is not Christ, but the replicated Christ, the Christ face or white wall/black hole system). Deleuze and Guattari (1987, p. 178) write:

> If the face is in fact Christ, in other words, your average ordinary White Man, then the first deviances, the first divergence-types, are racial: yellow man, black man, men in the second or third category. They are also inscribed on the wall, distributed by the hole. They must be Christianised, in other words, facialised.

There he sits, the Christ. You know his face so well. A close-up, innocent and pure, 'as in a Byzantine mosaic, with the black hole of the eyes against a gold background, all depth projected forward' (Deleuze and Guattari 1987, pp. 184–185). There he sits, Cecil John Rhodes, 'the thinker' – the European white man, the image of European thought structures – fashioned in the image of Christ. Like the Christ-face, he is positioned to enact two hierarchising operations: 'signifying biunivocalisation and subjective binarisation' (Deleuze and Guattari 1987, p. 180). Biunivocalisation, Deleuze and Guattari tell us, functions to divide societies, nations, cultures, genders and so on, into mutually opposed groupings: this *or* that, x *or* y, man *or* woman, heterosexual *or* homosexual, capitalist *or* communist, black *or* white, human *or* nonhuman (Deleuze and Guattari 1987, p. 177). The second hierarchising operation, namely binarisation, then functions to set a standard between these mutually exclusive groups so that one group is always measured against the other. X *is better than* Y; man *is superior to* woman; human *is above* nonhuman, lecturer *surpasses* student, and so on. Deleuze and Guattari refer to this as a 'yes-no' relation: yes you measure up, no you do not. 'At every moment, the [faciality] machine rejects the faces that do not conform or seem suspicious' (Deleuze and Guattari 1987, p. 177). What degree of deviance has occurred in relation to the average White-Man, Christ-face?

For faciality to take place, the face has to become separated from the body. So while the head is part of the body, coded by the body, the face is not and so ceases to be materially coded. Instead, the face becomes part of an abstracted, surface semiotic system – what Deleuze and Guattari (1987, p. 170) call the surface-holes, holey surface system. That is, the face becomes overcoded by the grammar of the

Face, or signifiance and subjectification, though the face is not reducible to these. Instead, it is 'subjacent to them and provides the substance necessary to them' (Deleuze and Guattari 1987, p. 180). Again, *it does not come ready-made.* It is produced by an abstract machine of faciality 'which produces them at the same time as it gives the signifier its white wall and subjectivity its black hole' (Deleuze and Guattari 1987, p. 168). Abstract machines 'operate within concrete assemblages' (Deleuze and Guattari 1987, p. 510), but are abstract because they do not consist of 'forms and substances' (Deleuze and Guattari 1987, p. 511). Rather, their functions are diagrammatic (negative or positive) so that they can be said to map out the field of subjective experience and possibility. In other words, abstract machines regulate the relations in and between machinic assemblages and cause different centres to resonate (Deleuze and Guattari 1987, p. 68; p. 223). This is important because subjectification, that is, forms of subjectivity, needs a node of resonance in order for binarisation and biunivocalisation to take place. Here is Christ, here is Rhodes, notice their similarities, notice the way in which they resonate. What degree of deviance do *you* exhibit?

Structural racism – faciality – has not, as the #Rhodesmustfall and #feesmustfall movements have clearly shown, been eradicated in any meaningful way from our education system. As local activist Pakama Ngceni (2015) writes, 'Racism in this country determines who has a voice, and who is otherwise constructed as the "angry black rabble".' The calm, pure Christ-face, the rational, erudite Rhodes, the angry black rabble. The standard and the judgement, binarisation and biunivocalisation, signifiance and subjectification, the white wall and black hole of faciality. '*The question then becomes what circumstances trigger the machine* that produces the face and facialisation?' (Deleuze and Guattari 1987, p. 170). And how can we combat facialisation, specifically in our education system, to instead effectuate socially just pedagogies? There are a number of aspects which need to be addressed here. The first is that there is 'more to the picture than semiotic systems' (Deleuze and Guattari 1987, p. 180). That is, besides semiotic systems, we also need to take into account assemblages of power which impose and uphold signifiance and subjectification. These systems include, for example, racism, colonialism (or at least the legacies of colonialism and Apartheid in South Africa), late capitalism, the State, the educational system, religious institutions, and so on. So how do these systems work, or, how are bodies 'materially differentiated into hierarchies in the first place' (Saldanha 2013, p. 7), and what effects and affects do they produce?

Here Deleuze and Guattari's 'nomadological and biophilosophical geology of morals can demonstrate that race is built upon fully contingent territorialisations of power and desire which could be disassembled and differently reassembled' (Saldanha 2013, p. 8). But while contingent, phenotypical differences – expressed especially through racism and xenophobia – now form necessary tendencies for the functioning of capitalism. It is, therefore, not necessarily in the interest of the government to grant free education to all South African citizens, as #feesmustfall demanded, because much of the country's economy, for example the mine industry, in fact relies on an unskilled and low-skill workforce. Consequently, besides taking account of semiotic systems and assemblages of power, we may need to concede that the education system, in its current form at least, needs facialisation, depends on it in fact. Curricula, too, continues to perpetuate a facialised pedagogy through colonial legacies of learning and ideas around, for example, knowledge production. As Jason J. Wallin (2015, p. 141) argues, for 'education to become adequate to posthuman thought necessitates its investment in the destruction of the face', opening itself to what Patricia MacCormack (2013, p. 13) terms a 'pedagogical grace', which is the unthinking of man simultaneous with the leaving be of the nonhuman – teaching ways to unthink the self in order to open up the thought of the world'.

When we look at recent news headlines and current curricula, we notice that this is not as yet the case. Not for the most part, at any rate. But something more is going on, because besides the obvious racial facialisation in Higher Education and the persistent inclusion of European humanism in syllabi, it was furthermore reported that #feesmustfall leaders at Wits University were 'being targeted by police' and placed 'under constant surveillance' (Whittles 2016a). Now faciality takes on another dimension – a very contemporary dimension – 'an ever-swelling grid of choices organised biunivocally' (Saldanha 2013, p. 18). We may think here also, for example, of border control and the racialised migrant problem facing Europe and the US, as well as how recognition software and social media are used for racial (and other) profiling, especially since 9/11. Facialisation is thus directly related to the biopolitics of disposability. As Deleuze and Guattari (1987, p. 177) write, 'You don't so much have a face as slide into one'.

Judith Butler (2009) approaches the biopolitics of disposability from a different angle when she asks: when is life grievable? She argues that there is an implicit understanding that life is grievable not only when a life has been led – that is, at the end of a life – but, also, according to the future anterior which supposes grievability at the beginning of a life. She writes: 'Without grievability, there is no life, or, rather, there is something living that is other than life. [. . .] The apprehension of grievability precedes and makes possible the apprehension of precarious life' (Butler 2009, p. 15). One of the effects of faciality, I would argue, is that some lives become more grievable and, in consequence, less disposable than others. According to the binary logic and biunivocal organisation of faciality, other lives are thus less grievable and more disposable. Here again the student protests are a case in point. We read, for example, of a student from the Tshwane University of Technology (TUT) who was reportedly shot with live ammunition in the leg (Magwedze 2016). At the University of the Witwaterand, Busiswe Seabe was also reported to have been shot, while a fellow student leader, Shaeera Kalla, was shot at least nine times at close range in the back, 'allegedly when her hands were raised' (Whittles 2016b). None of these students were white. Gamedze, in conversation with his brother GamEdze, writes: 'No matter the style of protest, whether music, art intervention, blockading, shit-pouring, or political education, the violence that meets black protestors is always the same – a hyper-masculine, physical brutality whose focus meets the viscerality of bodies with undue force' (GamEdze and Gamedze 2016). Bodies fully facialised, we notice here that all the features of biopower are in place too: 'property, sovereignty, division of labour, readiness for war, even multiculturalism' (Saldanha 2013, p. 21). Devalued, diminished, ungrievable lives. Similarly, in education, the dualist notions of man/woman, teacher/student, human/ nonhuman, and so on, continue to facialise pedagogical praxis. Is it possible, then, to dismantle faciality? Deleuze and Guattari would have it so, but with proviso. They write (Deleuze and Guattari 1987, p. 188):

> If the face is a politics, dismantling the face is also a politics involving real becomings, an entire becoming-clandestine. Dismantling the face is the same as breaking through the wall of the signifier and getting out of the black hole of subjectivity.

Probe-Heads, Disidentification and Defacialisation

If 'human beings have a destiny', write Deleuze and Guattari, (1987, p. 171) it is 'to escape the face, to dismantle the face and facialisations, to become imperceptible, to become clandestine ...' But faciality does not affect only the face and the body; it performs facialisation on all its surroundings too, as well as on objects, such as clothes (think of 'ethnic' clothing, for example, and the exoticism – orientalism we might even say – it gestures). Subjectivity, then, is not only about subjects, significance and subjectification, but also about milieus and landscapification (that is, the facialisation of milieus, like educational milieus). It is in this way, then, that we accumulate our symbols and weave our myths into the fabric of the universe. So begins the despotic, paranoiac regime of signifiance and the totalitarian regime of subjectification. So the 'trajectory merges', writes Deleuze (1997, p. 61), 'not only with the subjectivity of those who travel through a milieu, but also with the subjectivity of the milieu itself, insofar as it is reflected in those who travel through it'. How are we to rupture these regimes of signs and assemblages of power? Here Deleuze and Guattari propose that facialisation and landscapification be deterritorialised, put to flight, so that faces are exchanged for probe-heads (Deleuze and Guattari 1987 p. 190; p. 191; p. 301). We have seen many probe-heads during the protests of the past two years: new modes of organisation, new modes of thinking and calls for a decolonised pedagogy. I am reminded, in particular, of Shackville, a 'corrugated iron and wood protest structure which was erected on UCT's upper campus' (Africa News Agency 2016) to resemble the makeshift housing (or shacks) found in predominantly black neighbourhoods, such as Khayelitsha, Gugulethu and Soweto, and to protest the lack of accommodation close to or on campuses for black students. I remember, also, when the UCT Trans Collective disrupted the Rhodes Must Fall exhibition to protest the fact that, of the 1,000 plus images shown, only three featured trans people (see, for example, Hendricks, 2016). With their semi-naked and naked bodies painted with red paint, members of the collective lay down on the floor and blocked the entrances to the gallery. This return to the materiality of the body – the naked body, the animality of the body – at once deterritorialises the semiotisation of the face. In this sense, defacialisation can be seen as distinctly posthuman in that it situates the human in such a way that the concept *human* 'denotes a very particular (and historically specific) set of capacities, attitudes and knowledges' (O'Sullivan 2006, p. 309). Simultaneously, defacialisation can be seen as new materialist in that it pays attention to matter and mattering, as well as feminist, in that it requires the return to an ethics of care which is 'attentive to, and responsive/responsible to, the specificity of material entanglements in their agential becoming' (Barad 2007, p. 91).

But what is a probe-head? Simon O'Sullivan (2006, pp. 312–13) argues that 'this is an open question' to a large extent, and that it depends 'on the specifics of time and place, on the particular materials at hand – and on the concrete practices of individuals'. However, although probe-heads remain essentially undefined, I want to argue here that we can recognise them by certain characteristics and that these characteristics respond directly to Deleuze and Guattari's (1987, p. 22) social ontology, consisting of collective assemblages of enunciation (or discursive and symbolic orders and practices) and machinic assemblages of desire (or flows, bodies and processes, as well as their structurations and affects). In other words, I am arguing that, according to this ontology, probe-heads can be identified, first, by the fact that they are assemblages of collective enunciation and thus social, rather than personal or Oedipalised. At the same time, probe-heads are immanently political; we are reminded that Deleuze and Guattari (1987, p. 203) tell us that 'politics precedes being' and that dismantling the face is 'a politics involving real becomings' (Deleuze and Guattari 1987, p. 188). In other words, probe-heads deterritorialise the existing field of subjective possibilities and, through the material practice of mapping, diagram new potentialities, thus modifying the abstract machine of faciality. This process is marked by asignification and a disidentification with Oedipal apparatuses; that is, a rupturing of identity and representation. We could also say that it ruptures and deterritorialises existing machinic assemblages of desire so that desire no longer desires its own repression. In Deleuze and Guattari's (1987, p. 215) words:

> Desire is never separable from complex assemblages that necessarily tie into molecular levels, from microformations already shaping postures, attitudes, perceptions, expectations, semiotic systems, etc. Desire is never an undifferentiated instinctual energy, but itself results from a highly developed, engineered setup rich in interactions: a whole supple segmentarity that processes molecular energies and potentially gives desire a fascist determination.

Guattari (1995, p. 21) states this beautifully when he says that: 'The only acceptable finality of human activity is the production of a subjectivity that is auto-enriching its relation to the world in a continuous fashion.' As Gamedze (GamEdze and Gamedze, 2016) goes on to write:

> In this movement toward a different university, we need to start asking: in the future and in the present, where might this different university be located both geographically and intellectually? [...] So as we continue to shut down the university, let us continue to question and imagine beyond it and also remember that our fight is not merely for it [the university] but for a radically different society and a fundamentally different type of education.

This, then, is the crux for me: that socially just pedagogies in South Africa should not only seek to retrospectively address the social injustices stemming from Apartheid and the legacy of colonialism – a movement reaching towards history – but that it should, also, be reaching forward – into the future – calling forth 'a people to come'. But what does a pedagogy for a people to come look like? And why *a people to come*?

Effectuating Socially Just Pedagogies, or, Pedagogy for a People to Come

Deleuze and Guattari talk about a people to come in a number of their works, both collectively and individually. I want to highlight here a number of aspects I deem important for pedagogy and, specifically, for thinking about socially just pedagogies in Higher Education in South Africa, post #Rhodesmustfall and #feesmustfall.

In *Cinema II*, Deleuze (1989, p. 221) writes that 'because the people are missing, the author is in a situation of producing utterances which are already collective, which are like the seeds of the people to come, and whose political impact is immediate and inescapable'. We find here two aspects that I have already addressed: collective enunciation and politics. Accordingly, in thinking about a pedagogy for a people to come, it is imperative, I would argue, that we think about education as immediately politicised or radicalised. Posthumanism and new materialism have done much in terms of politicising ontology; that is, by questioning the primacy of human subjectivity and conceiving of agency in ways that is not solely 'tied to human action', thereby 'shifting the focus for social inquiry from an approach predicated upon humans and their bodies' to methods which examine, instead, 'relational networks or assemblages' (Fox and Alldred 2015, p. 399). However, while ontologies have been troubled, the ontological positionings of students and lecturers have remained largely unchanged in South African Higher Education, with teaching and learning viewed as 'the passing of knowledge, cognitive and static, a product, from one individual or group to another, via the medium of language or text' (Leibowitz 2016, p. 226). Typically, this passing is also seen and treated as moving from those with more authority to those with less.

One way of dealing with this in class, as I do in my Gender Theory module, is to include what Donna Haraway (1988) refers to as 'situated knowledges' so that each assignment is viewed as an attempt aimed at collaborative learning, knowledge production and experimentation. Instead of only asking students to answer questions on gender theory (which includes both African and 'Western' theorists), they are also asked to talk about their personal experiences of gender. For example, they are asked to think about how they feel about their own gender (affective responses); what internal and external pressures they perceive and how these inform their actions and emotions; how their gender is related to cultural and social norms and the tensions between these (or not); and so on. In this way, the personal stories (situated knowledges) of the students are viewed as knowledge production and their positioning as students with less authority than lecturers is challenged. As Donna Haraway (1988, pp. 586–7) states: 'The knowing self is partial in all its guises, never finished, whole, simply there and original; it is always constructed and stitched together imperfectly, and therefore able to join with another, to see together without claiming to be another'. In another postgraduate module in which students have to produce a research report, they are asked to do a desktop study on gender and body modification. This cultural-theoretical-material assemblage not only allows for an investigation into pertinent gender discussions, but also explores the ways in which culturally specific understandings are materially transformed, allowing for the defacialisation of specific subjectivities and knowledge. This defacialisation of education and subjectitivies, in turn, institutes a pedagogy for a people to come which itself *is* a socially just pedagogical praxis. That is, by challenging existing ways of knowing and the power attached to certain forms of knowledge through collective knowledge production, we can disrupt faciality and effectuate socially just pedagogies. It is, in short, a foregrounding of the intensive and affective, or asignifying; hence, a passing 'into sensation' (Deleuze and Guattari 1994, p. 176) so that binaries, such as subject/object, material/discursive, human/nonhuman, are dissolved and focus is placed on processuality rather than discreet events, facialised subjects, and landscapified milieus. It is a politics exterior to thought, 'the force that is always external to itself, or the final force, the *n*th power'. It is a force 'for which there is no possible method, no conceivable reproduction, but only relays, intermezzos, resurgences' (Deleuze and Guattari 1987, p. 377). It is apersonal, presubjective, precognitive, preverbal and, therefore, asignfying, and can be said to constitute those determinations of forces which allow for a mapping of that which is missing, that which is yet to come. Defacialisation, as a posthuman, new materialist, feminist praxis, thus allows for experimentation – 'a field of continuous intensities' (Deleuze and Guattari 1987, p. 134) – that which disrupts the formalised structure of education aimed at forging Oedipalised and fully facialised individuals. This is our destiny: to escape the face, to dismantle the face and facialisations, to imagine and enact a radically different, auto-enriching, hitherto unthought pedagogy, to call forth a people yet to come.

Conclusion

In this chapter I surveyed the current South African Higher Education landscape, looking in particular at the recent Fallist Movement and what it has brought to light about education fees, neoliberal policies, and the legacies of Apartheid and colonialism. I examined the structural violence of racism with reference to Deleuze and Guattari's notion of *faciality*, arguing for probe-heads as a material and posthuman practice – one which can map or diagram new subjective potentialities; the enacting of #itmustallfall. To effectuate socially just pedagogies in South African Higher Education, I highlighted four characteristics of probe-heads, namely defacialisation, becoming-molecular, the foregrounding of the intensive and affective, and exteriority. Finally, I suggested that in seeking to address the social injustices of the past, we also reach forward, into the future, so as to provoke a pedagogy for a people yet to come.

References

Africa News Agency (2016), '"Shackville" Erected at UCT to Protest Lack of Housing for Black Students', *eNCA*, 15 February. Available online: http://www.enca.com/south-africa/shackville-erected-uct-protest-lack-housing-black-students (accessed 3 November 2016).

Beckman, F. (2013), *Between Desire and Pleasure: A Deleuzian Theory of Sexuality*, Edinburgh: Edinburgh University Press.

Bignall S., Hemming, S, and Rigney D. (2016), 'Three Ecosophies for the Anthropocene: Environmental Governance, Continental Posthumanism and Indigenous Expressivism', *Deleuze Studies* 10(4): 455–478.

Butler, J. (2009), *Frames of War: When is Life Grievable?*, London, New York: Verso.

Deleuze, G. (1988), *Foucault*, trans. S. Hand, Minneapolis: University of Minnesota Press.

Deleuze, G. (1989), *Cinema II: The Time Image*, trans. H. Tomlinson and R. Galeta, Minneapolis: University of Minnesota Press.

Deleuze, G. (1997), 'What Children Say', in *Essays Critical and Clinical*, trans. D. W. Smith and M. A. Greco, 61–67, Minneapolis: University of Minnesota Press.

Deleuze, G. and Guattari. F. (1987), *A Thousand Plateaus*, trans. B. Massumi, London, Minneapolis: University of Minnesota Press.

Deleuze, G. and Guattari. F. (1994), *What is Philosophy?*, trans. H. Tomlinson and G. Burchell, New York: Columbia University Press.

Dlamini, K. and Shikwambane, N. L. (2016), 'Opinion is Still Split on the Library Fire at UKZN', *The Daily Vox*, 9 September. Available online: https://www.thedailyvox.co.za/opinion-still-split-library-fire-ukzn/ (accessed 18 October 2016).

Duncan, J. (2016), 'Why Student Protests in South Africa Have Turned Violent', *The Conversation*, 29 September. Available online: https://theconversation.com/why-student-protests-in-south-africa-have-turned-violent–66288 (accessed 22 October 2016).

Everatt, D. (2016), 'What must fall: Fees or the South African State?', *The Conversation*, 20 October. Available online: https://theconversation.com/what-must-fall-fees-or-the-south-african-state-67389 (accessed 22 October 2016).

Evron, B. (1982), 'Les interprétations de l'Holocaust: Un danger pour le peuple juif', *Revue d'Etudes Palestiniennes* 2: 36–52.

Fox, N. J. and P. Alldred (2015), 'New Materialist Social Inquiry: Designs, Methods, and the Research-Assemblage', *International Journal of Social Research Methodology* 18(4): 399–414.

GamEdze and Gamedze. (2016), 'Concerning the Politics and Approaches to Shutdowns', *The Daily Vox*, 28 October. Available online: http://www.thedailyvox.co.za/concerning-politics-approaches-shutdowns/ (accessed 5 November 2016).

Guattari, F. (1995), *Chaosmosis: An Ethico-Aesthetic Paradigm*, trans. P. Bains and J. Pefanis, Bloomington, Indianapolis: Indiana University Press.

Haraway, D. (1988), 'Situated Knowledges: The Science Question in Feminism and the Privilege of Partial Perspective', *Feminist Studies* 14(3): 575–599.

Hendriks, A. (2016), 'Rhodes Must Fall Exhibition Vandalised in UCT Protest', *GroundUp*, 10 March. Available online: http://www.groundup.org.za/article/rhodes-must-fall-exhibition-vandalised-uct-protest/ (accessed 1 August 2016).

Herman, P. (2016), 'Don't destroy your futures, Max Price tells protesting students', *News24*, 28 September. Available online: http://www.news24.com/SouthAfrica/News/dont-destroy-your-futures-max-price-tells-protesting-students-20160928 (accessed 2 November 2016).

Leibowitz, B. (2016), 'In Pursuit of Socially Just Pedagogies in Differently Positioned South African Higher Education Institutions', *South African Journal of Higher Education* 30(3): 219–234.

MacCormack, P. (2013), 'Gracious Pedagogy', *Journal of Curriculum and Pedagogy* 10(1): 13–17.

Magwedze, V. (2016), '[Update] TUT Student Shot in Leg', *Eyewitness News*, 13 October. Available online: http://ewn.co.za/2016/10/13/TUT-students-shot-with-live-ammunition (accessed 2 November 2016).

Naidoo, J. (2016), 'Guilty as Charged: Burning Universities are a Mirror of Our Country", *Daily Maverick*, 18 October. Available online: http://www.dailymaverick.co.za/opinionista/2016-10-09-guilty-as-charged-burning-universities-are-a-mirror-of-our-country/#.WBMpOOB94_4 (accessed 18 October 2016).

Ngceni, P. (2015), 'What #Feesmustfall Teaches Us About Racism', *Vanguard*, 5 November. Available online: http://vanguardmagazine.co.za/what-feesmustfall-teaches-us-about-racism/ (accessed 1 November 2016).

Ngcobo, Z, Manyanthela, C. and Bateman, B. (2016), '#Feesmustfall Protests Turn Violent, Bus Set Alight in JHB CBD', *Eyewitness News*, 10 October. Available online: http://ewn.co.za/2016/10/10/Bus-set-alight-during-Wits-protests (accessed 1 November 2016).

O'Sullivan, S. (2006), 'Pragmatics for the Production of Subjectivity: Time for *Probe-Head*', *Journal for Cultural Research* 10(4): 309–322.

Petersen, T. (2016), '3 Buildings Torched at Rhodes University', *News24*, 26 October. Available online: http://www.news24.com/SouthAfrica/News/3-buildings-torched-at-rhodes-university-20161026 (accessed 1 November 2016).

Pitts-Taylor, V. (2016), *Mattering: Feminism, Science and Materialism*, New York, London: New York University Press.

Saldanha, A. (2013), 'Bastard and Mixed-Blood are the True Names of Race', in A. Saldanha and J. M. Adams, (eds), *Deleuze and Race*, 6–34, Edinburgh: Edinburgh University Press.

Svrluga, S. (2016), 'Slurs, Blackface, and Gorilla Mask: The Academic Year Opened With Racial Ugliness', *The Washington Post*, 7 October. Available online: https://www.washingtonpost.com/news/grade-point/wp/2016/10/07/slurs-blackface-and-gorilla-masks-the-academic-year-opened-with-racial-ugliness/ (accessed 20 October 2016).

Wallin, J. J. (2015), 'The End of the Anthropocene', in N. Snaza and J. Weaver, (eds), *Posthumanism and Educational Research*, 134–147, London, New York: Routledge.

Whittles, G. (2016a), 'Police Hunt Down Student Leaders', *Mail & Guardian*, 14 October. Available online: http://mg.co.za/article/2016-10-14-00-police-hunt-down-student-leaders (accessed 2 November 2016).

Whittles, G. (2016b), 'Student Leader Shot in the Back Thirteen Times', *Mail & Guardian*, 21 October. Available online: http://mg.co.za/article/2016-10-21-00-student-leader-shot-in-the-back-13-times (accessed 2 November 2016).

2

Feminism and Feminist Studies in Neoliberal Times: Furthering Social Justice in Higher Education Curricula[1]

Rosemarie Buikema and Kathrin Thiele

Due to the increasing prevalence of contemporary economic and ethnocentric narratives, a major concern of twenty-first-century feminist activism and pedagogies is that achievements of the movement for liberation are in danger of becoming disconnected from their initial manifestations of equality for all – understood as transnational solidarity. Instead, the outcome of different feminist waves – at least in a Western European and American context – often seems to serve neoliberal capitalism and the concomitant individualisation and ethnocentrism of the process of emancipation and social participation. As Nancy Fraser (2013) suggested in a timely summary in *The Guardian*, this risk of empowerment becoming the handmaiden of global neoliberal capitalism might even have been implicated in the movement from the very start. Western feminist goals and strategies in the end seem to have been ambivalent and thus susceptible to two different elaborations: An initial, deeply political, commitment to participatory democracy and social justice, which in turn leads to results simultaneously serving the neoliberal ethnocentric vocabulary of autonomy, choice, and meritocratic advancement. Thus, contrary to the feminist de- and postcolonial projects that situate subjectivity as submitted to patriarchal, racist, and capitalist structures (hooks 2013), current neoliberal articulations of feminism serve the status quo rather than question it.

In this chapter we aim to elaborate upon and contextualise this problem by focusing on feminist studies and its task of furthering social justice discourses in higher education today. However, rather than discussing feminist pedagogies *per se*, we intend to foreground the terrain upon which such pedagogies can further build. A primary goal of our contribution is, therefore, to open the discussion on the ambivalence of (Western) feminist achievements towards the following question:

How, within the university as a public institution and the institutionalised spaces of Gender Studies, can we counter-act these current trends and thereby once more enable different futures for social justice in which transnational solidarity can emerge? By also approaching the issue from a feminist (new) materialist/critical posthuman(ist) perspective, in the second part of the chapter we especially attend to the question of how curricular spaces of feminist knowledge production and queer/feminist theorising can be envisioned as always/already *practical* engagements with the world.[2] They are – to use Karen Barad's terminology – ethico-onto-epistemological endeavors, in which matters of consequentiality, ac/countability, solidarity and response-ability do not come second – i.e. only after the fact. Rather, as she suggests, 'knowing *is* a material practice of engagement as part of the world in its differential becoming' (Barad 2007: 83). To counter the current output- and impact-driven neoliberalised academic climate in universities in so many places on the globe, we stress the sociopolitical significance of what it means 'to think today', and from there also what it means for us in our feminist curricula to teach critical thinking as a *worlding practice* (Thiele 2015). We argue for the potential of feminist (as queer/de-/postcolonial/critical race) studies to continually allow for such speculative practical curricular spaces in which the powers of our imagination to envision 'another world' – 'to imagine otherwise' – become trained and practiced in view of greater sustainability, solidarity, and social justice (Buikema 2017).

Looking Back into the Future: Feminism and Neoliberalism

First and second wave Western European and US feminists struggled to realise full access to citizenship and the creation of a participatory democracy that ensured social solidarity for all citizens. As a direct result of the struggles of these twentieth-century activists, twenty-first-century women in Western Europe and the US have access to higher education, the right to vote, are able to retain control over property and capital, combine motherhood and work, receive (not quite) equal wages for equal work, pay taxes, and enjoy reproductive rights and gender-specific care. However, it is also important to realise that of course the majority of these rights, accessible now for three or four generations of specifically Western women, still prove elusive in many other contexts.[3]

First of all, as exposed by all feminist activism, attaining any semblance of first class citizenship is obstructed by many more factors than legislation alone. Achieving full access to citizenship for women and then enabling those women to become an integral part of democratic systems of representation is an ongoing, complex process that requires changes to occur on many different levels simultaneously – empirical, institutional, and symbolical. Building upon first-wave gains in access to the public sphere, so-called second-wave feminists (i.e. radical feminists and/or feminisms of difference) made the symbolic dimensions of the phallocratic and racialised order into one of their explicit *political* goals, raising awareness of the feminist mantra that 'the personal *is* political'. These feminists argued that personal experiences of marginalisation and unequal power balances are the result of entangled political and societal structures and thus, as also already suggested by Carby (1982) and Irigaray (1985), for as long as we do not implement structural changes we will remain prey to our own oppression and exclusion. Further to this, second-wave feminism revealed how personal experiences of marginalisation and submission were shared by women in comparable geopolitical situations and positions. Whilst tensions should of course never be overlooked, the second-wave feminist movement in all its diverse manifestations – radical, black, Marxist, equality, and difference, to name but a few – managed to maintain this central concern of specific 'situatedness' (Haraway 1988), and therefore worked for nothing less than the transformation of the societal *and/as* the symbolical order. All these strands of feminism saw the division of gendered positions as the result of a history of societal conventions and geopolitics, founded by patriarchal, racialised, and colonial systems, and supported and reproduced by sociopolitical structures: law, religion, and the class system.

Both with – and in – their manifold struggles, one could therefore argue that second wave feminist activisms managed not only to playfully perform, but also to embody, the deployment of solidarity as a gesture of both equality and difference. Further, as the process of the diverse feminist activisms in the broader social context – specifically also in its curricular and educational manifestations – illustrate, the intersection of the personal and the political can only ever be successfully realised if it also includes a thorough analysis of the multi-layered situatedness (here to be understood as *intra-active* constellation in the Baradian sense [Barad 2007]) of empirical and symbolic dimensions. Or, as also already explained by Gayatri Spivak in her agenda-setting article *Can the Subaltern Speak?*: it is in a complex material-discursive approach that global feminisms meet – be it by means of rebellious humor, political radicalism, onto-theoretical analysis, or the struggle for further emancipatory measures (1988: 280).

Popular contemporary discussions on the societal effects of the different feminist waves – especially in a Western context – invariably involve key indicators of societal changes either as visible achievements or as measurements of an emancipation or equality reached. Commonly, debates in the public arena focus on questions such as: What is the proportion of women in full-time employment? What are career opportunities for leading positions? Where is the glass ceiling in Western European society? What childcare facilities are available, and what are the continuing pay differences between men and women? These questions illustrate that the emphasis on economic differences and an empowerment of the individual in some contexts, results in reductive identity politics; an identity politics that obscures both persisting inequalities in the distribution of politico-economic infrastructures and the shared experiences of oppression that could potentially lead to the strengthening of a more inclusive feminist solidarity.[4]

As we have already argued supporting Nancy Fraser, the outcome of successful feminist and queer challenges to the normative order run the risk of serving neoliberal capitalism and ethnocentric nationalisms far too well (see also Scott, 2011). The dual feminist enterprises of analysing uneven societal structures, and strengthening transnational solidarity might therefore become seriously under-theorised in today's mainstreaming of feminist 'achievements'. As such, the feminist movement in its current formation risks being instrumental in creating what it initially aimed to dismantle: inequality and social injustice. Or, as Wendy Brown has recently argued: feminism itself now seriously risks the gradual replacement of the *homo politicus* with the *homo oeconomicus* (2013; 2015). It is here that feminist pedagogies and the necessity of curricular awareness in higher education have a major role to play, and the critical question for feminism in neoliberal times (especially in higher education, in which Gender Studies as a discipline has fully 'arrived') becomes also very much directed at feminists and/or queer teachers and/as activists themselves. In view of this politically intricate situation, the question for us as critical thinkers must become the following: How can feminist studies mitigate the risks of women's and 'other other's' recognition and empowerment simply becoming the handmaidens of a global neoliberal capitalism and neoliberalised educational practices? Or, to formulate it with Virginia Woolf's *Three Guineas*: '[W]e have to ask ourselves, here and now, do we wish to join that procession, or don't we? On what terms shall we join that procession? Above all, where is it leading us, the procession of educated men?' (1966: 62).

Returning to the Matter of Thinking as Mattering for Social Justice

After setting the stage in these broad terms, we now zoom in on what we see as the task for those practicing feminist pedagogies in the university today, in order to distinguish more clearly between a neoliberal feminism – one focused mainly on economic gains (and thereby following the white, bourgeois, Western concept of the subject) – and the rich and diverse strands of a liberating, i.e. critical feminism that is still alive in these neoliberal times. In the spirit of a recent public intervention by the Dutch cultural theorist Mieke Bal (2015) – a publication based on a lecture she held in the context of the 2015 student occupation of the University of Amsterdam, entitled 'Power to the Imagination!' – we first of all claim that higher education is still one of the most important public spheres in contemporary societies in which such counter-action could (again) find a beginning. Yet, for such actions to happen the higher education curricula need to return themselves more thoroughly to one of their classical core businesses: the *matter of thinking as the power to imagine*. Thinking, as a practice to be trained in, is not to be misunderstood as the positivist scientific definition of merely finding the correct definition of, or answer to, the issues and the questions at stake. Rather, what we want to stress by making thinking a matter of explicit curricular and pedagogical concern, is that thinking has to be approached as an event – that is, a transformative encounter with something that makes us think. It is to be practiced in the specific sense of an affirmative critical thinking; as something that does not just happen by itself or that 'we' as humans simply have a natural capacity for.[5] Instead, thinking has to be emphasised as a *complex action*, in the way in which also hooks writes in *Teaching Critical Thinking*: 'Thinking is an action. For all aspiring intellectuals, thoughts are the laboratory where one goes to pose questions and find answers, and the place where visions of theory and praxis come together' (2010: 7). Thus, countering the often-repeated reductive image that thinking means abstract reflection of, and therefore withdrawal from, praxis as 'real' reality, affirmative critical thinking as a feminist/queer and de-/postcolonial practice is always already an active engagement with the world. In this sense, it is an action that provides a place in which theory and praxis (can) come together. When acknowledging such an active approach to thinking – and in the following subsection we will explicate such entangled practice of thinking in detail – it can also be claimed that no practice can actually do without theory or theorisation, in as much as no thinking could be without intra-acting with/in material practices.

To help undo the current neoliberal political culture that is based on the hegemony of economic efficiency and a renewed – and heightened – ethnocentrism, we suggest that such a complex manner of thinking is required to better understand what thinking *is* beyond its dominating discourses structured by the dualist tradition of Western Cartesianism, that is the heritage of 'imperialist white supremacist capitalist patriarchy' (hooks 2013: 4). It is here that we also see contemporary critical posthuman(ist) and feminist (new) materialist interventions – as critical approaches to pedagogy in higher education curricula – as very fruitful endeavors. At their heart, and in the entangled constellation of ethico-onto-epistemology, both critical posthuman(ist) and feminist (new) materialist approaches deconstruct the foundational dichotomous and/or dualistic simplicities that far too often still serve as 'initial conditions' (Kirby 2012) within dominant thought traditions, and therefore also still haunt feminist critical scholarship. The present moment – the year 2017 – gives very clear signs that emergent feminist discussions *yet again* need to influence a way of understanding and envisioning the world we live (in). It is important that we as feminist scholars and pedagogues dare to contest the 'lazy patterns of thought' (Bal 2015: 68) that we are offered by both the political powers and the increasingly powerful administrators in our very own work and teaching environments. As Bal states in her lecture given in support of the student protests in Amsterdam: 'When culture is diminished or disappears, put under threat by binary thought, we all know what happens, because it is happening today. Such destruction is not only culturally, but also economically a terrible and irreversible waste' (2015: 71).

In order to illustrate more thoroughly this question of 'thinking as action' as a specific contribution to socially just pedagogies as feminist task, in what follows we focus our attention upon the matter(s) of thinking directly and move to the essential function of the powers of imagination for social transformation in today's neoliberal societal framework by bringing into a diffractive conversation two different thought traditions and feminist times. From an ethico-onto-epistemological perspective we aim to return to the question of thinking with Hannah Arendt, who already in her work on *The Human Condition* from 1958 addresses the game-changing replacement of (early modern) *homo politicus* with (late modern) *homo oeconomicus* very effectively. Most significant for us here is that Arendt makes her point by focusing precisely on the mattering historical shifts in what it means 'to think'. Whilst philosophically more aligned with idealism rather than materialism, Arendt as a political, interventionist thinker defies any such limiting categorisation. Therefore, she can help us again today to envision further imaginative weapons and thus create an affective 'conceptual toolbox' for feminist pedagogical endeavors in the academy and beyond.[6]

Practicing Critical Thinking *and/as* Diffraction: (Post)human(ist) Interventions

Let us first turn then to the 'agential realist' (Barad 2007) framework, which allows us to approach the matter of thinking as an always/already ethico-onto-epistemological phenomenon, thereby foregrounding pre-established dualist splittings that are otherwise far too often still found on the level of the question of what thinking itself actually *is*. One key focus in current *queer/feminist* (new) materialist discussions is an engagement with the phenomenon of diffraction as a methodological instrument for what is termed the production of 'a different difference', with the continued claim that such different difference will have transformative powers within, and for, the realities we live (in). The phenomenon of diffraction – be it in its optical (Haraway 1997) or quantum (Barad 2003; 2007) theorisation – transforms the hegemonic theoretical framework of difference as opposition and dichotomy into 'the production of difference patterns' (Haraway 1997: 34). It is then understood as an *onto-epistemological* phenomenon which, in Barad's words, is itself 'part of the world in its differential becoming' (2007: 89). To approach difference as diffraction, therefore, can act as a critical methodological strategy helping to transform the persistent oppositional and dualist framework of thinking. For, in its onto-epistemological change of initial conditions – patterns and superposition of intra-acting forces instead of oppositions and antagonisms of pre-existing entities – the phenomenon of diffraction transforms theory/thought and its supposed 'other' – praxis – into one entangled, i.e. mattering, theory-practice, in which 'agential separability' (ibid.), as Barad writes, rather than categorical separation is the rule. In this vein, the phenomenon of diffraction helps to articulate how theorising *is always/already (part of) worlding* and also how worlding *is always/already theorising*. Barad's quantum version of queer/feminist theory stresses arduously that 'knowing, thinking, measuring, theorising, and observing *are material practices* of intra-acting within and as part of the world' (Barad 2007: 90, emphasis added).[7] Yet, to carry this conclusion through – i.e. to not only 'know it' as an epistemological 'truth', but let it become something to be practiced as ontology and *ethos* within the curricular spaces in which knowledge production and feminist theorising are at stake, offers a very promising dimension to queer/feminist classroom discussions. As Barad continues, in knowledge production '[w]e do not uncover preexisting facts about independently existing things as they exist frozen in time like little statues positioned in the world. Rather, we learn about phenomena – about specific material configurations of the world's becoming' (ibid.). By understanding diffraction as such ethico-onto-epistemological entanglement, everything – 'us' included – is always/already taking part with/in the world *as* its differential becoming ('worlding').

The argumentative turn in the context of different onto-epistemological initial conditions that we present here is important: what we gain by bringing the conceptual insights embodied by the phenomenon of diffraction to our discussion of the matters of thinking, is an approach to those matters that transforms any categorical segregation of theory and thinking from what is supposed to be mattering in a practical sense into an *ethico-onto-epistemological entanglement*. Within this diffractive (and diffracting) constellation, the most common hierarchical – and hence 'mattering' – split between that which is called thinking – as *reflection on* and *abstraction from* the world – and that which is seen as this 'real world' or proper 'reality' is undone. This consequential splitting is that which structures both the currently so virulent academic neoliberal 'pragmatisms' and therefore also the study curricula taught therein; in as much as it governs the scientific research projects funded today and the institutional training offered for those projects to succeed.[8] Within the different onto-epistemological framework suggested here, instead of the repetition of this consequential splitting, theory itself is approached as a praxis that *diffracts (with) other practices in a thinking, measuring, and accounting manner*. What might be marked with theory and thinking as diffractive praxis in contemporary feminism is the capacity to imagine and work with different onto-epistemological beginnings (e.g. using patterns rather than oppositions; superposition rather than dichotomies as starting points). Such different initial conditions, as Kirby argues (2012), do not so much lead to new fields of discovery, but instead instigate a re-turn(ing) to – and of – everything we already do. With regard to Barad's quantum philosophy, Kirby writes: '[I]f we look closely at the work of physicist Karen Barad, the tantalizing provocation in her argument is that she is not challenging us to learn physics so that we can understand complexity. Instead, what informs her reworking of interaction as 'intra-action' is the suggestion that we are already practicing physics' (2012: 204). Taking further this re-evaluation of thinking as ethico-onto-epistemological force and applying it now directly to the question of curriculum creation raises the following questions: What if we could make again a feminist claim out of the challenge to engage with *all kinds of practices as material engagements*, and do not stop short on their theoretical side? Such 'stopping short' seems to us one of the most direct consequences of the current neoliberal discursive climate, in which it has become far too common to claim that theories and 'thinking' are needed only if applied to something, and that nothing is gained by 'merely theorising'. Yet, what might be the outcome if 'thinking' were to *be practiced with/in and amongst other practices*?

We will return to this question again towards the end of this chapter. For now, let us move a little further into the matters of thinking itself – its mattering dimensions in the ethico-onto-epistemological sense – and attend also to the work of Hannah Arendt, who in a very comparable manner positions the power of thought as both action and worlding practice. It is in her investigations into the relation between thought and practice more than half a century ago that Arendt made a very similar claim in respect to the matters of thinking as practice in, or practicing, the world. In her work on *The Human Condition* (1958), one of Arendt's specific points in respect to the worlding force of thought/thinking is that the major transformation (*Umstülpung*) occurring with what is called the Modern Age (*Neuzeit*) might not be the actual dethronement of the (pre-modern) *vita contemplativa* by the (modern) *vita activa* as the guiding reality for people's lived experience. Instead – and this is still most important for understanding our contemporary neoliberal structures – the true 'reversal', as she also calls it, i.e. the much more foundational change is that the activity of thinking itself is from now on subjugated to the *economic* logic of production and manufacture (*Herstellen*). To delve deeper into this idea, let us examine a short passage from her work in which she discusses this significant shift:

> Actually, the change that took place in the seventeenth century was more radical than what a simple reversal of the established traditional order between contemplation and doing is apt to indicate. The reversal, strictly speaking, concerned only the relationship between thinking and doing, whereas contemplation in the original sense of beholding a truth, was altogether eliminated.
>
> Arendt 1958: 291

Arendt's point here is not to merely complain (in a dogmatic idealist or a narrow humanist fashion) about the changes occurring in sociopolitical realities on the threshold of 'modernity'; that *vita activa* (doing) actually becomes the dominant practice, replacing the habit (and privilege) of a *vita contemplativa* (contemplation). Instead, what is far more significant in relation to that question of 'what it means to think' is Arendt's contention that the 'modern' threshold was accompanied by an inherent process in which certain activities become marked as relevant and important for the 'new' times to come, whilst others – because they are seemingly useless and therefore of no value, just like contemplation – fall from sight completely. The older (and much more than merely Western) understanding that thinking is contemplation but as a doing, an action, and a practice, becomes thereby *unthinkable*. It is substituted once and for all by an oppositional logic, the reductive opposition of *vita contemplativa* versus *vita activa*, both of which now obey the demands of use-value and production; and therefore producing 'us' as *homo oeconomicus*.[9] Arendt shows the loss of recognition for an understanding of thinking as *worlding action* – of thought as active engagement *with/in* this world – as one of the major characteristics of 'modernity'. Thereby she can be read alongside new materialist and/or posthuman(ist) critiques of precisely this concept of modernity as one that is based on a dichotomous order, enforcing the splitting of the subject and the object, followed by the emergence of a detrimental theory/practice divide. And to go one step further with Arendt here, so that the political dimension of this ethico-onto-epistemological claim is also emphasised: It seems to be her conviction that the powers of thought and the praxis of thinking are *mattering* in order to enact different kinds of world(ing)s. It is this conviction which also makes her conclude most provocatively in 1963 in her *Report of Eichmann in Jerusalem* that it was Eichmann's *in*capacity and *un*willingness to think (understood now in the strong sense as an *a/effective doing*) that has become the shocking truth of what she termed 'the banality of evil' (Arendt [1963] 2006).[10]

The Powers of Feminist Imagination in Neoliberal Times

In a final step, we now aim to return this diffraction pattern of what thought as action does to the question of how to further social justice in feminist studies curricula. Feminist approaches provide us with a dynamic canon of knowledges that we (re)claim as a most important force with which to counteract current neoliberal frameworks in both our societies at large and in the universities in which we teach and research. Feminist thinking and the genre of 'feminist theory' is all about (societal) change. By arguing both with Arendt's civic necessity 'to think' and with (new) materialism's/critical posthuman(ist) or agential realist approaches to thought as 'intra-acting within and as part of the world', we have exemplified how a re-turn to, and of, the powers of the imagination in current curricular engagements can be undertaken. When we ask ourselves – with, for example, Elizabeth Grosz – 'What is feminist theory?', we are primarily addressing the question of how to intervene into this world by 'thinking differently [and] innovatively' (Grosz 2011: 77); and maybe, '[a]t its best, feminist theory has the potential to make us become other than ourselves' (ibid.: 87). The concerns of social justice can once more be strengthened within higher education if we start again to effectively counter persistent underlying dualist splittings of most *entangled relations*. In a feminist (new) materialist/ critical posthuman(ist) key, what this means is that by taking seriously an intra-active and diffractive ethico-onto-epistemological approach to our teaching situation and its 'initial conditions', the hierarchical framework of theory *versus* practice, currently still all too often seen as separate endeavours, becomes foundationally transformed. That theory and practice are never separate is, of course, one of the most original feminist claims, and thus, it could be argued it is not unique to this 'newer' feminist works. Yet, what *is* apt to argue is that it is contemporary (new) materialist and critical posthuman(ist) feminist discussions that once again remind us – also in the established discipline Gender Studies – that merely the correct application of 'our theories' cannot suffice. What needs to come again to the fore in our feminist, post-/decolonial, critical race and queer discussions is the necessarily *political* thought-dimension underlying all scientific and/as pedagogical endeavours. The return of scientific positivism (be it with respect to quantitative data analysis or a hyper-attention to what is called 'empirical realities') has also taken hold of feminist discourses and the public reception of feminism. The misleading – but rather common – presupposition that the concepts, ideas, or the knowledges we use are 'above' the analyses and objects we investigate, and the assumption that they are abstractions from, or objective reflections on, the world we live (in), need to be transformed into a multi-sited constellation of always/already *theoretico-practical,* and therefore mattering *actions*. As initial conditions of further practicing and acting, they directly shape sociopolitical realities (and how we approach them). In the neoliberal times in which we live – and in which we are therefore also implicated – it might indeed be this practicing of thinking itself that could produce another opening 'for all', *if* – and this is for sure directly addressing us in the universities – we allow, and also reclaim, the societal space to think as worlding practice into our classrooms. Rosi Braidotti emphasises such concern in to us, a similar manner when she rehearses the very kernel of feminist thinking, of which her own work is exemplary: 'Faith in the creative powers of the imagination is an integral part of feminists' appraisal of lived embodied experience and the bodily roots of subjectivity' (2011: 36). To think – that is to learn, to analyse, and to practice an argument and, in this very process, to transform ourselves – is an always *embodied doing* that needs to again receive much greater attention in our curricular work. In order to rebuild the university as a civic institution furthering societal discourse on social justice and 'freedom for all', we still need to find a place for this practicing of our world within our teaching and learning environments. Even more so than in Arendt's time, ours is a reality that is driven by the rhetoric of use and consumption, i.e. by purely economic concerns, with all the dehumanising and exclusivist consequences we currently witness. In times such as these, the dream for new feminist knowledges – to have more time to practice thinking as action again within the university as a place to work for social justice – needs greater support. We see it as an urgent and forceful path towards a 'freedom for all' that would also allow us to again differentiate between a neoliberal feminism and a critical transformative feminism in neoliberal times.

Notes

1 This chapter is based on two individually published articles by the authors, see: Buikema 2016, and Thiele 2015. While certain elements in the text can be already found in these earlier publications, the argumentative turn towards the question of socially just pedagogies is originally developed in this co-authored work.

2 We will use this double formula throughout this article in order to signal the difficulty of correct 'labelling' in this new field of research, as well as to be inclusive of the specific feminist articulations in the field of (new) materialisms and critical posthumanisms.

3 By using 'Western' in its most common and classical sense here, we want to bring to the fore once more the important argument that Stuart Hall made in his seminal text 'The West and the Rest: Discourse and Power' (1992) with regard to this problematic geopolitical distribution. Hall explains that 'the West and the Rest' is how global relations became represented in (post)colonial times. However, Hall also claims, we need to remember that these concepts represent very complex ideas and have no single or simple meaning (1992: 185).

4 Our concern with neoliberalism's consequences for feminism lies therefore both with the visible tendencies of individualisation on the political right and the political left.

5 Gilles Deleuze's elaboration on the question of thought/thinking in his third chapter in *Difference and Repetition* entitled 'The Image of Thought', is here still very much to the point: 'It cannot be regarded as a *fact* that thinking is the natural exercise of a faculty, and that this faculty is possessed of a good nature and a good will' ([1968] 1994: 133). As can be seen in the seminal works of authors such as Rosi Braidotti, Claire Colebrook, or Elizabeth Grosz, the feminist reception of Deleuze's philosophy

emphasises precisely the affirmative critical quality as the powers of thought. For a short recapitulation of affirmation as a critical tool, see also: Thiele 2017.

6 This phrasing of 'conceptual weapons' is inspired by Elizabeth Grosz's call for (new) feminist theorisations in 'The Future of Feminist Theory: Dreams for New Knowledges' (2011).

7 See Collins 1991; Harding 1991; and Haraway 1988.

8 See also José Esteban Muñoz's discussion of the neoliberal dimensions of dominant pragmatism in his book *Cruising Utopia* (2009).

9 One of the blind spots of Arendt's historical analysis in this book is that she does not account for the history of colonialism that lies at the heart of the process of 'modernisation' in 'the West' and in Europe specifically. This omission is especially unfortunate, since what has traditionally been counted as human is so dependent on the European/Western history of enslavement and the colonial expansion processes. For a resonating history of 'Man', also thinking through the thresholds of *homo politicus* and *homo oeconomicus* in the process of 'modernisation', yet decisively from a decolonial perspective, see the work of Sylvia Wynter (e.g. 2003; Wynter and McKittrick 2015). And for Arendt's own very insightful discussion of colonialism, racism, imperialism, see Arendt ([1951] 2017), esp. Part 2.

10 After the public turmoil that followed the publication of *The Report of Eichmann in Jerusalem*, Arendt further worked on this ethico-political question of what it means to think. See e.g. 'Some Questions of Moral Philosophy' (1994), which can also be read as a response to her critics from the Eichmann trial book; and *The Life of the Mind* ([1971] 1978) that devotes the first volume to 'Thinking'. For the use of 'a/ effective' in our characterisation of Arendt's approach to thinking as a doing, see also the discussion of an ethics of becoming in: Thiele 2008. Here, the folding together of 'affect' and 'effect' is argued for in a Spinozian manner, according to which effects are produced via the capacity to affect and to be affected.

References

Arendt, H. ([1951] 2017), *The Origins of Totalitarianism*, New York: Penguin.

Arendt, H. (1958), *The Human Condition*, Chicago: The University of Chicago Press.

Arendt, H. ([1963] 2006), *Eichmann in Jerusalem: A Report on the Banality of Evil*, New York: Penguin Press.

Arendt, H. ([1971] 1978), *The Life of The Mind*, New York: Harcourt Inc.

Arendt, H. (1994), 'Some Questions of Moral Philosophy', *Social Research*, 61(4): 739–764.

Bal, M. (2015), 'Power to the Imagination!', *Krisis: Tijdschrift voor actuele filosofie*, 2: 68–74. Available online: http://krisis.eu/the-new-university/ (accessed 27 May 2017).

Barad, K. (2003), 'Posthumanist Performativity: Toward an Understanding of How Matter Comes to Matter', *Signs: Journal of Women in Culture and Society*, 28(3): 801–831.

Barad, K. (2007), *Meeting the Universe Halfway: Quantum Physics and the Entanglement of Matter and Meaning*, Durham: Duke University Press.

Braidotti, R. (2011), 'Interview with Rosi Braidotti', in R. Dolphijn and I. van der Tuin (eds), *New Materialism: Interviews & Cartographies*, 19–37, Ann Arbor: Open Humanities Press.

Brown, W. (2013), 'Reclaiming Democracy: An Interview with Wendy Brown on Occupy, Sovereignty, and Secularism (an Interview with Robin Celikates and Yolanda Jansen)', *Critical Legal Thinking*, 30 January. Available online: http://criticallegalthinking.com/2013/01/30/reclaiming-democracy-an-interview-with-wendy-brown-on-occupy-sovereignty-and-secularism/ (accessed 27 May 2017).

Brown, W. (2015), *Undoing the Demos: Neoliberalism's Stealth Revolution*, Cambridge MA: The MIT Press.

Buikema, R. (2016), 'Women's and Feminist Activism in Western Europe', in N. Naples et al. (eds), *The Wiley Blackwell Encyclopaedia of Gender and Sexuality Studies*, 1–5, Oxford: Wiley-Blackwell.

Buikema, R. (2017), *Revoltes in de Cultuurkritiek*, Amsterdam: Amsterdam University Press.

Carby, H. (1982), 'White Woman Listen: Black Feminism and the Boundaries of Sisterhood', in Centre for Contemporary Cultural Studies (ed.), *The Empire Strikes Back: Race and Racism in 70s Britain*, 212–235, London: Routledge.

Collins, P. H. (1991), *Black Feminist Thought: Knowledge, Consciousness, and the Politics of Empowerment*, New York: Routledge.

Deleuze, G. ([1968] 1994), *Difference and Repetition*, trans. P. Patton, New York: Columbia University Press.

Fraser, N. (2013), 'How Feminism Became Capitalism's Handmaiden', *The Guardian Online*, 14 October. Available online: https://www.theguardian.com/commentisfree/2013/oct/14/feminism-capitalist-handmaiden-neoliberal (accessed 27 May 2017).

Grosz, E. (2011), 'The Future of Feminist Theory: Dreams for New Knowledges', in *Becoming Undone: Darwinian Reflections on Life, Politics, and Art*, Durham: Duke University Press.

Hall, S. (1992), 'The West and the Rest: Discourse and Power', in S. Hall and B. Gieber (eds), *Formations of Modernity*, 185–225, Cambridge: Polity Press.

Haraway, D. (1988), 'Situated Knowledges: The Science Question in Feminism and the Privilege of Partial Perspective', *Feminist Studies*, 14(3): 575–599.

Haraway, D. (1997), *Modest_Witness@Second_Millennium.FemaleMan_Meets_ OncoMouse: Feminism and Technoscience*, New York: Routledge.

Harding, S. (1991), *Whose Science? Whose Knowledge?*, Ithaca: Cornell UP.

hooks, b. (2010), *Teaching Critical Thinking: Practical Wisdom*, New York: Routledge.

hooks, b. (2013), *Writing Beyond Race: Living Theory and Practice*, New York: Routledge.

Irigaray, L. (1985), *Speculum of the Other Woman*, Ithaca: Cornell UP.

Kirby, V. (2012), 'Initial Conditions', *Differences: A Journal of Feminist Cultural Studies*, 23(3): 197–205.

Muñoz, J. E. (2009), *Cruising Utopia: The Then and There of Queer Futurity*, New York: NYU Press.

Scott, J. W. (2011), *The Fantasy of Feminist History*, Durham: Duke University Press.

Spivak, G. (1988), 'Can the Subaltern Speak?', in C. Nelson and L. Grossberg (eds), *Marxism and the Interpretation of Culture*, 271–313, Urbana, IL: University of Illinois Press.

Thiele, K. (2008), *The Thought of Becoming: Gilles Deleuze's Poetics of Life*, Berlin: Diaphanes.

Thiele, K. (2015), 'Theorizing is Worlding – Teaching Feminist New Materialism in Contemporary Feminist Theory Courses', in P. Hinton and P. Treusch (eds), *Teaching with Feminist Materialisms*, 101–111, Utrecht: ATHENA/Utrecht University.

Thiele, K. (2017), 'Affirmation', in M. Bunz, B.M. Kaiser and K. Thiele (eds), *Symptoms of the Planetary Condition: A Critical Vocabulary*, 25–30, Lüneburg: Meson Press.

Woolf, V. ([1938] 1966), *Three Guineas*, New York: Harcourt Inc.

Wynter, S. (2003), 'Unsettling the Coloniality of Being/Power/Truth/Freedom: Towards the Human, After Man, Its Overrepresentation – And Argument', *CR: The New Centennial Review*, 3(3): 257–337.

Wynter, S. and K. McKittrick (2015), 'Unparalleled Catastrophe for Our Species? Or, to Give Humanness a Different Future?: Conversations', in K. McKittrick (ed.), *Sylvia Wynter: On Being Human as Praxis*, 9–89, Durham: Duke University Press.

3

Practicing Reflection or Diffraction? Implications for Research Methodologies in Education[1]

Vivienne Bozalek and Michalinos Zembylas

Dissatisfied with epistemological practices of reflexivity grounded in representationalism, scholars immersed in feminist science studies began to raise questions about the theoretical assumptions and consequences of reflexivity. Donna Haraway (1997), a pioneer in these debates, proposed the notion of *diffraction* as an alternative to reflexivity. As she expressed her misgivings at the time: 'Reflexivity has been much recommended as a critical practice, but my suspicion is that reflexivity, like reflection, only displaces the same elsewhere, setting up worries about copy and original and the search for the authentic and really real' (1997, p. 16). Haraway suggested instead that, '[w]hat we need is to make a difference in material-semiotic apparatuses, to *diffract* the rays of technoscience so that we get more promising interference patterns on the recording films of our lives and bodies' (ibid, added emphasis). Thus, diffraction for Haraway was suggested as a metaphor and a strategy for making a difference in the world that breaks with self-reflection and its epistemological grounding, which she regarded as problematic as it lures us into a reductionist way of thinking about things and words (Haraway, 2000).

The notion of diffraction has been taken forward in the work of Karen Barad (2007, 2010, 2014, 2015) who does not only regard diffraction as an optical metaphor; but also as a *method* and a *practice* that pays attention to material engagement with data and the 'relations of difference and how they matter' (Barad 2007, p. 71). Diffraction is understood by both Barad and Haraway as a process of being attentive to how differences get made and what the effects of these differences are. Barad's notion of diffraction is derived from the physical phenomenon of diffraction which she extends to other forms of knowledge production.[2] Diffraction from her perspective can be used to acknowledge the influential role of the knower in knowledge production and particularly how we learn about 'material configurations of the world's becoming' (p. 91). For Barad, diffraction is a useful tool highlighting the entanglement of material-discursive phenomena in the world. Diffraction is thus predicated on a *relational ontology*, an ongoing process in which matter and meaning are co-constituted.

Our point of departure in this chapter is Haraway's and Barad's suggestion that diffraction constitutes an alternative methodology to reflexivity. From their perspective, reflexivity remains caught up in sameness because of its mirroring of fixed positions, whereas diffraction is specifically attuned to differences and their effects in knowledge-making practices. In addition, diffraction is not only epistemic, but also ontological and ethical (Barad, 2007; 2014). We therefore consider in this chapter what the methodological implications of *both* this metaphor *and* method would be for doing research in education. We acknowledge that there have already been important efforts so far to theorise what a diffractive analysis would imply for research in education (e.g. see Davies, 2014a and 2014b; Hoel and van der Tuin, 2012; Hultman and Lenz Taguchi, 2010; Jackson and Mazzei, 2012; Juelskjaer, 2013; Lenz Taguchi, 2012; Lenz Taguchi and Palmer, 2013; Palmer, 2011). Our analysis joins and builds on these efforts, focusing in particular on how these two practices – reflection and diffraction – differ from each other and/or intersect and what consequences such understandings might have for research methodology in education.

In the first part of the chapter we briefly discuss the concept of reflection, its different meanings and the epistemological, ontological and methodological premises on which it is grounded. We do the same for diffraction and then discuss their convergences and divergences, emphasising in particular the historical continuity between reflection and diffraction and at the same time the break that has come with diffractive methodology. The chapter ends with a brief discussion on the methodological implications of this analysis for educational research.

Reflection – What is it?

Reflection as the physical phenomenon of mirroring has been used as a metaphor to express an inner mental activity in which someone is taking a 'step back' and looking into his or her self for the purpose of thinking about one's life and perhaps changing it (Barad, 2007). In late and advanced modernity, 'reflexivity' has become a major concept in sociological discussions, expressing the ability and practice of a person to change his or her life in response to knowledge about their social circumstances. The work undertaken by sociologists like Beck and Giddens has become a central point of reference in debates about how reflexivity is relevant to social transformation. The concept of reflexivity has grown to encompass different meanings among different research traditions and disciplines, often lacking a distinction among the different terms used such as reflection, reflexivity and critical reflection, to name a few. To show this, we briefly discuss various meanings of reflexivity and then focus more specifically on the practice of reflexivity in research methodology.

In their review of the social work literature on the different meanings of 'reflexivity', D' Cruz, Gillingham, and Melendez (2007) identify three variations. It is valuable to briefly revisit each variation because they show precisely the different nuances as well as the epistemological and ontological assumptions embedded in each manifestation. The first variation regards reflexivity as an individual's response to his or her social circumstances; Giddens' and Beck's work are included in this variation. This definition of reflexivity emphasises the ability of the individual to make choices, hence individuals are considered responsible for problems they experience. Definitions in this variation, suggest D' Cruz and her colleagues, assume that reflexivity is developed as a skill which can be used to master the forces that shape one's life; reflexivity, then, is understood as a competence that can be taught and is offered as a means of emancipation and self-actualisation.

The second variation defines reflexivity as an individual's self-critical approach that questions how knowledge is generated and how power relations influence the process of knowledge production. Feminist research in particular has developed and explored notions of 'reflexivity' and 'critical reflection' to highlight the multiple interrelations between power and knowledge in the research process. For example, Sandra Harding's (1996) concept of 'strong objectivity' recognises and responds to the entanglement of power and knowledge in the research process. In this regard, reflexivity and critical reflection constitute practices of interrogating knowledge, including the role of the researcher's own subjectivities. Feminist researchers have applied the practices of reflexivity and critical reflection to interrogate reflexivity itself (Daley, 2010). As Daley explains, feminist research has particularly examined the role of the researcher in addressing methodological dilemmas of interpretation and representation, calling attention to emotions, relationality, discourse, and women's bodies (Gray, 2008; Holmes, 2010).

Finally, the third variation is aligned to the second variation in that it is based on a critical examination of the factors that influence knowledge production (D' Cruz, et al., 2007). What it adds, according to D' Cruz and her colleagues, is the acknowledgement of the role of emotions in the process of reflexivity and the 'emotionalisation' of reflexivity, as Holmes (2010) calls it. By using this term, Holmes refers not only to the theoretical attention to emotion, but also to the exploration of how individuals can increasingly draw on emotions in assessing themselves and their lives. Holmes and others (e.g. Zembylas, 2014) argue that emotions are crucial to how the social and the political are reproduced through power relations.

The notion of 'critical reflection', in particular, has emerged as an approach that unpacks how power relations influence the processes of knowledge production in teaching and learning, including the process of reflexivity itself (Harrison and Lee, 2011). Mezirow (1990) acknowledged that there is more to reflection than simply thinking about experiences, pointing out that critical reflection involves a critique of our held assumptions and values. Brookfield (1995) used the term 'critical reflection' to distinguish the difference with instrumental reflection, suggesting that critical reflection involves critical thinking, which links personal experience with social and power arrangements. Fook (2002) added that critical reflection involves thinking about one's practice and critically deconstructing how we have developed these skills and how some of these discourses might work against us (see also, Fook and Gardner, 2007).

Finally, concerning research methodology and more specifically qualitative research, reflexivity has been defined as a generalised practice in which researchers attempt to acknowledge their influence on research (Gentles, Jack, Nicholas and McKibbon, 2014; Mruck and Mey, 2007). The idea of reflexivity in qualitative research, according to these authors, has largely evolved from methodological critiques regarding problems of representation in research, such as claims of objectivity and relativism and the influence of the researcher in what is being researched. They suggest that the general objective of reflexivity is to increase transparency and trustworthiness in research, yet there have been several criticisms pointing out either the dangers of excessive reflexivity, the uncritical adoption of it and its consequences in really producing better research (Pillow, 2003; Schneider, 2002) or criticisms about the inadequacy of reflexive methodology because it involves ambivalent practices (Davies et al., 2004) and produces partial accounts (Gentles et al., 2014).

Diffraction – What is it?

What attracted Haraway to the notion of diffraction is the affordance it provides for patterns of difference and heterogeneity through interference rather than *sameness* – which reflection and reflexivity tend to signify. Haraway (1992) initially defined diffraction as 'a mapping of interference, not of replication, reflection, or reproduction.' 'A diffraction pattern does not map where differences appear, but rather maps where the effects of difference appear' (p. 300). The possibility of including non-humans together with humans was another advantage of using diffraction rather than reflection. Diffractive patterns which reveal that there is light in darkness and dark in lightness are similarly fluid and provide an understanding of how binaries can be queered, and how differences exist both within and beyond boundaries (Barad, 2014).

Barad (2007) builds on Haraway's ideas of diffraction as a metaphor, trope or figuration. She proposes diffraction as a methodological approach focusing on difference and the entanglement of matter and meaning, using ideas from Niels Bohr's quantum physics. She does not only see diffraction or interference as a metaphor or as a category but also as a *physical phenomenon* which is part of wave behaviour – whether it is light, water, or sound waves. Diffraction is where waves 'combine when they overlap and the apparent bending and spreading out of waves when they encounter an obstruction' (Barad, 2007, p. 28). In combining, waves can be amplified by being superimposed upon one another. Barad uses this physical process of diffraction as a methodology which engages affirmatively with difference.

Barad (2014) thus posits that diffraction is more than merely a metaphor – it is a method or methodology. She notes that it is not just quantum physics which has played a part in developing diffractive methodology – feminist theorising about difference has in itself made a significant contribution to its development. In a diffractive methodology the details of one discipline (in this case quantum physics) are read attentively and with care through another (feminist queer theory) in order to come to more creative insights. Barad proposes a diffractive methodology rather than critique, which she regards as passé (Latour, 2004) and a potentially epistemologically damaging process of distancing, othering and putting others down (Juelskjær and Schwennesen. 2012). A diffractive methodology in contrast, is not setting up one approach/text/discipline against another but rather a detailed, attentive and careful reading the ideas of one through another, leading to more generative 'inventive provocations' (Dolphijn and van der Tuin, 2012, p. 50) and the possibility of a true transdisciplinarity rather than interdisciplinarity.

In diffraction, material-discursive phenomena, matter and meaning are seen as entangled. As Barad notes in her interview with Adam Kleinman on intra-actions for *Mousse* magazine, matter is not just things or bodies but 'substance in its iterative intra-active becoming – not a thing, but a doing, a congealing of agency. It is morphologically active, responsive, generative, and articulate. Mattering is the ongoing intra-active differentiating of the world' (Kleinman, 2012, p. 76). Barad also equates matter with meaning or sense-making which she refers to as 'mattering' or as 'material-discursive' (Barad, 2007, 2014, Kleinman, 2012). For Barad, matter is not just of the head but also of the heart and hands; it has to do with a scholarly engagement with care, social justice and seeing oneself as part of a world. Diffraction is also then about issues of taking responsibility, or as Barad refers to it – response-ability, of a yearning for social justice (Barad, 2007) and towards possible worlds (Haraway, 1997). Diffraction is thus seen as both a process and as a result – ontologically a being and becoming. Barad's approach entails a relational ontology which is not separated from epistemological and ethical domains – she refers to it as an *ethico-onto-epistemological* approach.

This methodology as described by Barad has been put to creative use by educational theorists and practitioners such as Jackson and Mazzei (2012) who use diffractive methodology to examine the same set of data from different poststructural concepts of Derrida, Spivak, Foucault, Butler, Deleuze and Barad herself. Lenz Taguchi (2012; 2013) has used a diffractive methodology to differently conceptualise early child development and her collaborative data analysis work with her PhD students. Bronwyn Davies (2013) analysed anger using a diffractive methodology at a Swedish preschool and Phillips and Larson (2012, 2013) have used a diffractive methodology to analyse data from a teacher–student writing conference as an entanglement of the discursive and the material. This emerging work of analysing data in educational research highlights that diffractive analysis can make visible new kinds of material-discursive realities that have important epistemological, ontological and methodological consequences. It is to these consequences that we turn in our discussion now.

Reflection and Diffraction: Continuities and Breaks

For both Haraway and Barad, 'diffractive analysis constitutes an alternative methodology to critical reflection' (Lenz Taguchi, 2012, p. 268). Why is this so? Haraway, Barad as well as education scholars who have recently used diffractive analysis (e.g. Davies, 2014a and b; Hultman and Lenz Taguchi, 2010; Jackson and Mazzei, 2012; Juelskjær and Schwennesen. 2012; Larson and Phillips, 2013; Lenz Taguchi, 2010, 2012; Lenz Taguchi and Palmer, 2013; Palmer, 2011) argue that reflexivity is not sufficient any more on two important grounds. First of all, as it is suggested, reflexivity starts off with preconceived assumptions of binaries rather than investigating how boundaries or binaries are produced through the methodology itself. In reflexivity, there is a researcher as an independent subject who is actually the locus of reflection, whereas in diffraction there is no such distinction as subjects and objects are always already entangled. Thus, from a diffractive perspective, subjects and objects such as nature and culture are not fixed referents for understanding the other but should be read through one another as entanglements.

Also, as Lenz Taguchi (2012) and Jackson and Mazzei (2012) point out, the perennial goal for interpretation falls into the representational trap of trying to figure out what a subject really means. Lenz Taguchi explains that, 'As an act of thinking, interpretation in reflexive analysis is about reflecting sameness (as in mirroring), or identifying differences from something previously identified and acknowledged; a thing, an identity, a category, a discursive theme or a subject position' (2012, p. 269). Reflection remains fundamentally an inner mental activity in which the researcher supposedly takes a step back and reflects at a distance from the outside of the data (Hultman and Lenz Tagushi, 2010). Reflection is thus based on the assumption of an 'I' who is different and exterior to that which is conceptualising, an 'I' who is separate from the world (Lenz Taguchi, 2010). The slip into the subject 'I' is important in understanding reflection and diffraction, since in the latter there is no researcher as independent subject – in diffraction the intra-action and connections between human and non-human phenomena are foregrounded. Rather than pondering on the meaning of texts or events, a diffractive methodology focuses on what these phenomena do and what they are connected to (Grosz, 1994). This interconnectedness and relationality between all organisms and matter is important to bear in mind, as the taken-for-grantedness of the coherent 'I' in reflexivity needs to be constantly challenged in diffractive methodologies (Lenz Taguchi, 2010). To summarise then, Haraway, Barad, and education scholars propose a diffractive methodology as a way of troubling dualisms: me and not me, discourse and matter, words and things.

A second ground on which reflexivity is considered insufficient is that it does not pay attention to the materiality of data and the entanglements and interdependencies in processes in which different kinds of bodies are co-constituted. Barad (2007) outlines a number of differences between reflection and diffraction in her relational ontology which forms the basis for her 'posthumanist performative account of material bodies (both human and nonhuman)' where 'a relationality between specific material (re)configurings of the world through which boundaries, properties, and meanings are differentially enacted' (p. 183). She proposes diffraction as a way out of seeing the world from an individualist, humanist and representationalist perspective in which a distinctly separate, atomistic individual man, seen as the 'measure of all things', the centre of the universe is able to reflect from a distance on the world, as is assumed in reflection or reflexivity. From a posthuman perspective, Barad (2007), Braidotti (2013) and Snaza and Weaver (2015) see this humanist view of the world as being so deeply rooted in current thought that it is difficult to extricate thoughts from the taken-for-grantedness of the tenets of humanism and of how human subjects are constituted.

Bronwyn Davies (2014a), in her explanation of why she uses a diffractive rather than a reflexive methodology for qualitative research, indicates how a diffractive methodology causes a profound rethinking of the research process (see also Davies & Gannon, 2013). This process of questioning qualitative research methodology has not come out of nowhere, of course. Similar to what Liz Stanley and Sue Wise (1983) were already putting forward in the 1980s, Sofia Villenas (1996), Davies et al (2004), and Wanda Pillow (2002) (to name a few scholars), have already raised important issues with regard to the epistemic privilege of researchers within a reflexivity paradigm of research (see Pillow, 2015 for an in-depth discussion of reflection and reflexivity as well their different modalities and contributions in research methodologies). Davies, in particular, notes that reflexivity represents what exists outside, a preexisting world, such as an object which is independent of the researcher and can be pinned down by the researcher's gaze. As she observes, reflexivity 'is implicitly based on the phenomenon of a pattern of light that reflects an actual object or entity' (Davies, 2014a, p. 2). While reflection can document difference, diffraction, on the other hand, is a process of *producing* difference.

Implications of Diffractive Analysis for Research Methodology

We now turn our attention to issues of methodology, focusing in particular on the aspects of diffractive analysis which are particularly useful; and at the same time we wish to acknowledge the contributions that have been made by the paradigm of reflexivity and especially critical reflection. Thus, we agree with the points raised about the value of using diffractive analysis, but we want to avoid setting up a binary between reflection and diffraction. Undoubtedly, reflexivity might not have been sufficient for some of the reasons discussed earlier; however, if we want to be fair to the theoretical and methodological developments that have been made over the years, we might need to acknowledge that the 'entanglement' of reflexivity and diffraction is one that includes continuities and breaks rather than a 'story' of one versus the other.

First, we need to acknowledge that the concepts of reflection, reflexivity and critical reflection are often used interchangeably, implying that they have the same meaning (Fook and Askeland, 2006). Yet, we need to recognise the nuance in these terms; reflection, reflexivity and critical reflection are not the same thing (Pillow, 2015). Although they are all grounded in the 'ideology of representation' as Woolgar (1988) would say, some forms of reflexivity have covered considerable ground in terms of interrogating the representational paradigm and its consequences.

For example, the notion of critical reflection has been developed and explored over the years, especially in the context of critical theory, poststructuralist and feminist literature, as an approach that recognises and responds to power structures and relations in reflection processes (Brookfield, 2009; Harding, 1991; Pillow, 2015). Collectively, this work emphasises that there is something more to critical reflection as an alternative to mere reflection. Critical reflection involves critical thinking about our experiences within their social and political context and also a deeper understanding of how to use this knowledge to improve our practices in the future (Hickson, 2011).

Therefore, we agree with Fook and Askeland (2006) that the distinction among different terms is important enough, if we don't want to fall into the trap of treating these terms in the same manner. Haraway and Barad, correctly in our view, focus their critique on reflexivity (as they are concerned with the wider sociological process of change), whereas some of their followers (e.g. Lenz Taguchi, 2012, p. 161) jump from 'reflection' (as a method and metaphor) to 'critical reflection' without making a clear distinction between them. However, although critical reflection is useful in that it begins to recognise at least the entanglement of issues of power relations in the process of knowing, it is still located in the linguistic turn which foregrounds language and discourse – assuming that reality is constituted through language and that objects and language are separate from each other, thus holding the material world at a distance.

Diffraction moves a step further in that it assumes a direct material engagement and incorporates both things and words – the material-discursive.

The primacy of materiality in diffractive analysis is grounded in a solid onto-epistemological framework (Barad, 2007). Diffraction is not constituted as an inner mental activity inside a separated human being; rather it is an inter-connected activity that entangles the human and the non-human (Hultman and Taguchi, 2010). To engage in diffractive analysis means to study the practices of knowing as they are enacted in the materiality of the world, in a state of interdependence with other parts of the world. This onto-epistemological thinking, as Barad (2007) calls it, decentres the researcher as knowing subject and takes us 'beyond the dominating subject/object, human/non-human, as well as the discourse/matter and nature/culture dichotomies' (Hultman & Lenz Taguchi, 2010, p. 539).

Furthermore, a diffractive analysis diverges from a self-reflective, phenomenological or interpretive reading of data, because it moves beyond the representational trap of trying to figure out what a participant really meant by what she or he said (Lenz Taguchi, 2012). A diffractive reading of data goes against interpretivism, as 'interpretation in reflexive analysis is about reflecting sameness (as in mirroring), or identifying differences from something previously identified and acknowledged, a thing, an identity, a category, a discursive theme or a subject position' (Lenz Taguchi, 2012, p. 269). Difference in interpretivism is grounded in an ontological essentialism between identified categories (man/woman, working class/middle class, white/black etc.). Rather, a diffractive analysis views difference as a relational ontology, that is, an effect of connections and relations within and between different bodies, affecting other bodies and being affected by them (Lenz Taguchi, 2012). Diffraction can then be regarded as an ethical and socially just practice, in that it does not do epistemological damage, pitting one theory/position/stance against another, but carefully and attentively doing justice to a detailed reading of the intra-actions of different viewpoints and how they build upon or differ from each other to make new and creative visions.

All in all, a turn to diffraction as a metaphor and methodology requires an important onto-epistemological and ethical shift in our thinking so that we begin to take notice of the differences and transformations that emerge in specific events. As Hultman and Lenz Taguchi (2010) argue, this will make us investigate and do educational research and write our analyses in a very different way, using quite a different language that is more evocative and perhaps poetic. Choosing to enact a diffractive analysis will also create new opportunities for ethical and political connections and transformations that were previously unimaginable (e.g. new social and interpersonal relations).

Conclusion

This chapter has taken the debate regarding the intersections and differences of diffraction and reflection as metaphors and methodologies further, particularly with respect to educational practice and research. We have noted that both methodologies acknowledge the situatedness of knowledge, and offer a more enlarged perspective of the research process. Diffraction alerts us to the entanglement of the apparatus in addition to the embedded and embodied researcher, who is seen as part of the world. Diffraction provides additional affordances through its connection of the discursive and the material, with knowledges making themselves intelligible to each other in creative and unpredictable ways. Barad's (2007) combination of the onto-ethico-epistemological revitalises the research process, making it methodologically powerful through its enlarged vision of making a difference in the world with ethics being an integral part of it (Mazzei, 2014, p. 743). One of the important propositions that this chapter makes is that diffraction is an affirmative methodology which has a great deal to offer for reconfiguring liberal humanist practices used in research methodology.

Although diffraction and reflection differ both as methodologies and as practices, being grounded in different ontologies, epistemologies, and ethics, there is some continuity in the historical development of ideas from one to the other (see, for example, Campbell's 2004 discussion of Haraway's notions of reflexivity and diffraction). This chapter emphasises the prospects of the notion of diffraction as a tool of analysis, for attentive and detailed reading of a text intra-actively through another for the consequential differences that matter. It is suggested that a diffractive analysis goes beyond the idea of reflexivity and interpretation and produces new entangled ways of theorising and performing research practices, co-constituting new possibilities of strengthening and challenging knowledges. The time has come for educational researchers to reconsider the metaphor and methodological implications of reflection and explore the ethico-onto-epistemological potentiality of diffraction in the historical continuities and breaks with the traditions of reflection.

Notes

1   This chapter is based on our previously published article Bozalek and Zembylas (2017).

2   Simply stated, the physical phenomenon diffraction is unique to waves – such as
    water, sound and light waves. Diffraction refers to the behaviour of waves which
    combine when they overlap, and bend and spread out when they encounter an
    obstacle (see Barad, 2007, pp. 74–85 for an extended explanation). In contrast to
    reflecting apparatuses (e.g. mirrors), which produce images, which are more or less
    faithful to the objects placed in front of them, thus producing sameness, diffraction
    patterns mark differences in the relative characters (i.e. amplitude and phase) of
    individual waves as they combine.

References

Archer, M. S. (2003), *Structure, Agency and the Internal Conversation*. Cambridge:
    Cambridge University Press.

Archer, M. S. (2007), *Making Our Way Through the World: Human Reflexivity and Social
    Mobility*. Cambridge: Cambridge University Press.

Archer, M. S. (Ed.), (2010), *Conversations About Reflexivity*. London: Routledge.

Barad, K. (2007), *Meeting the Universe Halfway: Quantum Physics and the Entanglement
    of Matter and Meaning*. Durham & London: Duke University Press.

Barad, K. (2010), 'Quantum Entanglements and Hauntological Relations of Inheritance:
    Dis/continuities, SpaceTime Enfoldings, and Justice-to-Come', *Derrida Today*, 3(2):
    240–268.

Barad, K. (2014), 'Diffracting Diffraction: Cutting Together-Apart', *Parallax*, 20(3):
    168–187.

Barad, K. (2015), 'TransMaterialities: Trans*/Matter/Realities and Queer Political
    Imaginings', *GLQ: A Journal of Lesbian and Gay Studies,* 21(2–3): 387–422.

Beck, U. (1992), *Risk Society*. London: Sage.

Beck, U. (1994), *Ecological Enlightenment: Essays on the Politics of the Risk Society*.
    Amherst, NY: Prometheus Books.

Bozalek, V. and Zembylas, M. (2017), 'Diffraction or Reflection? Sketching the Contours
    of Two Methodologies in Educational Research'. *International Journal of Qualitative
    Studies in Education*, 30(2), 111–127.

Bradbury, H., N. Frost, S. Kilminster and M. Zukas (eds), (2010), *Beyond Reflective
    Practice: New Approaches to Professional Lifelong Learning*. New York: Routledge.

Brookfield, S. (1995), *Becoming a Critically Reflective Teacher*. San-Francisco: Jossey-
    Bass.

Brookfield, S. (2009), 'The Concept of Critical Reflection: Promises and Contradictions',
    European Journal of Social Work, 12(3): 293–304.

Brookfield, S. (2010), 'Critical Reflection as an Adult Learning Process', in N. Lyons (ed.),
    *Handbook of Reflection and Reflective Inquiry: Mapping a Way of Knowing for
    Professional Reflective Inquiry*. Dordrecht, The Netherlands: Springer, 215–236.

Campbell, K. (2004), 'The Promise of Feminist Reflexivities: Developing Donna Haraway's Project for Feminist Science Studies', *Hypatia*, 19(1):162–182.

D' Cruz, H., P. Gillingham and S. Melendez (2007), 'Reflexivity, Its Meanings and Relevance for Social Work: A Critical Review of the Literature', *British Journal of Social Work*, 37: 73–90.

Daley, A. (2010), 'Reflections on Reflexivity and Critical Reflection as Critical Research Practices', *Affilia: Journal of Women and Social Work*, 25(1): 68–82.

Davies, B. (2014a), *Listening to Children: Being and Becoming*. London and New York: Routledge.

Davies, B. (2014b), 'Reading Anger in Early Childhood Intra-Actions: A Diffractive Analysis', *Qualitative Inquiry,* 20(6): 734–741.

Davies, B. and S. Gannon (2013), 'Collective Biography and the Entangled Enlivening of Being', *International Review of Qualitative Research*, 5(4): 357–376

Davies, B., J. Browne, S. Gannon, E. Honan, C. Laws, B. Mueller-Rockstroh and E. Bendix Petersen (2004), 'The Ambivalent Practices of Reflexivity', *Qualitative Inquiry*, 10(2): 360–390.

Deleuze, G. (1988), *Spinoza: Practical Philosophy*. San Francisco, CA: City Lights Books.

Denzin, N. (1997), *Interpretive Ethnography: Ethnographic Practices for the 21st Century*. Thousand Oaks, CA: Sage.

Dewey, J. (1933), *How We Think: A Restatement of the Relation of Reflective Thinking in the Educative Process*. New York: D.C. Heath and Company.

Dolphijn, R. and I. van der Tuin (2012), *New Materialism: Interviews & Cartographies*. University of Michigan Library: Open Humanities Press.

Edwards, A. (2015), 'A Tool for Public Services Research and Development', *International Journal of Public Management*, 11(1): 21–33.

Edwards, G. and G. Thomas (2010), 'Can Reflective Practice Be Taught?', *Educational Studies*, 36(4): 403–414.

Elliot, A. (2002), 'Beck's Sociology of Risk: A Critical Assessment', *Sociology*, 36(2): 293–315.

Fendler, L. (2003), 'Teacher Reflection in a Hall of Mirrors: Historical Influences and Political Reverberations', *Educational Researcher*, 32(3):16–25.

Fook, J. (2002), *Social Work: Critical Theory and Practice*. London: Sage.

Fook, J. (2010), 'Beyond Reflective Practice: Reworking the "Critical" in Critical Reflection', in H. Bradbury, N. Frost, S. Kilminster and M. Zukas (eds), *Beyond Reflective Practice: New Approaches to Professional Lifelong Learning*. New York: Routledge, 37–51.

Fook, J. and F. Gardner (2007), *Practicing Critical Reflection: A Resource Handbook*. London: Open University Press.

Fraser, N. (2009), *Scales of Justice: Reimagining Political Space in a Globalizing World*. Columbia University Press.

Gentles, S., S. Jack, D. Nicholas and A. McKibbon (2014), 'A Critical Approach to Reflexivity in Grounded Theory' *The Qualitative Report*, 19: 1–14.

Giddens, A. (1990), *The Consequences of Modernity*. Cambridge: Polity Press.

Giddens, A. (1991), *Modernity and Self-identity: Self and Society in the Late Modern Age*. Stanford, CA: Stanford University Press.

Gray, B. (2008), 'Putting Emotion and Reflexivity to Work in Researching Migration', *Sociology*, 42: 935–952.

Grosz, E. (1993). 'A Thousand Tiny Sexes: Feminism and Rhizomatics', *Topoi* 12(2): 167–79.

Haraway, D. (1991), 'A Cyborg Manifesto: Science, Technology, and Socialist-feminism in the Late Twentieth Century', in D. Haraway (ed.), *Simians, Cyborgs and Women: The Reinvention of Nature*, New York, NY: Routledge, 149–181. Retrieved from http://faculty.georgetown.edu/irvinem/theory/Haraway-CyborgManifesto. htmlhttp://faculty.georgetown.edu/irvinem/theory/Haraway-CyborgManifesto.html (accessed 4 December 2017).

Haraway, D. (1992), 'The Promises of Monsters: A Regenerative Politics for Inapproporiate/d Others', in L. Grossberg, C. Nelson, P A. Treichler (eds), *Cultural Studies*, New York: Routledge, 295–337.

Haraway, D. (1997), *Modest_Witness@Second_Millenium: FemaleMan_Meets_ OncoMouse : Feminism and Technoscience*. New York: Routledge. http://books.google. nl/books?id=ftO4jLQ2RM8C&printsec=frontcover&dq=modest+witness+at+secon d+century&hl=en&ei=QUvfTuqpH4ye-wa-udCvBQ&sa=X&oi=book_result&ct=res ult&resnum=1&ved=0CDAQ6AEwAA – v=onepage&q=modest%20witness%20 at%20second%20century&f=false (accessed 4 December 2017).

Haraway, D. (2000). *How Like a Leaf: An Interview with Thyrza Nichols Goodeve*. New York and London: Routledge.

Harding, S. (1991), *Whose Science? Whose Knowledge? Thinking from Women's Lives*. Milton Keynes, UK: Open University Press.

Harding, S. (1996), 'Rethinking Standpoint Epistemology. What is "Strong Objectivity"?', in E. Fox Keller and H. E. Longino (eds), *Feminism and Science* Oxford, UK: Oxford University Press, 238–248.

Harrison, J. K. and R. Lee (2011), 'Exploring the Use of Critical Incident Analysis and the Professional Learning Conversation in an Initial Teacher Education Programme', *Journal of Education for Teaching*, 37(2): 199–217.

Hickson, H. (2011), 'Critical Reflection: Reflecting on Learning to be Reflective', *Reflective Practice*, 12(6): 829–839.

Hoel, A. S., and I. van der Tuin, (2012), 'The Ontological Force of Technicity: Reading Cassirer and Simondon Diffractively', *Philosophy & Technology*, 26(2):187–202.

Holmes, M. (2010), 'The Emotionalization of Reflexivity', *Sociology*, 44(1): 139–154.

Hultman, K. and H. Lenz Taguchi (2010), 'Challenging Anthropocentric Analysis of Visual Data: A Relational Materialist Methodological Approach to Educational Research', *International Journal of Qualitative Studies in Education*, 23(5): 525–542.

Jackson, A. Y. and L.A. Mazzei (2012), *Thinking with Theory in Qualitative Research: Viewing Data Across Multiple Perspectives*. London: Routledge.

Jackson, A. Y. and L.A. Mazzei (2013), 'Plugging One Text Into Another: Thinking With Theory in Qualitative Research'. *Qualitative Inquiry*, 19: 261–271.

Juelskjær M. and N. Schwennesen (2012), 'Intra-active Entanglements: An Interview with Karen Barad', *Kvinder, Koen og Forskning*, 21(1–2):10–23.

Juelskjaer, M. (2013), 'Gendered Subjectivities of Spacetimematter', *Gender and Education*, 25(6):754–768.

Kleinman, A. (2012), *Intra-actions. Mousse*, 34: 76–81.

Korthagen, F., J. Kessels, B. Koster, B. Lagerwerf and T. Wubbels (2001) *Linking Practice and Theory: The Pedagogy of Realistic Teacher Education*. Mahwah, NJ: Lawrence Erlbaum Associates.

Larson, M. and D. Phillips (2013), 'Searching for Methodology: Feminist Relational Materialism and the Teacher-Student Writing Conference', *Reconceptualizing Educational Research Methodology*, 4(1): 19–34.

Latour, B. (2004), 'Why Has Critique Run out of Steam? From Matters of Fact to Matters of Concern', *Critical Inquiry*, 30: 225–248.

Lenz Taguchi, H. (2010), *Going Beyond the Theory/Practice Divide in Early Childhood Education: Introducing an Intra-Active Pedagogy*. London & New York: Routledge.

Lenz Taguchi, H. (2012), 'A Diffractive and Deleuzian Approach to Analysing Interview Data', *Feminist Theory*, 13(3): 265–281.

Lenz Taguchi, H. and A. Palmer (2013), 'A More "Livable" School? A Diffractive Analysis of the Performative Enactments of Girls' Ill-Well-Being With(in) School Environments', *Gender and Education*, 25(6): 671–687.

Lyons, N. (ed.) (2010), *Handbook of Reflection and Reflective Inquiry: Mapping a Way of Knowing for Professional Reflective Inquiry*. Dordrecht, The Netherlands: Springer.

MacLure, M. (2013), 'Classification or Wonder? Coding as an Analytic Practice in Qualitative Research', in R. Coleman and J. Ringrose (eds), *Deleuze and Research Methodologies* Edinburgh: Edinburgh University Press, 164–184.

Mezirow, J. (1990), 'How Critical Reflection Triggers Transformative Learning', in J. Mezirow (ed.), *Fostering Critical Reflection in Adulthood: A Guide to Transformative Emancipatory Learning*, San Francisco, CA: Jossey-Bass, 1–20.

Moon, J. (1999), *Learning Journals: A Handbook for Academics, Students and Professional Development*. London: Kogan Page.

Mruck, K., & Mey, G. (2007), 'Grounded Theory and Reflexivity', in A. Bryant and K. Charmaz (eds), *The Sage Handbook of Grounded Theory* (pp. 515–38). London, UK: Sage.

Murris, K. (2016), *The Posthuman Child: Educational Transformation through Philosophy with Picturebooks*. London and New York: Routledge Contesting Early Childhood Series.

Palmer, A. (2011), '"How Many Sums Can I Do?" Performative Strategies and Diffractive Thinking as Methodological Tools for Rethinking Mathematical Subjectivity', *Reconceptualizing Educational Research Methodology*, 1(1): 3–18.

Phillips, D. K., and M.L. Larson (2012), 'The Teacher–Student Writing Conference Entangled: Thinking Data With Material Feminisms', *Cultural Studies? Critical Methodologies*, 12(3):225–234.

Phillips, D. K., and M.L. Larson (2013), *The Teacher-Student Writing Conference Reimaged: Entangled Becoming-Writing Conferencing*. Retrieved from http://digitalcommons.linfield.edu/educfac_pubs/8 (accessed 4 December 2017).

Pillow, W.S. (2003), 'Confession, Catharsis, or Cure: The Use of Reflexivity as Methodological Power in Qualitative Research'. *International Journal of Qualitative Studies in Education*, 16(2):175–196.

Pillow, W. (2015), 'Reflexivity as Interpretation and Genealogy in Research', *Cultural Studies? Critical Methodologies*, 15(6): 419–434.

Pollard, A. (2002), *Reflective Teaching: Effective and Evidence-Informed Professional Practice*. London: Continuum.

Schneider, J. (2002), 'Reflexive/Diffractive Ethnography', *Cultural Studies? Critical Methodologies*, 2(4): 460–460.

Schön, D. (1983), *The Reflective Practitioner*. New York: Basic Books.

Schön, D. (1987), *Educating the Reflective Practitioner: Toward a New Design for Teaching and Learning in the Professions*. New York: Basic Books.

Van De Putte I. and M. Verstichele (2013), 'Recognition and Difference – A Collective Biography', *International Journal of Qualitative Studies in Education*, 26(6): 680–691.

Villenas, S. (1996), 'The Colonizer/Colonized Chicana Ethnographer: Identity, Marginalization and Co-optation in the Field', *Harvard Educational Review*, 66(4): 711–731.

Snaza, N. and J. Weaver (2015), 'Introduction: Education and the Posthumanist Turn', in N. Snaza and J. Weaver (eds), *Posthumanism and Educational Research*, Routledge: London, 1–14.

Zeichner, K. M. and D.P. Liston (1996), *Reflective Teaching: An Introduction*. Mahwah, NJ: Lawrence Erlbaum Associates.

Zembylas, M. (2014), 'The Place of Emotion in Teacher Reflection: Elias, Foucault, and Critical Emotional Reflexivity', *Power & Education*, 6(2): 210–222.

4

The Politics of Animality and Posthuman Pedagogy

Delphi Carstens

Introduction

This chapter critically examines negative anti-human, as well as more affirmative posthuman and new materialist gestures that help to explode the anthropocentric conceit that the world or cosmos is as it is for us only. A sensory pedagogy and politics of animality utilises such moves to generate aesthetic corridors of 'disorientating affects' that enable 'new conditions for thought and action'. Scientific narratives of extinction, cosmological and evolutionary deep-time scenarios, Deleuzo-Guattarian trickster cartographies, vibrant materialisms, sonic fictions and speculative fabulations (both visual and textual) provide potentially useful affect-laden classroom tools, the author argues, for crafting an 'anti-speciesist pedagogy' appropriate to the new conditions of the Anthropocene.

Thinking with the uncanny

There seems to be a pressing need in education for new modalities that are less entangled in the anthropocentric conceits of modernity; aesthetic orientations that might help us find new relationalities through which pedagogy might be transformed. Despite a recent proliferation of human-animal studies and other environmentally-orientated interdisciplinary courses in tertiary institutions across North and South America, Europe, South Africa and the Antipodes, many educational praxes still find themselves adhering, often by default, to a reductionist pedagogy that boxes in how subject fields should be taught, thought and practised (Stengers 2015; Wallin 2014). Underpinning such reductionist pedagogical schemas is the often unquestioned assumption that the category 'human' constitutes privileged life or *bios*, contrasted against the 'bare life' or *zoe* of non-human others and of humans who find themselves 'animalised' and consequently available for exploitation (Sassen 2014). To counter such destructive enclosures and conceits, posthumanism suggests a 'deconstruction of the humanist subject as well as the attributes normally associated with it such as free will, self-determination and mastery' (Fernández 2016, p. 275). New materialist theories extend this premise, drawing on a multidisciplinary approach to investigate the multiple 'interrelations between technological, biological, environmental and social processes' (Fernández 2016, p. 275). Both posthumanism and new materialisms consider animal and other non-human subjectivities on equal terms with human ones, rendering untenable the 'ontological distinctions between organic and inorganic, animate and inanimate, human and animal, individual and environment' (Fernández 2016, p. 275). Building on this confluence of the human and non-human, Brian Massumi suggests a politics and pedagogy of animality, expressing the hope that, as he writes (2014, p. 3):

> We might move beyond our anthropocentricism as regards ourselves: our image of ourselves as humans standing apart from other animals; our inveterate vanity regarding our assumed species identity, based on the specious grounds of our sole proprietorship of language, thought and creativity.

The onset of the Anthropocene, the geological 'age of man', has brought with a kind of troubling knowingness 'of a horrific human-caused drive toward a sixth mass extinction of species'; a cognisance that is as corrosive towards the anthropocentric schema of privilege as it is illuminating towards the 'neocolonial arrangements of material and energy extractions around the globe' that this schema has enabled (Parikka 2015, p. 6). Visually, the reality of the Anthropocene emerges in various arresting and uncanny ways, for example the 'manufactured landscape' images of artists like Edward Burtynski, which make for compelling and affect-laden classroom viewing. Panoramas of vast factory floors, mounds of e-waste, dead river deltas, enormous oceanic trash-zones, massive toxic open-cast mines, dead agricultural land, and burning rainforests denote a necrotically bounded image of the human, a monster of *bios* at the apex of creation and at the brink of an awful terminus of extinction. 'That the human must [now] become something else to survive is a moot point,' writes Jason Wallin, 'as is the obsolescent conceit that the world is *as it is for us*' (2014, p. 158). To ignore the anthropocentric conceit in our pedagogy is to resign ourselves to a future of climate disasters, resource wars, continued rampant environmental and social expulsions, and the reality of extinction (not only of nonhuman others, but of humans also). Through the use of uncanny visual and written materials, as well as stimulating debates, an animalistic 'anti-speciesist pedagogy' seeks to move away from an anthropocentric educational paradigm that has obfuscated 'the affective potentials' of human subjects for forming productive (as opposed to destructive) 'material connections' with other animals and things (Wallin 2014, p. 147). This chapter asks what strategies we might employ in our pedagogical practices to move beyond the 'blackening' of affective multispecies relationality that has taken place through pedagogy's unwitting affirmation of 'the presumption that there is but one life' that matters, 'and that it is a human one' (Wallin 2014, p. 146). A pedagogy of animality, I will suggest, begins by exploding the anthropomorphic conceit that the world or cosmos is as it is for us only by invoking, in the context of the classroom, various uncanny affects and effects.

The uncanny, which may be defined as 'the familiar suddenly made strange, the everyday when it takes on the numinous aura of the otherworldly', has various stimulating pedagogical functions (Ramey 2013, p. 181). Joshua Ramey believes that invoking the uncanny in the classroom via images, texts and discussion might constitute 'a genuinely communicative' and productive pedagogical strategy (2013, p. 188). To this end, he argues that using the uncanny as a pedagogical aid might help bring about a radical redefinition of 'human well-being in broader [and more inclusive and less destructive] terms' (2013, p. 192). Instead of reflexively retreating from the uncanny, he argues that education needs, at all costs, to embed itself in 'an ethos where we might find ourselves at home in the *unheimlich*' (2013, p. 193). As Wallin writes, 'the disidentification of the world as given' to humans the creation of a new ethico-aesthetic paradigm, will take place only through the uncanny; through the creation of aesthetic 'corridors of disorientating effects and affects' in order to 'create new conditions for thought and action' (2014, p. 152). We might begin to articulate this new paradigm in the classroom by confronting, with the help of science, what Brian Massumi refers to 'aporetic complexities produced at the limits of traditional logic under the sign of the negative' (2014, p. 117).

Arche-fossils, aporias and anti-humanism

The world in which we live and of which we are a part has become increasingly unthinkable. To fully and truly encounter it 'is to confront an absolute limit to our ability to adequately understand the world,' writes Eugene Thacker, proposing that pedagogues employ a kind of aesthetic relation premised on the affective play of cosmic horror (2011, p. 1). With its ability to induce a kind of *horror vacui* or 'dread of infinitude', Quintin Meillassoux's concept of the 'arche-fossil' (2009) constitutes one such 'aporetic complexity' or contradiction that works at the sheer outer limits of a politics of 'bare life' or animality with which we can confront our students. While science is as deeply caught up in the anthropocentric conceit as any other human system, it also happens to offer, according to Meillassoux, compelling direful challenges. It now has the ability, for instance, to describe multiple inhuman vectors, such as the formation of the Milky Way galaxy, the beginnings of biological life, mass-extinction events, the death of the sun, or even scenarios that will occur after the universe has reached a state of absolute entropy. These 'arche fossils', as Ray Brassier (2007, p. 40) explains, form an 'aporia or contradiction' that strikes at the heart of the traditional 'correlationist' frameworks of Western humanist philosophy which presumes that 'nature is a repository of anthropomorphically accessible meaning', and that challenge the anthropocentric assumption that the world exists only to the extent that humans exist to think it.

Philosophy (including 'natural philosophy' or science) and pedagogy should, writes Brassier, 'be more than a sop to the pathetic twinge of human self-esteem' which suggests that nature is our home, exists for our benefit, and is our 'beneficent progenitor' (2008, p. xi). The myth of modernity, which Heidegger identified as the myth that nature is a boundless stockpile of resources available on demand (in Davis 1998, 144), is part of this world view that cannot conceive of the worth of anything outside of the human framework of reference. Under these circumstances, we must embrace at all costs the realist conviction that there is a mind-independent reality which, as Brassier writes, 'is indifferent to our existence and oblivious to the "values" and "meanings" which we would drape over it in order to make it more hospitable' (2008, p. xi). The more science understands the vastness of the universe (even at the quantum level) and the immense timescales of evolution, or theorises about the inevitable evolutionary morphogenesis (i.e. the evolutionary redundancy) of humanity, the more we approach what Schopenhauer refers to as the *nihil negativum*, or the absolute horizon of human thought (in Thacker 2011, p. 47). This is an uncanny horizon that we need to bring into play in our pedagogy. Knowledge from the life-sciences and geo-sciences, particularly about the realities of extinction have, like thermodynamics or cosmological deep time scenarios, present conundrums that erode anthropocentric certainties. As McCarthy and Rubidge note, 'the long record of both normal and mass extinctions reveal that, in the grand scheme of things, *Homo sapiens* may not be very special' and that our emergence was, in all probability, purely accidental (2005, p. 300). More shocking to anthropocentric thought, perhaps, is the uncanny possibility that, despite our depredations, 'life will go on,' albeit in radically different forms, 'with impersonal ambivalence for human concerns or nostalgias' (Wallin 2014, p. 158). Thacker explains the ongoing conundrum of all these aporias: 'we are increasingly more and more aware of the world in which we live as a non-human world [but] we cannot help but to think of the world as a human world, by virtue of the fact that it is we human beings that think it' (2011, p. 47).

Science's capacity for revealing a universe entirely indifferent to or completely unrelated to human existence, forms the basis for a kind of radical anti-humanism/ahumanism that, as Rosi Braidotti points out, tends to 'dismiss the need for a subject altogether', along with a sense of 'ethical or political accountability' (2013, p. 102). To counter the absence of responsible ethics inherent in some forms of radical anti-humanism, Braidotti proposes a more affirmative project of '*zoe* egalitarianism' that, while remaining attentive to the corrosive contradictions of science, overturns the *bios/zoe* relation by veering off in the direction of the 'simultaneously materialist and vitalist force of [bare] life itself, *zoe* as the generative power that flows across all species' (2013, p. 103). While urgently considering the aporias of infinitude and the paradoxes of human consciousness, a more generative *zoe* egalitarian politics of animality also attempts to reclaim the hidden world of vital affects that anthropocentric science has so resolutely ignored (and which consumer-driven capitalism has so shamelessly exploited). It does so by paying close attention to the uncanny entanglements between *res cognisans* (the 'privileged' realm of cognition) and *res extensa* (the other, lesser material, affective 'things' which are supposedly 'not mind,' 'without volition' and the traditionally excluded subjects of *zoe*, or 'bare life'.

An ethico-aesthetic paradigm orientated toward *a* life

Deleuze and Guattari, as Massumi explains, conceive of a new ethico-aesthetic paradigm that resumes and re-intensifies 'the nature-culture/human-animal continuum to invent unrepresentable movements of singularisation constituting a revolutionary [multispecies] democracy in the act' (2014, 108). These philosophers conceive of affect, the provinance of *zoe*, in terms of 'immanence and pre-personal intensities' (Vermeulen 2011, p. 181). Although this approach is closely attentive to the aporias of contemporary science, it also conceives of a committed aesthetic response that relates affect to the body's capacity to act, to engage, and to connect in new ways with the world. As Patricia Ticinto Clough observes, in the writing of Deleuze and Guattari, a diversity of living animal intensities, immaterial artistic interventions, technological devices and scientifically-mediated 'hyperobjects' (such as nebulae, galaxies, black holes, etc.) are imagined as 'allowing us to "see" affect and to produce [new] affective bodily capacities' (2007, p. 2). Not only does such an approach blur the boundaries between disciplines of learning, between humans and things, between material and immaterial, between natural and the artificial, but it also 'inserts the immaterial into felt vitality, the felt aliveness given in the pre-personal bodily capacities to act, engage, and connect – to affect and be affected' (2007, p. 2). This 'affective turn', therefore, indicates a shift toward articulating a new configuration of bodies and matter, based around what social scientist and media theorist Nigel Thrift describes as a 'processual sensualism', which emphasises 'the materiality of thinking [and] material culture', while engaging sensually with an entanglement of embodied subjects, both human and non-human (2006, p. 140). What this sense of affect attempts to achieve, as Wallin writes, is to free *zoe*, or bare 'life itself', from predetermined anthropocentric limits, to open the body to relations and forms of desiring production beyond the human (2014, p. 158).

In the classroom, we can teach with *zoe* egalitarianism by calling attention to the affective world of non-verbal communicability and attention that we share with our animal kin. Yet how do we begin to articulate this slippery world in order to teach with the animal and with affect? According to David Abram (1997, 14), the embodied 'sensual world' we share with animals is an 'elemental terrain of contact', an 'inexhaustible field of unmediated experience', of textures and smells, 'fields of rippling and raucous sounds, shifting shapes and colors'. Deleuze and Guattari conceptualise this terrain as a shifting and immanent zone of perpetual becomings, 'where modes of individuation very different to that of a person, a thing or a subject' operate (1988, p. 261). This interzone is pervaded by haecceities and transports of haecceities; 'a climate, a wind, a fog [...] an hour, a season, an atmosphere, an air, *a life*', entering into perpetually shifting relations of 'speeds and slownesses' (1988, p. 262). This is also the world that we, as humans, 'have most thoroughly forsaken' in our privileging of mind over matter (Abram 1997, p. 15).

A politics of animality takes it for granted that science, philosophy, art, pedagogy and even cognition itself have only ever taken place with the help of 'insensate' things: 'the turning stars, apples which fall, turtles and hares, rivers and gods, cameras and computers' (Muecke 2007, p. 1). A pedagogy that pays close attention to this uncanny relationality (between that which thinks and that which supposedly does not) is a trickster pedagogy. Tricksters, after all, are mediators that bridge between *heimlich* and *umheimlich*, between the homely of the comfortably human and the unhomely wilderness of affects that we perplexingly share with animals, things, landscapes, ambiences and other forces beyond our ken. A pedagogy of animality, then, is rhizomatic. Concerning itself with the *intermezzo*, the in-between, it finds itself, like the trickster, at home with the altogether difficult to determine. Such a pedagogy engages with, and does not shy away from, difficult or uncomfortable knowledge, seeking out, as tricksters invariably do, the uncanny agency of 'things' (whether these things are human, animal, material or immaterial), as well as their capacity to affect and be affected, to enter into multispecies assemblages and admixtures. This is a pedagogy, as Wallin writes, that teaches using 'the filthy lesson of symbiosis', namely, 'that we have never been humans proper by fact of our constitution by microbial and amoebic intelligences that are not our own', and that we 'share significant similarities in genetic makeup' with other life forms as divergent as 'orangutans and pumpkins' (2014, p. 155). Overturning anthropocentric conceits such a pedagogy of animality calls for a prismatic multimodal ecological praxis that mediates, as tricksters do, between different becomings, some violent and sad, some hadean and hidden, some trans-corporeal, joyful and productive. The 'bare-life' assigned to the anthropocised 'animal' is based on the premise that language and cognition belong solely to the human. Such an assumption 'submerges our capacity for relatedness', granting us humans 'a freedom of a paradoxical nature, the freedom to modernise' (Franke 2010, p. 48). Turning aside from this, a politics of animality turns towards the more productive *a life* assigned to the posthuman or new materialist animal.

Massumi, in *What Animals Teach Us About Politics* (2014), convincingly demonstrates the relation between human language and animal play, exploding the founding conceit of anthropocentrism, namely that complex communicability is something that only humans do. Animal play, he writes, forms a prototype for human language through its complex formulations of an 'enactive cartography' that plays with existential territories through 'ludic gestures', as well as 'categorical and vitality affects' in order to 'establish an instantaneous back and forth between present and future' (2014, p. 23). There is a kind of non-cognitive, affective language at work in animal play, an intensity of feedback that is forever in the process of becoming, aimed in the direction of the future, yet thoroughly *in* the world rather than affectively disengaged from it. Deleuze introduces the concept of '*a life*' to indicate this process of enmeshment that we share with animals as an antidote to the alienation of modernity, using the indefinite article to indicate that 'a life' indicates a 'pure subjective current' (1997, p. 3). Simultaneously, 'a life', as Jane Bennet explains in *Vibrant Matter* (2010), also names something general; 'a restless activeness, a destructive-creative force . . . a vitality proper not to any individual but to pure immanence' (2010, 54). Not life, therefore, or *the* life or even the 'self', but rather that which remains uncannily removed from the 'self'; that which is indeterminate, undefined, and forever unfolding – a sense of affect that, as Bennet writes, can manifest sometimes as 'beautitude', or sometimes as sheer 'terror' (Bennet 2010, p. 53).

What, then, is the nature of 'a life'? This is a question frequently asked by artists and writers whose work embodies an ethics of *zoe* egalitarianism. The question of 'a life' is one we may pose to our students – by way of novels, poems, images, theoretical praxes and projects – as a way of teaching them to think beyond the conceits of anthropocentrism and also to inculcate in them a new ethico-aesthetic paradigm grounded in concepts of social and environmental justice. South African novelist, Nthikeng Mohlele, for instance, provides a wonderful teaching aid for exploring notions of 'a life' in his novel *Rusty Bell* (2014). Mohlele asks what a life is 'when its possibilities suddenly become ostensibly finite; given rather than chosen' (Gray van Heerden 2014, p. 1). Moreover, 'what is to be expected from a life; at once vibrant yet so unknowable?' (Mohlele 2014, p. 139). These questions are both posed and answered in a rather humorous fashion in the novel by a talking trickster cat, who appears to Mohlele's chief protagonist during a self-imposed fast. This 'prankster' tells tales (as we should in our classrooms), about the perils of speciesism, nomenclature and anthropocentrism, the affective nature of 'a life' and what animal familiars can teach us about being in immanence.

For Deleuze and Guattari, nurturing and encouraging an 'aesthetico-existential' process via the notion of 'a life' is crucial for a philosophical practice that aims to operate *in* the world rather than in some transcendent realm of ideals and abstractions. Their onto-epistemology, although it pays heed to science, does not turn to scientific reductionism for its praxis. As Félix Guattari explains in *The Three Ecologies* (2000, p. 20), 'in order for us to extend our existential territories we must abandon scientific (or pseudo-scientific) paradigms and return to aesthetic ones [...] like a performance, one must construct [a life], work at it, singularise it'. Singularity, it must be noted, is for Guattari *not* the same as conventionally understood individuality; rather it involves pre-personal, pre-individual affects. 'Affect', as Massumi (1988, p. xvi) writes, echoing Mohlele's imaginative insights in *Rusty Bell*, does not denote a 'personal feeling' but rather 'a pre-personal intensity corresponding to the passage from one experiential state to another'. In *Rusty Bell*, the role of the animal trickster is to serve as guide through the paradoxical passage of a life. Mohlele's talking cat who, 'with admirable skill and exactitude, narrated terrors suffered at the hands of sadistic humans', helps his narrator to overcome his own personal sufferings at the hands of the same by instilling a 'reckless gallantry'; a keen animal awareness of life's passions and intensities, its beauty and terrors, its myriad potentialities and inevitabilities (2014, p. 122).

Affect is often expressed via the spectral agency of the uncanny (Massumi 2002, 30). The body, as Mohlele observes throughout *Rusty Bell*, has its own experience of sensation and intensity that is abstruse and resists the logic of language. Of course, the point at which the talking trickster cat enters the narrative is also an uncanny moment, both cognitively out of time and firmly 'in time' from the perspective of affect; a moment of 'delirium', a certain 'nowness' when a 'strange lucidity' suddenly enters the deterritorialised frame induced by the narrator's fast (2014, p. 113). Deleuze and Guattari, who derive their interpretation of affect from Spinoza, write that affect denotes 'relations of movement and rest, speed and slowness' (1988, p. 260). Affect, as Mohlele demonstrates, lies at the core of a life; a type of non-conscious experience of intensity, a resonance transmitted between bodies and across the human-animal divide. This is something we tend to notice only when we step, for an uncanny moment, out of the frame of our thoroughly modernised lives.

As Royle (2003, p. 2) suggests, such moments of stepping out are uncanny moments, involving a sense of creeping strangeness; a strangeness located in ontological and epistemological disturbance – 'a crisis of the natural, touching upon everything that one might have thought was "part of nature": one's own nature, human nature, the nature of reality and the world'. As Mohlele's narrator realises, the uncanny materialises when we realise that we are caught up and implicated in the very processes we are trying to comprehend. The uncanny has to do with the sense of being 'lost in the world' that assaults us when the familiar is rendered unfamiliar, when the boundaries that separate nature from culture, animate from inanimate, individual from collective, living from dead, embodied from disembodied, or the future from present or past are suddenly agitated (Royle 2003, p. 2). These are all extremely useful points of aesthetic departure when attempting to teach with a politics of animality, and they are suggested by the narrator of *Rusty Bell* – a seemingly ordinary human who finds himself suddenly embroiled in a strangeness given to dissolving all assurances about stable identity. The uncanny, as Royle (2003, p. 10) explains, manifests when 'one tries to keep oneself out [of the trouble], but one cannot … [when] the escape clause is confounded'.

It is not only the occasional work of literature like *Rusty Bell* that finds itself, uncannily, in the affective world of the animal. All art, literature, philosophy, science and music, as Deleuze and Guattari, write, find themselves 'continuously haunted by the animal' and the 'melodic, polyphonic and contrapuntal conception of nature' that animals invoke in us terms of their creative 'language' of precepts and affects; their markings of territories through smell, posture, colours of display and songs in counterpoint (1994, p. 185). From the Deleuzo-Guattarian perspective, a pedagogy of animality is, therefore, a pedagogy of 'survival' and of 'creativity'; of 'being on the [continuous] lookout', as our animal cousins are, for the differential relations of speeds and scales, the 'shocks or vibrations, which must give rise to thought in thought' (in Stivale 2014, p. 69). For pedagogues, this means being on the lookout for unexpected connections, mixing together insights from different disciplines of knowledge production, continuously bringing the unexpected and the uncanny into the classroom, as well as experimenting with different styles and subject matters in order to find whatever works. If something does not work, a pedagogy of animality will, trickster-like, attempt a different model or graft together a new assemblage of possible relations. Like the *intermezzo* praxis of the trickster, the art of pedagogy requires, like all art does, a strange coupling of order and chaos. As Elizabeth Grosz (2007, p. 3) writes, the affects that a trickster pedagogy needs to explore are 'non-human becomings' that connect the 'lived phenomenological body [...] with fields "outside" that the body itself can never experience directly'. Immersing itself in the chaos of life, art is one handy, and often uncanny, pedagogical tool with which we might disrupt and frame chaos by 'rendering it sensory' (Deleuze and Guattari 2009, p. 204). Aside from art works, we have the literary adventures of science fiction/speculative fabulation/sonic fiction (sf) – all of which keenly express the question of *a* life by framing its chaos ('at once vibrant yet so unknowable') in relation to the transport of affects or haecceity.

Dark haecceities, sonic ecologies of fear and transformative panic

While a politics of animality pays close attention to formulating a *zoe* egalitarianism along the lines of joyous and exuberant energies, it cannot ignore the darker and more shadowy side of affect that I have already referred to.

Sometimes it needs to undertake 'a mad vector', a flight 'on a witch's broom' into trickster cartographies in which 'House and Universe, *Heimlich* and *Unheimlich*, territory and deterritorialisation' are commingled (Deleuze and Guattari 2009, p. 186). For us as pedagogues to gain a foothold on such slippery, potentially unproductive territory, we need to consider how becomings-animal modulate between relations of speed. We need to teach about the glacial slowness of geological/evolutionary time and contrast it with the vertiginous speeds of human/animal lives and immaterial forces (such as the speeds of light or sound). There are also the extreme and reactive affective speeds of joy/terror or sluggish creep of tedium/unease that we need to explore more creatively through examples of art and aesthetic relations. These speeds and slownesses, as well as their intermingling, are what define the notion of a haecceity (namely the sense of thisness/hereness/nowness). As far as bodies are concerned, haecceity expresses 'nothing but affects and movements, differential speeds [that impact] the ability to affect and be affected [. . . something] that directs the metamorphosis of things and subjects' (Deleuze and Guattari 1988, pp. 261–262). As Erin Manning (2013, p. 30) expresses the radically embodied, transmissive and collective nature of affects and haecceities thusly:

> The body, a haecceity: the thisness of experience active as a singularity in the dephased now. Not individual but individuation. Not subject but collectivity [...] the body before the subject, in advance and always toward subjectivity (rarely there), the body as transindividuation, the body as resonant materiality, the body as the metastable field before the taking-form of this or that. The body, always more than one, replete with the force of life.

Sonic theorists Steve Goodman (2009) and Kodwo Eshun (1998, 2003) are, like Manning, keenly interested in the affective potential of bodies. They identify an uncannily embodied trickster frequency in Afrofuturistic 'sonic fictions' (musical styles such as Jungle, Kwaito, Dubtechno, Detroit-techno, etc.) that seek to collectively and sonically galvanise bodies in a quest for new relations of affect and transports of haecceity. As with many Afrofuturistic experimentations (literary, visual and auditory), the intention behind these 'styles of encounter' is 'to defy the violent imposition' of a 'tyrannical, taxonomical order of seeing' into the 'bodies of those' who, like animals, have been 'made into specimen' (Gains and Segade 2008, p. 146). The work of artists like Wangechi Mutu, writers like Octavia Butler, sonic collectives like Drexciya, or performance-based social justice activists like Detroit's Complex Movements, through their active identification with the alien and non-human, mobilise and create novel aesthetic relationalities out of abject dystopian and alienating affects. Their often shocking and violent affects and effects are intentionally located 'differentially [and] on the edge' where, as Manning writes, 'the force of life meets life itself' (2010, p. 30). Discerning modernity as 'the condition of alienation, understood in its most general sense, as a psychosocial inevitability', Afrofuturism uses 'extraterrestriality and space exploration' as platforms for 'speculation' and 'hyperbolic tropes' (Eshun 2003, p. 299). Mapping the 'imposed dislocations and forcible mutations' that characterise the laying waste of biopower (slavery, forced migration, genetic engineering, ecological devastation, etc.) across time and space, Afrofuturism manufactures distance from the Enlightenment conceptions of what it means to be human, 'manufacturing tools' for 'critical intervention' within the brutalising schemas of Anthropocene expulsions (Eshun 2003, p. 301).

Locating the potential for a pedagogy and ethics of animality in a contemporary Afrofuturist musical scene dominated by electronic hardwares and softwares that produce schizophony (sounds without recognisable natural sources) may seem outlandish. Yet, as design theorist Anthony Dunne points out, the contemporary 'electroclimate' of electronically produced music, 'defined by wavelength, frequency and field strength' arises from 'a confluence between natural and artificial landscapes' – a convergence that first appeared in the 'electronic fictions' of avant-classical or Jazz composers such as Sun-Ra and Stockhausen, who sampled and expressed electromagnetic frequencies in order to open themselves 'to a music of the whole earth' (2009, pp. 103–104). In exploring this vibrational ocean, writes Dunne, contemporary electronic artists have employed the affective terrain of horror and abjection to sensually explore the contours of the uncanny merger between the natural and artificial, the human and the animal, as well as the mysterious nature of the 'world-in-itself' and the impenetrable limits of human cognition (2009, p. 104). This sonic experimentation finds its most convincing and visceral expression in the abstract 'rhythmachine' of countercultural dance-floor orientated 'urban machine musics', which graft a more complete vocabulary of animal affects (sounds, gestures, groupings, markings/graffiti) to 'reverse engineer what bodies can do' (Goodman 2010, p. 198). As Ramey (2012, p. 153) writes:

> Some kind of deep apprehension of the vibratory state of matter seems to be occurring in [electronic] music, when [sonic artists] explore the interior life of tonality, breaking sound out of cliché, neutralising timbre through electronic instruments, through the production of uncanny, cosmic mantras.

While music brings us close to a world of vital and vibrant materiality, there is much more than simple affirmation at stake with the 'black noise' of Afrofuturist sf. The uncanny or *umheimlich* requires us to not only consider the cosmic fullness of life, but also its turbulence. People and animals cannot always piece their lives back together after exposure to what Bennett terms the 'terror' and 'meaninglessness' of 'world-annihilating violence' that 'make us numb' and induce us to 'lose touch with life' (2010, p. 53). To this we might add the violent and often senseless devastation of habitats, the 'dead land and dead water [. . .] sites marked by the expulsion of biospheric elements from their life space' that Saskia Sassen (2014, p. 150) records alongside the multiple social expulsions of capitalism. Violence and alienation speak to the contemporary sense of a dark haecceity that we need to bring to our pedagogies. Rather than being vehicles of nihilist capitulation, 'in its most convincing formulations, the negativity of a politics of [electronic] noise is twisted into an engine of construction', an affirmative form of *zoe* egalitarianism, 'a reservoir of rhythmic potential, a parasitic probe beckoning toward the future', directed at an audience yet to come (Goodman 2010, p. 192). Teaching with and through the theorists and practitioners of Afrofuturist sf may, therefore, form a crucial part of the search for a future-orientated politics, ethics and pedagogy of animality that, as Ramey suggests, is engaged in a process of 'learning with the uncanny' (2013, p. 181).

Conclusion: pedagogical science fictions

A politics of animality plays with the possibilities inherent in contemporary sf and other diverse avenues of artistic, theoretical and pedagogical experimentations that extend beyond the human. As Donna Haraway observes, today 'we are talking seriously mutated worlds that never existed on this planet before [. . .] and it's not just ideas, it's the new flesh' (cited in Kunzro, 1995, p. 3). The 'new flesh' that Haraway refers to is, of course, the immediate concern of bio-power, namely genetic manipulations and other novel technological platforms, such as computing, that are learning fast from advances in the life-sciences. Software programmers, for instance, have begun to mimic the behaviour of slime-moulds in generating adaptive code, grafting the dynamics of biological evolution, namely, 'mix, mutate, evaluate, repeat [. . .] and experiment' into a new computing paradigm (Johnson 2001, p. 171). Such an expansion of technological processes and techniques into the sphere of life itself has, of course, enabled greater degrees of social control, exploitation, extraction and environmental destruction (Sassen 2014). Pedagogy therefore needs to pay attention to and teach about these potentially parasitic developments and their uncanny implications. It also needs to urgently explore the more affirmative possibilities of symbiosis inherent in creative multi-modal syntheses. Afrofuturist sf, as well as the numerous interventions of affect-orientated posthumanisms and new materialisms to which I have alluded, are already exploiting such uncanny transdisciplinary potentials to shift attention to a more inclusive vision of the human/animal informed by a more hopeful programme of *zoe* egalitarianism. In the contexts of these new posthuman theoretical/speculative forms, the 'new flesh' is no longer the exclusive domain of biopower, but rather a radically affective domain open to transversal code-sharing between divergent fields of knowledge, cultures, bodies and species. By eschewing anthropocentrism, a pedagogy informed by these affective/posthuman/new materialist turns in theory will, as I have argued, attempt to reconceptualise questions of nature and culture, rethinking the relations between technologies, societies, time, and the ontologies of bodily matter. We live in a world in which 'the spaces in which humans and animals can be together have progressively increased in scale as new forms of materials, which are also new forms of spacing, have allowed new kinds of eco-social relations to exist' (Thrift 2006, p. 143). These relations constitute the core of my suggested pedagogy of animality. Goodman and Eshun's sonic collectives, for instance, spring immediately to mind as excellent teaching aides for exploring how new forms of space/spatial exploration and material interrelation are already manifesting in popular culture at large.

References

Abram, D. (1997), *The Spell of the Sensuous*. New York: Vintage Books.

Bennet, J. (2010), *Vibrant Matter: A Political Ecology of Things*. Durham: Duke University Press.

Braidotti, R. (2013), *The Posthuman*. Cambridge, UK: Polity.

Brassier, R. (2007), *Nihil Unbound: Enlightenment and Extinction*. New York: Palgrave MacMillan.

Davis, E. (1998), *Techngnosis: Myth, Magic + Mysticism in The Age of Information*. London: Serpents Tail.

Deleuze, G. (1997), 'Immanence: A Life', *Theory, Culture, and Society,* 14(2): 3–7.

Deleuze, G. and F. Guattari (1988), *A Thousand Plateaus: Capitalism & Schizophrenia*. Translated by Brian Massumi. London: Continuum.

Deleuze, G. and F. Guattari (2009), *What is Philosophy?* Translated by Hugh Tomlinson and Graham Burchill. London: Verso.

Dunne, A. (2009), *Hertzian Tales: Electronic Products, Aesthetic Experience, and Critical Design*. Cambridge, Massachusetts: MIT Press.

Eshun, K. (1999), *More Brighter Than The Sun: Adventures in Sonic Fiction*. London: Quartet Books.

Eshun, K. (2003), 'Further Considerations on Afrofuturism', *The New Centennial Review*, 3(2): 287–302.

Fernández, M. (2016), 'Posthumanism, New Materialism and Feminist Media Art', *Proceedings of the 22nd International Symposium on Electronic Art*. Hong Kong: ISEA, 275–278.

Franke, A. (2010), 'Much Trouble in the Transportation of Souls', in A. Franke (ed.), *Animism Volume 1*. London: Sternberg Press, 11–53.

Gaines, M. and A. Segade (2008), 'Tactical Collage', in D. Singleton (ed.), *Wangechi Mutu: A Shady Promise*. Bologna: Damiani, 145–146.

Gray van Heerden, C. (2014), 'Treatise on a Life', Slipnet. Available online: http://slipnet.co.za/view/reviews/treatise-on-a-life/ (accessed 15 May 2015).

Grosz, E. (2007), *Chaos, Territory, Art*. New York: Columbia University Press.

Guattari, F. (2000), *The Three Ecologies*. Translated by Paul Sutton and Ian Pindar. London: Athlone Press.

Haraway, D. (1991), 'Cyborg Manifesto', *Simians, Cyborgs, and Women: The Reinvention of Nature*. London: Free Association Books, 149–181.

Johnson, S. (2001), *Emergence*. London: Penguin Books.

Kolbert, E. (2011), 'The Age of Man', *National Geographic*. March: 70–76.

Kunzro, H. (1995), 'You Are Cyborg: An Interview with Donna Haraway', *Wired*. Available online: http://www.wired.com/wired/archive/5.02/ffharaway.html?person=donna_haraway&topic_set=wiredpeople (accessed 5 June 2015).

McCarthy, T. and B. Rubidge (2005), *The Story of Earth & Life: A Southern African Perspective on a 4.6-Billion-Year Journey*. Johannesburg: Kumba Resources.

Manning, E. (2013), *Always More Than One*. Durham: Duke University Press.

Massumi, B. (2014), *What Animals Teach Us About Politics*. Durham: Duke University Press.

Meillassoux, Q. (2009), *After Finitude: An Essay on the Necessity of Contingency*. London: Continuum International Publishing Group.

Mohlele, N. (2014), *Rusty Bell*. Pietermaritzburg: University of KwaZulu-Natal Press.

Muecke, S. (2007), 'The cassowary is indifferent to all this', *Rhizomes*, 15 (Winter). Available online: http://www.rhizomes.net/issue15/muecke.html (accessed 5 September 2015).

Parikka, J. (2015), *The Anthrobscene*. Minneapolis: The University of Minnesota Press.

Ramey, J. (2012), *The Hermetic Deleuze: Philosophy and Spiritual Ordeal*. Durham: Duke University Press.

Ramey, J. (2013), 'Learning the Uncanny', in D. Masny and I. Semetsky (eds), *Deleuze and Education*. Edinburgh: Edinburgh University Press, 177–195.

Royle, N. (2003), *The Uncanny*. Manchester: Manchester University Press.

Sassen, S. (2014), *Expulsions: Brutality and Complexity in the Global Economy*. London: The Bellknap Press.

Stengers, I. (2015), 'Accepting the Reality of Gaia: A Fundamental Shift', in C. Hamilton, C. Bonneuil and F. Gemenne (eds), *The Anthropocene and the Global Environmental Crisis: Rethinking Modernity in a New Epoch*. London: Routledge, 134–144.

Stivale, C.J. (2014), '*Etre Aux Augets*: Deleuze, Creation and Territorialisation', in P. MacCormack (ed.), *The Animal Catalyst*. London: Bloomsbury, 69–80.

Thacker, E. (2010), *In The Dust of This Planet: Horror of Philosophy Vol.1*. Winchester, UK: Zero Books.

Thrift, N. (2006), 'Space', *Theory, Culture & Society*. 23(2–3): 139–155.

Wallin, J. (2014), 'Dark Pedagogy', in P. MacCormack (ed.), *The Animal Catalyst*. London: Bloomsbury, 145–162.

Part Two

Ethics and Response-ability in Pedagogical Practices

5

Each Intra-Action Matters: Towards a Posthuman Ethics for Enlarging Response-ability in Higher Education Pedagogic Practice-ings

Carol A. Taylor

Introduction

Critical posthumanism dislocates traditional ideas of the human as centre and ground of ethical understanding. Instead, in posthumanist/new materialist mode, ethical considerations become a matter of relations, engagements, and entanglements, and ethical relations become materialised in and through activations, attunements and instantiations. Ethics are about practices that matter or, to be more precise, ethics emerges as the moment-by-moment material doings which activate matterings which include more than the human.

For Braidotti (2013, p. 48), a posthuman ethics proposes 'an enlarged sense of inter-connection between self and others, including the nonhuman or "earth" others'. This enlarged sense of ethics emerges when ecology and environmentalism are included in considerations of what matters and who counts. It 'requires and is enhanced by the rejection of self-centred individualism. It produces a new way of combining self-interests with the well-being of an enlarged community, based on environmental inter-connections' (Braidotti 2013, p. 48). For Barad (2007, p. 142) a posthuman/new materialist ethics is as 'ethic of worlding' as an in situ in-relational attunement to the 'dynamism of becoming' which emerges through 'specific material reconfigurings of the world'. Haraway (2016) speaks of 'response-ability' – which recognises the moral force of the other to respond in a move which shifts away from 'us' (humans) 'speaking for' the other. This chapter deploys these relational orientations and the ethical practices they promote to consider a pedagogic instance from my higher education teaching.

This deployment indicates how posthuman ethics can provide powerful motivation for widening the orbit in considering who and what matters and who and what counts in higher education. However, conceptualising and doing pedagogy and ethics in the enlarged sense of ethics that Braidotti speaks of, requires 'us' (humans) to give some things up as well as doing some hard work to develop new, unfamiliar and sometimes difficult ways of being, doing and thinking.

The chapter deals with what I think we have to give up first: 'our' anthropocentric egocentricity and its imbrication in a humanist ethical framework that has served 'us' (albeit not very well if you count how many wars are going on right now in the world and how many species have disappeared over the past 50 years) since the Enlightenment. Following this, I discuss the contours of a posthuman ethics and its relational imperatives in a little more detail, and argue that Barad's (2007) ethico-onto-epistemology, Haraway's (2016) response-ability and Braidotti's (2013) affirmative ethics have their necessary location in practices that are more humble, more halting, and more concrete than we have been led to believe and think ethics and morality 'ought' to be. The posthuman/new material feminist ethical frames I draw on emphasise a need to focus on actual, material practice – or, rather, what I think of as practice-ings, because all practice occurs as an unfinished unfolding. I then tease out some of the consequences of this recasting of ethics through a particular pedagogic instance involving a class trip to a University Holocaust Memorial Day exhibition on an undergraduate module I teach. The main thread of my argument is that activating posthuman/new materialist relational ethics can help shape more expansive pedagogic practice-ings which may (just may) be productive of new modes of responsibility, accountability and commitment. But first:

Why we need to exit the cul-de-sac of humanism

I have been pondering the need to get out of the ethical cul-de-sac that humanism has led 'us' into for some years now (Taylor 2016). This need revolves around a number of key problems. The first problem is the relation humanism sets up between the individual and the universal. Humanist ethics locates moral conceptions in individual human bodies while, at the same time, positioning ethics within abstract, universalising and human rights-based discourses. In sliding between these two poles of the individual and the universal, philosophical discussions distinguish between morality – which is said to be about personal character and the moral principles of an individual, group or tradition – and ethics – which is used to refer to the study of morality in social systems and how moral principles are put into action (Taylor and Robinson 2014). However, from a posthuman stance, the individual-universal dichotomy actually serves to obfuscate ethical issues of responsibility and acts as a sleight of hand to (arguably quite complacently) cover up the astonishingly lamentable state of worldly affairs that humans fail to/ have to take responsibility for.

To add a little background: the individual-universal duality which both shapes humanist ethical thinking and enables 'us' to evade ethical actions came about as a result of Enlightenment, European philosophical allegiance to the traditions of deontological and consequentialist ethics. Deontological ethics, also known as the 'ethics of principles', originated with Immanuel Kant, who proposed that humans are rational, autonomous beings whose existence is shaped by moral laws which are universal, general and unconditional. Kant proposed that such laws are equitable, have universal applicability, and can be articulated in frameworks, codes and procedures to regulate ethical conduct. This way of thinking will be familiar to many who have submitted research proposals to Institutional Ethics Review Boards and research councils, or whose profession is regulated by codes of conduct. In contrast to this, consequentialist ethics originate with Jeremy Bentham, whose 'utilitarian ethics of consequences' maintains that taking consequences into account is the best route to ensuring the greatest well-being for the greatest number. The central argument here is that focusing on the effects of actions impels us to consider their beneficence and impact on others. As an ethics of particular situations, consequentialist ethics might seem ostensibly more helpful to a posthumanist ethics in that they can put deontological ethics to the test by asking difficult questions about how universal principles apply in specific situations for particular people (Taylor 2015). However, like deontological ethics, consequentialist ethics are oriented to the regulation of human affairs. Ethics is circumscribed to the human realm because it is grounded in a philosophical view that humans, as sovereign subjects in possession of reason, will use their reason – the highest and god-given faculty man (*sic*) has – to arrange the world in a reasonable manner. In humanism, then, man figures as an ethical, political person from whose ego, rational certitude and boundaried body ethical action emanates. Ethics is directed 'at' others with whom man interacts or perhaps more precisely, *on whom* he acts; ethics grounds a disposition in which man can (quite literally) dispose of the world, nature and all the creatures who inhabit it from his indisputable location as centre, source and authority of ethical reasoning.

Ethics formulated in this humanist vein gives rise to a second problem: that the supposedly 'universalistic' values presumed to be a 'god-given birthright' turn out to be quite partial in the end, deriving as they do from particular, historical and questionable Western epistemologies. As feminist, postcolonial, Black, queer, intersectional and indigenous scholars have amply shown, these epistemologies are normatively-based on the outlooks and viewpoints of the 'standard' political citizen – that is, one who is male, White, Western, able-bodied and heterosexual. The Enlightenment ideals they encode – rationality, objectivity and scientific progress – have acted as a powerful impetus for Western individual-universalist ethical frameworks, but the unmasking of this epistemology as a founding fantasy of power-over is both welcome and overdue. And this is the second reason why I think humanism has led us into an ethical cul-de-sac: it fundamentally functions through practices of othering. It positions every being not made in the image of 'Mr Normal' as aberrant, unequal and, therefore, able to be discounted. Ethics and morality, then, as functions and outcomes of liberal humanism, work as white, male, colonialist exclusionary practices aimed at securing hegemony for some and delivering only partial benefits for only some 'others'. Indeed, it is the case that when particular groups of people (and never nonhumans) have progressively, often via emancipatory narratives or violent political struggle, or the latter mingling with the former, been accorded some share in the Enlightenment narrative of 'progress', then this has been specifically because they have been deemed by those White, male power-brokers as having demonstrated sufficient developed rational human qualities to have 'graduated into humanhood' (Spivak, cited in Wolfe 1998, p. 43–4) from their formerly 'uncivilised' and 'natural' state.

There is an additional, third reason why we need to exit the humanist ethical cul-de-sac: the principle and practice of human exceptionalism which presumes that humans are the most important beings in the world is based in the presumption that the world, its natural resources and all other creatures which inhabit it, are available for use by humans for their particular ends. This humanist disposition puts the world is at his – man's – disposal. Human exceptionalism is, therefore, another othering, via the institution of a binary – human as 'culture', nonhumans and the inorganic world as 'natural other' which justifies varying modes of species-specific violence, from zoos and the misery of captivity, to approximately 1.5 million animals euthanised in animal shelters in the USA each year, to intensive dairy farming, to destruction of land and marine habitats. The logic of humanist exceptionalist ethics makes these violences not only possible but necessary for securing 'our' 'natural' place as insurmountably superior and different, and for enabling us to obtain the resources 'we' need to inhabit the planet at the level of 'comfort' and 'ease' we require. Human exceptionalism, in unholy alliance with technocracy, capitalist expansion, and necro-politics, has, therefore, enabled 'us' humans to arrogate to ourselves the ethical right to dispose of nonhuman bodies in any way we wish – a train of ethical thinking that has undoubtedly led to the suffering and extinction of nonhuman animals on a vast scale.

The three reasons outlined above are underpinned and cross-cut by a fourth reason why it is necessary to exit the humanist ethical cul-de-sac: the presumption that objectivity is obtainable, desirable and required to guarantee Truth and therefore ensure human progress. Daston and Galison (2007, p. 371) have shown, however, that 'the emergence of [objectivity] is recent and contingent', and that the 'stranglehold' of objectivity on the epistemological imagination is a recent 'rupture' occasioned by modernity and its humanist centerings. Interestingly, they argue that the elevation of objectivity as the one and only epistemic virtue is grounded in fear – a fear that knowledge based in subjectivity may give rise to errors, errors borne of passion, sensuousness, imagination. For the scientific imagination to succeed, objectivity has to be pitted against the 'weakness' of subjectivity and subjectivity has to be controlled and corrected by efforts of will, sacrifice and renunciation. As feminist scholars of science (Fox Keller 1985; Haraway 1988; Harding 1993) have long known and admirably demonstrated, and as Daston and Galison (2007, p. 374) underline, 'the demands [objectivity] makes on the knower outstrip even the most strenuous forms of self-cultivation, to the brink of self-destruction'. Adherence to objectivity both shapes the image of the idealised knower as he who has overcome all his sensuous frailties in pursuit of Truth (most emphatically with a capital 'T') *and* has divorced knowledge irrevocably from the body. Subjectivity is a cardinal sin in Enlightenment, humanist epistemology.

From a posthuman, new materialist perspective, enthroning objectivity and reason as epistemic virtues *par excellence* does some neat ethical work to bifurcate the world into a series of binaries (male/female, reason/emotion, mind/body, self/other), accord privilege to the former term in the couplet, and denigrate the second term. But, as these binaries and the discussion above show, an epistemology is not separate from an ethics, an aesthetics and an ontology. Haraway (1988) was right to argue that humanist universalism, individualist egocentrism, and scientific objectivity, grounded in and emanating from an epistemology which separates the knower (man) from the known (the world and all its 'others') is a 'god trick', a showy bit of plate spinning, a means to separate the 'clean' body of the mountebank on stage from the unwashed, smelly bodies of his audience. Posthumanist, new materialist ethics bring this (rather extended) bout of shadow-boxing with reality to an end: there is no impersonal place of knowing 'outside' the messiness that emanates from embodied and sensory forms of knowing, and distance is neither desirable nor possible in mutually entangled futures on a shared planet. Instead of a dis-engaged ethic of use it proposes an entangled ethics of relation, the features of which I now outline.

Posthuman Ethics/Relational Orientations

Earlier, I suggested that the frameworks proposed by Karen Barad, Rosi Braidotti and Donna Haraway could be helpful in reconceptualising ethical being, doing and thinking. In this section, I expand on this and propose that posthumanist, new materialist ethics entails five relational orientations. After that, I discuss how these orientations informed an instance of pedagogic action in higher education.

Orientation 1: Posthuman/new materialist ethics are affirmative in respecting and valuing all bodies

In the posthuman ethical frame, *all* bodies, not just human bodies, matter and count and it is this more expansive and inclusive orbit that can begin to undo the problem of selfishness and self-centred individualism that humanism has wedded 'us' to for so long. Braidotti (2013, p. 49) writes that the rejection of individualism is also a rejection of nihilism and defeatism and, in their place, promotes 'an ethical bond of an altogether different sort from the self-interests of an individual subject'. What follows, she argues, is an 'enlarged sense of inter-connection between self and others' (*ibid*, 49). This point is supported both by Wolfe (2010) – who argues that forging 'trans-species affinity' is part of the hard moral work that needs to be done to forge a less violently exclusionary posthuman ethics – and by MacCormack (2012, p. 10) – who proposes that posthuman ethics have to 'de-establish' the human as 'a site both of a certain reality and the way the concept of the human has been privileged in constituting all reality at the expense of those who do not count as human'. These ethical re-orientations provide a welcome impetus to do away with the binaries which have produced and held denigrated categories of being in place for so long. Such doing away with isn't necessarily easy though: as Chiew (2014) notes, it seems relatively easy to include dogs, cats and zebras, for example, in trans-species affinities, but what about viruses, microbes, snakes, lice and cyborgs?

Orientation 2: Posthuman/new materialist ethics propose a logic of entanglement

The rather difficult question about inclusion raised just now provides a push to consider a second aspect of posthuman ethics: the role played by entanglement. Barad (2007) develops the concepts of entanglement and intra-activity to draw attention to the fact that there are no separate and clearly bounded entities in nature, but that entities come into existence through the act of making agential cuts, and that these cuts both institute boundaries to separate things off from each other (cf. the dualisms of humanism) and bring things together in new relations (cf. human-animal relations). The notion that entities do not pre-exist their relations, that they are constituted *through* their relations and are therefore always entangled together in an ongoing and dynamic process of emergent mattering, poses a severe challenge to humanist deontological and consequentialist ethics, with their representationalist ethical logics. If 'we' are already entangled with all and any 'others', such that the categories of I/you, we/them, us/other are rendered redundant, then there can be no ethical speaking 'of' or doing 'for' 'others' in the relational ontology proposed by Barad, because ontology *is* relationality. 'We' (humans) *are* microbes, lice, cyborgs, viruses etc – apparently 90 per cent of the human body is made up of the microbiome: nonhuman, microscopic organisms which regulate metabolism, digestion, immunity and even mood. Matter is agentic, and matter and meaning are mutually constituted and ontologically inseparable. Hence, there can be no separation of ethics from epistemology and ontology; instead, there can only be 'ethico-onto-epistemology' in which, *contra* Descartes, knowledge is knowing-and-becoming-in-relation' to/with matter and meaning. As Barad (2007, pp. 392–393) says, 'we (but not only "we humans") are always already responsible to the others with whom or which we are entangled, not through conscious intent but through the various ontological entanglements that materiality entails'. Ethics is an ongoing act of accountability in an ongoing relational process of 'worlding' which works outside dualist understandings of ethics.

Orientation 3: Posthuman/new materialist ethics are powered by an affective politics

Just as ethics are not separate from epistemology, aesthetics or ontology, neither can ethics be separated from politics. Of course, in posthuman/new materialist vein, politics is reconceptualised in relational mode and affect provides a valuable conceptual-practical resource to re-think ethics as an affective politics. Here,

Spinoza's notion of affect as power, passion, desire and action is relevant. For Spinoza, affect is not emotion and is not localised in individually separable bodies; affect is multiple, it is a force, a vitalist power, a capacity to act and to be acted upon; affect traverses all bodies and binds them together via cross-cutting flows. MacCormack (2012) notes that affect is an incarnate relation. The importance of this in developing a posthumanist ethics is that where Descartes split body from mind, Spinoza reintegrates them. For Spinoza, there is 'no body without mind, no individuality without connection, no connection without another dividuated life with its own concomitant reality, no affect without expression, will as appetite beyond consciousness and, perhaps most importantly, no thought or theory without materiality' (MacCormack 2012, p. 4). Ethics powered by an affective politics figures bodies as porous, as open to each other; as bodies experiencing other bodies in encounters and in relations. This point is well made by Massumi (2015, p. 57) who explains that a politics of affect works by triggering cues 'that attune bodies while activating their capacities differentially', thereby opening 'minor lines' of 'political potential' which emerge as 'an active part of the constitution of [the] situation' (Massumi 2015, pp. 56–57). Furthermore, because affective politics are inherently collective, and dynamically traverse all bodies, they bring new potentials for in-forming those bodies in ways which can re-modulate and re-form situations. A politics of affect is, therefore, in Massumi words, an 'alter-politics', which carries the capacity to potentialise new modes of ethical becoming and doing in opposition to conformity.

Orientation 4: Posthuman/new materialist ethics activate an ethic of concern

Posthumanist, new materialist ethics enact a shift from an ethic of care to an ethic of concern, which, in effect, is a shift from responsibility to response-ability. This is not a play on words but a recasting of the terms of who/what matters and what/who counts in ways which revitalise understandings of what is at stake in ethics in relational mode. Chiew (2014, p. 53) notes that the pervasive assumption of traditional humanist ethics is that 'the originating source of responsibility is a human duty of care that is (or ought to be) extended toward other entities who will receive, rather than enable it.' An ethic of care is about care *for* the other. Many who advocate better treatment of animals, for example, remain centred in a humanist ethic of care discourse which presumes that animals are more vulnerable than humans, are unable to articulate their needs, and have a weak sense of agency in comparison with humans. Animals are, thus, seen as dependent on humans; they are 'living things' which have to be taken care of (Taylor 2017). Likewise, feminist discourses have a long affiliation with an ethic of care. Feminist ethics of care have focused on participants in the context of their lives and communities, and have sought to ask what constitutes compassionate and caring action for specific groups perceived as disadvantaged and on the receiving end of unequal treatment (Taylor and Robinson 2014). While these feminist ethics of care efforts are laudable in trying to move beyond any easy sense of 'empowerment' as a passing of the baton of power back to dispossessed and unequal individuals or groups, it is still the case that the ethical focus remains on humans as responsible and rational cognitive agents doing things for other humans, often within the orbit of rights-based legislative discourses.

Therefore, while an ethic of care remains a human affair, an ethic of concern, founded in response-ability, shifts beyond this human framing. Here, Whitehead's process ethics, with their founding presumption that there are no hierarchical differences between subject (human) and object (animal), is useful. This presumption enables Whitehead (1929) to argue that 'each occasion is an activity of concern' in which 'concern' figures as 'a weight upon the spirit. When something concerns me, I cannot ignore it or walk away from it. It presses upon my being, and compels me to respond' (Shaviro 2008, p. 1). And concern, as an involuntary experience of being affected by others, 'opens me, in spite of myself, to the outside' (Shaviro 2008, p. 1). As noted above, this 'affective tone' is a non-personal fusing of subject-and-object in-relation. Concern conceived in this way as a relational, connective force is affiliated with Stengers' (2005, p. 188) recasting of responsibility as a non-linear, non-causal attentiveness which shift ethics away from general principles to specific acts of 'tak[ing] the time to open your imagination and consider this particular occasion', and in which 'paying attention as best you can' is the most valuable (and ethically useful) thing to do. It is also affiliated to Haraway's (2016) notion of 'response-ability' as an empirical ethical practice which emerges as a mode of obligation in the meetings between nonhuman and humans. Concern and response-ability, based in an ontology of reciprocity, active co-presence, sensitivity and receptive openness, provide useful reorientations for the generation of a posthuman ethics.

Orientation 5: In posthuman/new materialist ethics each intra-action matters

An active, open relational ethics of concerned companionability and response-ability requires attunement to particular bodies in relation in the here-and-now.

This has been implicit in the preceding discussion and is made explicit in Karen Barad's (2007, p. 185) comment that 'each intra-action matters'. If Barad is right to say that each intra-action matters – and I think she is – then the challenge posed by posthuman ethics is profound, both for what we do in our higher education pedagogic practices, and in how we live our lives to enable the flourishing of all beings. Indeed, these two things are not separable. As Barad (2007) notes, in an agential realist account, 'the primary ontological unit is not independent objects with inherent boundaries and properties but rather phenomena', whereby 'phenomena are the ontological inseparability/ entanglement of intra-acting agencies'. Ethics is always an intervention – or, better, an *intra-vention*. Envisaging ethics in this way recasts ethical agency as an enactment-in-relations amongst all bodies, and not as a 'thing' possessed by a sovereign and boundaried human subject which can be deployed 'on' or 'towards' 'others' as if 'they' were somehow 'outside' the self, a point I made earlier. But more than this it focuses on posthuman ethics as being about materialising in the minutiae of our ongoing relations 'an ethical obligation to intra-act responsibly in the world's becoming' (Barad 2007, p. 178). And it is here that the clear difference between posthumanist ethics and consequentialist ethics becomes apparent. While both focus on ethics as situational, specific and unique, consequentialist ethics remain in thrall to human agency, posthuman ethics – in urging the need for attending to capacities, affective flows, and relational response-ability in which all living bodies are the site of ethical address – recognises that the call to response-ability issued by our entangled connectivity occurs across space and time. Posthuman ethics do not separate out space and time but, instead, enfold past-present-future in 'thicker "moment[s]" of spacetimemattering' (Barad 2014, p. 169), which may produce possibilities for new diffraction patterns – new material matterings – to take hold. A posthuman ethical call, then, erases philosophical disputations about the individual and universal, referred to above, and summons ethics as a life-affirming practice into being.

The five posthuman ethical orientations outlined above have, in my view, the capacity to help shift ethics into a different key and suggest ways of doing ethics differently in higher education pedagogy. In what follows, I offer a pedagogic instance of how this may happen. I focus on this instance as an example of pedagogic practice-ing, that is, as an emergent intra-active pedagogy of material moments and movements which matter, which may, just may, have worked to enlarge the ethical sense-abilities and response-ability of those involved.

Friday 27 January 2017

This email arrives in my inbox on 10 January 2017 at 15:03:

Subject: Holocaust Memorial Day

Dear colleagues

Attached is a flyer about this year's civic commemoration of Holocaust Memorial Day that will take place on Thursday 26 January in the Winter Garden.

Here at the University there will be a small exhibition on display in Heartspace throughout the day on Thursday 26 January and Friday 27 January – more information will follow shortly about this.

Please feel free to forward this information to anyone you know who might be interested.

If you would like to find out more about Holocaust Memorial Day, please go to www.hmd.org.uk

Kind regards

I am teaching a module called *Experiencing Space, Embodying Education* to second year undergraduates on Friday afternoon. But this email touches me bodily; it closes my throat with instant tears; it issues an ethical call I cannot ignore. I have planned my 11 weekly three-hour sessions diligently in advance, scaffolding theories and activities into a structure which carefully builds students' knowledge and skills. Going to the exhibition – inviting students to take time out of class to visit it properly and then consider what emerges from it – would throw that plan out somewhat. But remembrance of the Holocaust – and of other systematic genocides of peoples under various political regimes – has to – *must* – interfere with any planned schedule. I go off into a slight daze sitting at my desk, work forgotten momentarily, as I recall Mary Daly's (1978) work on the European witch-craze of the middle-ages in which, she estimated, up to 11 million women, children and men were killed (burned, drowned, dismembered) or tortured as witches. My mind bumps to the girls kidnapped by Boko Haram, efforts to release them stymied; and then onto the everyday violence against women and girls and the horrific figures on domestic abuse, rape and sexual assault in the UK and elsewhere in the world. I know these don't count as a Holocaust but, as a feminist, I also know they are part of a continuum of death, violence, denigration and control of women that is entwined within unjust power relations, political lack of will, and institutional arrangements that produce privilege along lines of gender, race, class, and able-bodiedness. Holocaust = Death + Destruction. Only some bodies matter. Only some people count. I click on the webpage in the email and notice Hope Azeda's words in the scrolling bar at the top of the Holocaust Memorial Day Trust website: 'There is nothing we can do about the past, but we can do a lot about the present and the future' (http://www.hmd.org.uk).

So, on Friday 27 January 2017, we work in class for an hour then visit the exhibition, which is ten minutes walk away. We stay for 30 minutes, reading the narratives, looking at the photos, some stand together and talk, some go to sit nearby with a coffee and talk, some remain alone. We head back to class in small groups, talking along the way. The last part of the lesson is a discussion that spins around and off from what we have seen and experienced, where we have just been, and where we are now. These spinnings are wide-ranging discussions which include: the importance of individual stories and names in memorialising what happened; the impossibility of representing the Holocaust on screen, apart from a few notable examples such as the Claude Lanzmannn film, *Shoah*, and the László Nemes film, *Son of Saul*; the experience of going on a school visit to Auschwitz and Birkenau; the nature of political control over populations; the ability of ruling political elites to dispose of the bodies of the populace through war, genocide, forced labour, poverty and starvation; the machinic nature of killing on an industrial scale; how bodies and minds are (literally) marked by the legacy of racism. Spinnings which also included: questions about how such things keep happening, looking the other way, thinking it's not happening here, pondering how to survive *in extremis*. And more spinnings: Brexit, Palestine, France and the far right, President Trump, tuition fees, education as output, credentialism and qualification not learning, nationhood, identity, animal rights, bridges not wall. Then and there. Here and now. Us and them. Folded spinnings of theory, practice, politics and ethics that would not have been possible without the exhibition, without walking out of the classroom to visit the exhibition, without a willingness to open oneself up to the exhibition.

Pedagogic Practice-ings for Enlarging Ethical Sense-abilities and Response-abilities

Massumi (2015, p. 57) notes that 'the event cannot be fully predetermined. It will be as it happens'. The session plan went out of the window that Friday afternoon. It had to. The Holocaust Memorial Day Exhibition – those words and images printed on display boards in a university atrium on 27 January 2017 – reverberated, emitted forces, and generated affects which diffracted the normal clocked, coded and scheduled time of pedagogy (the timetabled Friday afternoon session) into an emergent spacetime of connected matterings, as those materially present came into relation with absent bodies, ghostly presences, the bodies of the disappeared – none of whom have, of course, disappeared. How could they? They are waiting for justice to be done. As Derrida (1994 cited in Barad 2010, p. 241) said:

> If I am getting ready to speak at length about ghosts, inheritance, and generations, generations of ghosts, which is to say about certain *others* who are not present, nor presently living . . . it is in the name of *justice* . . . It is necessary to speak *of the* ghost, indeed *to the* ghost and *with* it.

A pedagogic event is not one but many. It is a multiplicity of iterations, it does not sit still, and it keeps making connections, albeit that these may be minor, unbidden and unknown. Its topology is discontinuous, its enfolds past-present-future, and threads multiple matterings together in a connective, layered mesh (Barad 2010). The matted, in/tangible, felt-ing of the event considered here – a class visit to the Holocaust Memorial Day Exhibition – was sensed-known-experienced as an iterative, intra-active becoming of spacetimemattering in which 'we' became entangled with all those ghostly others who called us near so that we might hear them, reckon with them, in the (our) present moment. 'They' hailed us so that, in relation to-and-with them, we were changed, and continue changing. Such meetings with ghosts, I contend, change the 'we', continually reconstitute the 'we', and resituate the 'we' in ethical frame by drawing the responsibilities of the past into the orbit of the present, by engendering sense-ings and provoking glimmers of new modes of response-ability. In this, the 'idiot wind' of history does more than blow through the dust on our shelves (to appropriate Bob Dylan's lyrics), it whirls up a windy space of happening for entangled ethical relationalities: a spacetime for 'alter-politics', for being-with the ghosts of all those others because they matter, and because they show 'us' (who are lucky enough to be alive still) that we are accountable – continually and perpetually – for the cuts we make which inaugurate differences that matter. As Barad (2010, p. 264) says: 'only by facing the ghosts, in their materiality, and acknowledging injustice without the empty promise of complete repair (of making amends finally) can we come close to taking them at their word.'

Considering the Holocaust Memorial Day class visit as a posthuman ethical pedagogic practice-ing created an ethico-onto-epistemological space for students to get a 'feel' for, and affectively apprehend, what is entailed in entangled ethical response-ability. On the exhibition site, on the walk back to the classroom, and in the classroom we talked about genocide as the doing of evil, greedy, paranoid, perhaps insane men (of course it is), AND about genocide as the horrific and ultimate manifestation of political regimes run riot with unlimited and unregulated power (it is that too, of course). What, then, can we do? This is where our various spinnings, mentioned above, led us: reason and objectivity – knowing 'about' something – is not sufficient: it did not prevent the biggest atrocities in history. Ethical action, then, has to mean there is no standing 'apart' at the side of the field, pretending you are not part of the game; what I do involves others – nonhumans (we discussed the christmas turkey sheds of factory farming, battery hens in tiny pens with wings they can't move, discarded dogs over-produced on pedigree puppy farms) and humans alike. Every action I take is co-implicated with and connected to other bodies. Ethics is not abstract; it is embodied practice-ing; it is engaged knowing; it is a materialisation of concern. What you do matters. The class visit to the Holocaust Memorial Day exhibition, the walk back and the discussion which followed provided the theory-practice springboard for the elaboration of the five relational orientations discussed above.

Conclusion

The pedagogic instance I have discussed in this chapter works, I suggest, as an emergent pedagogic practice-ing. As such, it is an activation of an intra-active pedagogy of material moments and movements which matter, and it bears the potential to enlarge the ethical sense-ability and response-ability of those involved. My hope is that it suggests ways in which posthuman, relational ethics may shape pedagogies for social justice and how the doing of pedagogic practice-ings reconstitutes what/who matters and what counts as social justice.

I have come to see the visit to the Holocaust Memorial Day exhibition as an example of a 'thicker moment', that is, as a condensed instance in which capacities, affective flows, sense-abilities, and relational response-ability are enfolded in an entangled connectivity occurring across space and time. Thicker moments, as emergent spacetimematterings productive of new possibilities, issue an ethical call to shift modes of being, doing and thinking in order that new material matterings may take shape. Thicker moments work via encounters with-amongst human-nonhuman bodies, and via attunements to detail, density and specificity which help us see more clearly that that 'each intra-action matters' (Barad 2007, p. 185) in the world's becoming. Thicker moments instantiate a pedagogy of alternative rhythms: a pedagogy which attends to a slower ontology, which opens towards a more care-full and concerned practice, and which offers a more contemplative stance. Doing posthuman ethics as a relational response-ability in pedagogic practice-ings means trying to remove the obstacles erected by self-centred individualism and aiming to promote practices oriented to a more positive affirmation of life. Flourishing is a vital matter of living well in the entangled, immanent relations of knowing and being, because 'meeting each moment . . . is an ethical call' (Barad 2007, p. 396).

References

Barad, K. (2007), *Meeting the Universe Halfway: Quantum Physics and the Entanglement of Matter and Meaning*, Durham: Duke University Press.

Barad, K. (2010), 'Quantum Entanglements and Hauntological Relations of Inheritance: Dis/continuities, SpaceTime Enfoldings, and Justice-to-Come', *Derrida Today* 3(2): 240–268.

Barad, K. (2014), 'Diffracting Diffraction: Cutting Together-Apart', *Parallax* 20(3): 168–187.

Chiew, F. (2014), 'Posthuman Ethics with Cary Wolfe and Karen Barad: Animal Compassion as Trans-Species Entanglement', *Theory, Culture & Society*. 31(4): 51–69

Daly, M. (1978), *Gyn/Ecology: The Metaethcis of Radical Feminism*, Boston, Mass: Beacon Press.

Daston, L. and Galison, P. (2007), *Objectivity*, Cambridge, Mass: Zone Books.

Fox Keller, E. (1985), *Reflections on Gender and Science*, New Haven: Yale University Press.

Haraway, D. (1988), 'Situated Knowledges: The Science Question in Feminism and the Privilege of Partial Perspective', *Feminist Studies*, 14: 575–599. Available online: http://www.jstor.org/stable/3178066. (accessed 4 December 2017).

Haraway (2016), *Staying with the Trouble*, Durham: Duke University Press.

Harding, S. (1993), 'Rethinking Standpoint Epistemology: What is "Strong Objectivity"?', in L. Alcoff and E. Potter (eds), *Feminist Epistemologies*, 49–82, London: Routledge.

MacCormack, P. (2012), *Posthuman Ethics: Embodiment and Cultural Theory*, Surrey: Ashgate.

Massumi, B. (2015), *Politics of Affect*, Cambridge: Polity.

Shaviro, S. (2008), 'Self-Enjoyment and Concern: On Whitehead and Levinas'. Available online: http://shaviro.com/Othertexts/Modes.pdf (accessed 18 April 2016).

Stengers' (2005), 'Whitehead's Account of The Sixth Day', *Configurations*, 13(1): 35–55.

Taylor, C. A. (2015), *A Guide to Ethics and Student Engagement through Partnership*. York: HEA. Available online: https://www.heacademy.ac.uk/resource/guide-ethics-and-student-engagement-through-partnership (accessed 4 December 2017).

Taylor, C. A. (2016), 'Edu-Crafting a Cacophonous Ecology: Posthuman Research Practices for Education', in C. A. Taylor and C. Hughes (eds), *Posthuman Research Practices in Education*. London: Palgrave Macmillan, 7–36.

Taylor, C. A. (2017), 'For Hermann: How Do I Love Thee? Let Me Count the Ways. Or, What My Dog Has Taught Me About a Post-Personal Academic Life', in S. Riddle, M. Harmes and P.A. Danaher (eds), *Producing Pleasure within the Contemporary University*, Rotterdam: Sense Publishers.

Taylor, C. A. and Robinson, C. (2014), '"What matters in the end is to act well": Student engagement and ethics', in C. Bryson (ed.), *Understanding and Developing Student Engagement: Perspectives from Universities and Students*. London: Routledge, 161–175.

Whitehead, A. N. (1929), *Process and Reality. An Essay in Cosmology. Gifford Lectures Delivered in the University of Edinburgh During the Session 1927–1928*, Macmillan, New York, Cambridge University Press, Cambridge UK.

Wolfe C. (1998), *Critical Environments: Postmodern Theory and the Pragmatics of the 'Outside'*, Minneapolis: University of Minnesota Press.

Wolfe C. (2010), *What is Posthumanism?*, Minneapolis: University of Minnesota Press.

6

A Pedagogy of Response-ability

Vivienne Bozalek, Abdullah Bayat, Daniela Gachago,
Siddique Motala and Veronica Mitchell

*Justice, which entails acknowledgment, recognition, and loving attention, is not
a state that can be achieved once and for all.*

Barad 2007, p. x

Introduction

This chapter sets out to examine how particular ethical dimensions identified in
feminist relational ontologies may be enacted by teachers in higher education who
are working towards social justice and flourishing in the contemporary South
African context. The legacy of apartheid persists to affect educational access and
success among students. The intersectionality of race, gender, class, religion and
sexual orientation (among other differences) render many of our students extremely
vulnerable while others continue to benefit from their privilege. The student protests
which both halted the academic project over months across South African Higher
Education institutions and have given voice to students, are an important reminder
of the stark inequalities that continue to impact on student learning and living with
multiple material and affective consequences.

The purpose of this chapter is to think about a pedagogy of *response-ability* by
diffracting the moral elements of a political ethics of care and posthumanist
ethics through each other, focusing specifically on *attentiveness and responsibility*,
and how those elements combine towards a responsive pedagogy. Diffraction is
used as a methodology to put care and posthuman ethics into conversation with
each other and use this to examine our teaching contexts and practices, as
discussed in interviews conducted with and between us for a research project on
social justice in education. We think with and through the work of feminist
theorists and philosophers Joan Tronto (1993; 2013), Karen Barad (2007; 2010;

2014) and Donna Haraway (2008; 2016), who have all written extensively about attentiveness and responsibility. In what follows we elaborate on these concepts by diffracting through each other the ideas of Tronto, Barad and Haraway, all of which are predicated on a relational ontology. We then use the superpositions emerging from these diffractions to envisage how a response-able pedagogy might work and be put to work. We draw on examples from our own practices in higher education institutions to more deeply examine each element.

We are five educators who met at professional development teaching and learning courses and who are located at differently positioned higher education institutions in the Western Cape, South Africa. Our connections and encounters through online engagement/writing, face-to-face meetings and different interdisciplinary pedagogical experiences have led to our common interest in queering what matters in teaching and learning in higher education. Our deliberations and readings about ontological approaches where pedagogy is seen as relational and ethical informs our work. More particularly, we consider how an affirmative and response-able pedagogy might be enacted – one which shifts beyond distancing and critique, with an openness towards new possibilities through relational responses of becoming-with and rendering each other capable (Haraway 2016). We examine our teaching processes where we are attempting to enact social justice in higher education through a response-able pedagogy. This writing is the result of many and sometimes intense conversations between the five of us, who are educators working in different fields of education: at the University of the Western Cape, Abdullah lectures in business and finance, Vivienne directs higher education teaching and learning; at the Cape Peninsula University of Technology, Daniela and Siddique have introduced digital storytelling in teacher education and geomatics respectively; and at the University of Cape Town, Veronica facilitates workshops in the Department of Obstetrics and Gynaecology. Differently positioned in terms of gender, race, religion, dis/ability, nationality, academic positioning and age, a common concern for enacting social justice in our work and curricula initially brought us together. Our continuing intra-actions across differences have emphasised the urgency of becoming response-able towards ourselves and Others, including the more than human forces influencing our becoming (Barad 2007).

Ethics of care and posthumanism as relational ontologies

We use a diffractive methodology[1] to read Tronto's political ethics of care (1997; 2003) through Haraway's notion of speculative feminism[2] and 'staying with the trouble' (2016) and Barad's agential realism (2007). The views of these three theorists are all based upon a relational ontology – one that rejects the view of individually bounded entities with 'inherent boundaries and properties' (Barad 2007, p. 333). All of these theorists are concerned with how to live as well as possible in the world, Tronto from a care ethics position which looks beyond the human and is inclusive of things and nature and Barad and Haraway from a position which challenges human-centeredness (posthumanism).

The chapter is structured as follows: first, we describe the different theorists' relational approaches to ethics. We then discuss the two major foci of the paper – attentiveness and responsibility, diffracting each element's meanings through the different theorists, and using each of these elements to envision a response-able pedagogy for social justice in higher education. We use superpositions from both of these moral elements – attentiveness, and responsibility – to examine our interview transcripts on socially just pedagogies for thinking about how a response-able pedagogy may be enacted in our southern context.

Tronto's Political ethics of care and Haraway's and Barad's posthuman perspectives

A political ethic of care regards care as both a *practice* and a *process* rather than a moral virtue. The definition of a political ethic of care according to Berenice Fisher and Joan Tronto is the following:

> From a general perspective, care is a species activity that includes everything that we do to maintain, continue and repair our world so that we can live in it as well as possible. This world includes our bodies, our selves and our environment, all of which we seek to interweave in a complex, life-sustaining web
>
> Tronto 1993, p. 103

This view is different from other views on care which focus more on human–human dyadic relationships (Noddings 2002; Ruddick 1989). The political ethics of care is more encompassing as it includes care of the world, material things, the environment as well as self-care. This definition can be seen to be similar to Barad's and Haraway's notions of living and dying or flourishing in the world – Fisher and Tronto refer to flourishing in the definition above as living 'in the world as well as possible'. Their definition of care is interesting when diffracted with Haraway's (2016) notion of *staying with the trouble* – 'learning to stay with the trouble of living and dying in response-ability on a damaged earth' (p. 2). Haraway (2016) believes that we need to form coalitions 'to recraft conditions of living and dying to enable flourishing in the present and in times to come' (2016, p. 137). She writes '[o]ur task is to make trouble, stir up potent response to devastating events, as well as to settle troubled waters and rebuild quiet places'. Similarly to Tronto, Haraway (2008) does not see ethics as a rules-based activity, but as sympoietic (made together with) imaginative playing and taking risks together and a 'propositional worlding activity' towards 'building something better' (p. 92).

Barad expresses her views of flourishing and intra-actions with the world in the following way:

> Intra-acting responsibly as part of the world means taking account of the entangled phenomena that are intrinsic to the world's vitality and being responsive to the possibilities that might help us and it flourish. Meeting each moment, being alive to the possibilities of becoming, is an ethical call, an invitation that is written into the very matter of all being and becoming.
>
> Barad 2007, p. 396

These definitions can be seen to be working towards flourishing and living (or dying) well from a position which surpasses human exceptionalism to include the environment and non-human and more-than-human others.

Tronto's (1993; 2013) political ethic of care, Haraway's speculative fabulation or staying with the trouble (2016) and Barad's (2007) agential realism are predicated on a relational ontology, which starts from the premise that entities do not preexist their relationships but rather come into being through relationships. In other words, there are no separate individuals/entities with discrete boundaries which precede and *interact* with other preexisting individuals/entities, but they rather *intra-act* and are entangled with each other across space and time as phenomena. We are all part of the world, and both matter and discourse are entangled as material-discursive phenomena, termed by Barad (2012) 'entanglements of spacetimemattering' (p. 32). A process of cutting together/apart in one move, through agential cuts, differentiates and entangles us as entities which come into being. This is different from Cartesian cuts which assume a separation between subject and object as entities. Barad's (2007) agential realism acknowledges the value of difference rather than engaging difference as a reductive process that seeks sameness. As Barad (2012, p. 46) notes 'empirical claims do not refer to individually existing determinate entities, but to phenomena-in-their-becoming, where becoming is not tied to a temporality of futurity, but rather a radically open relatingness of the world worlding[3] itself.'

The three theorists' concerns resonate with each other in a number of ways. First, they all emphasise practices, activities and processes rather than focusing on dispositions, and rule-based or principle ethics. Second, all three theorists are concerned with flourishing or living as well as possible in the world, although Haraway has now also added dying well as she is considering the damaged environment we are now living with. Third, all of them assume that we are part of the world and cannot extricate ourselves or view it from it at a distance. This means that we are implicated in everything and can never take a non-innocent position in relation to the world. Fourth, they all reject individualism and assume that we are entangled in a web of relationships. Fifth, all theorists emphasise the importance of staying with or being alive to what is happening in the world. Finally, all three theorists insist on the entanglement of ontology (being), epistemology (knowing), politics and ethics.

This chapter uses the resonances of these theorists' approaches as a potentially useful way of enacting pedagogies in our South African context, focusing specifically on their notions of attentiveness and responsibility for thinking about what a more response-able pedagogy could look like. We put the three theorists' notions of attentiveness and responsibility into conversation with each other, using these diffractions to re-imagine a pedagogy which is response-able and providing examples from our own practice to illustrate our ideas in this regard.

Attentiveness

Attentiveness is the moral element related to the first phase of care, according to Tronto (1993) and refers to the recognition that a need exists. Originating from the Latin word, *attendere* which refers to waiting and overlooking, attentiveness encapsulates the expectation of multiple ways in which needs are noticed. Attentiveness involves regarding and listening carefully, opening ourselves to being affected by the other and making an effort to suspend our own concerns (Tronto 1993). To be attentive, it is important to be able to recognise the other person's embodied difference – to be open to the other and also the other in oneself (Bozalek 2016).

Barad (2007, p. x) defines attentiveness as 'the ongoing practice of being open and alive to each meeting, each intra-action, so that we might use our ability to respond, our responsibility, to help awaken, to breathe life into ever new possibilities for living justly'. In many texts and in interviews, Barad refers to the importance of attentiveness for doing justice to the fine details of texts, especially in a diffractive methodology of reading one text or theory through another (see for example Dolphijn and van der Tuin (2012), Juelskjær and Schwennesen (2012)).

Attentiveness, according to Barad is also important for developing a transdisciplinary approach to research. Traditionally, research within the different academic traditions (such as the 'hard' and 'soft' sciences) has been done using methods and theory internal to the respective tradition. Barad foregrounds attentiveness for working across disciplinary boundaries in her diffractive methodology:

> My aim in developing such a diffractive methodology ... is to provide a transdisciplinary approach that remains rigorously attentive to important details of specialized arguments within a given field, in an effort to foster constructive engagements across (and a reworking of) disciplinary boundaries.
>
> Barad 2007, p. 25

Thus, attentiveness according to Barad (2007) engages with the fine details of texts and of arguments, but above all, for Barad, attentiveness requires respectful and care-full engagements with whatever one is examining.

Haraway's entire approach of speculative feminism/fabulation can be seen as a form of paying attention, as both the Latin and French roots of speculation pertain to attention (French *speculacion* meaning rapt attention and close observation and the Latin *speculationem* meaning close observation and contemplation) (Asberg Thiele and van der Tuin, 2015). Haraway (2016) foregrounds learning to pay attention to each other across species. This cultivation of attentiveness across difference leads to becoming-with, changing who and what the partners become. This is different from empathy which is trying to identify with another – to understand what they are thinking and feeling, but rather a relation of reciprocity and exchange (Despret, 2016). Haraway (2008, p. 19) sees attentiveness in the following way:

> To hold in regard, to respond, to look back reciprocally, to notice, to pay attention, to have courteous regard for, to esteem: all of that is tied to polite greeting, to constituting the polis, where and when species meet.

Haraway sees humans and animals tied together and living with each other in 'non-innocent bonds of respect'. For Haraway, these human and non-human animal companion species need to learn to pay attention to each other through playing together. She also refers to attentive practices of 'thought, love, rage, and care' (Haraway 2016, p. 56). By 'staying with the trouble' Haraway (2016) means learning to be truly present – 'meeting the look of the other, and in so doing facing oneself' (Haraway 2008, p. 88). This is important for attentiveness, as we cannot be attentive without being present.

An attentive pedagogy

What is the new, and what provocations can be gleaned from the diffraction of Tronto, Barad and Haraway's ruminations on attentiveness for higher education pedagogies? An attentive pedagogy would involve activating the 'sensibility of all our embodied faculties' (Lenz Taguchi 2012, p. 272), with a radical openness, so that we are alert and truly present to needs that exist and to the imbrications in our current contexts. Attentiveness is not possible without an openness towards the other (both human and non-human, and the other in oneself). Openness is also about creating material spaces which enable intra-actions and conversations to happen.

Attentiveness leads to a co-constitution or becoming-with the other, rather than a focus on self or the other in a binary manner. In an attentive pedagogy, learning from the other in practices of 'ontological and semiotic' creation and invention carries the potential to make something new happen (Haraway 2008, p. 232). Possibilities arise for both teachers and students to become attentive to complex histories of entanglement and to matters of justice. It is also necessary to be cognisant of asymmetrical reciprocity (Young 1997) in attentiveness, where difference in the other and in the self is respected rather than anticipating commonality and attempting to be empathic.

Applying an attentive pedagogy to our own context

Digital storytelling is one way of creating a space in a classroom to share stories of uniqueness, sameness and difference. This is a pedagogy that is based on transdisciplinarity, as it draws from the field of education, sociology and multimodality and harnesses the specificity of the students' lived experiences. Digital storytelling allows the student voice to be brought into the curriculum in a structured way, and provides a way of listening closely to student needs.

Both Daniela and Siddique have been using digital storytelling for a number of years with teacher education and geomatics students. The digital storytelling process they adopted emphasises collaboration and co-creation of stories, a *becoming-with* others rather than solitary creation of narratives that give a detailed account of students' everyday but often unseen and unheard lived experience.

Daniela: It's a very collaborative process – you could go and do the story by yourself but the process that we have adopted and modified and expanded, students [...] are advised that at least at the beginning, for the first few sessions to come and work in a collaborative way. They tell the story first in smaller groups to their peers, it's about sharing where they're coming from and often they are painful stories that people usually don't want to hear or that they don't even know exist – so it's about showing each other sides of themselves that they usually don't see ...

Siddique uses extensive group work to allow students to become attentive and respectful of their similarities but also differences, by interrogating issues of belonging:

... it's important to try and make them see that they belong to certain groups and those are not just the only groups that they belong to ... I try and do a lot of group work in my class where I put them together and I get them to talk about commonalities, differences, which I think is very important. And I try and get them to ... critique these groups that they belong to.

Digital storytelling is an attentive pedagogical tool, that creates an equitable space, where all students are given attention from multiple audiences, as Daniela explains:

.... and each story is shown and no story is more important than the other. So they all get the same kind of time, space, undivided attention from the whole class and everybody else who was there. It's a very democratic tool. And even if their stories are not of the same quality, it doesn't matter; everyone gets the same kind of audience attention.

Being attentive to all students in similar ways is often challenging, and more so with large class sizes. Students regularly tell stories of gender-based violence, domestic abuse, drugs, gangsterism, poverty and discrimination. Sharing such personal stories can help students to transcend limited personal paradigms and take on broader perspectives, and assist to facilitate intra-active connections across difference. This is an important aspect of a critical posthumanist pedagogy. However, sharing stories can also become a highly emotional experience, in particular, in a context such as South Africa, with its 'everyday trauma', or as Frankish (2009, p. 89) calls it, 'the systemic trauma of contemporary life'. To be able to be attentive to all students' needs requires a number of interventions such as negotiating rules of engagement to establish trust or training a group of peer facilitators in the digital storytelling process before the course starts. However, as Daniela reflects below, one of the major learnings of this project has been the acceptance of the indeterminacy of the process, of accepting one's own vulnerability and staying open to the trouble:

> Because we are so vulnerable in the process it is such a powerful process ... that process is highly challenging because I never know what's going to happen. It's not just the students who are out of the comfort zone, it's me as well – we put ourselves on the line every year because it's also a very emotional process, you never know what's going to happen.

Siddique picks up on that and shares how he uses his own fallibilities and shortcomings as a reciprocal pedagogical device:

> I was thinking about how do I treat my students; one has got to be compassionate and that probably means having unconditional positive regard towards students, but also being honest and being able to give freely – so in a sense it's related to charity; but also besides being able to give of yourself to your students, also being able to receive graciously ... it's important for me to show that I am fallible also, to my students, and I can be wrong. And I like to show that it affects me.

In this way as Low, Brushwood Rose and Salvio (2017, p. 18) write, the digital storytelling model that we apply in our teaching allows for a listening that is *attentive,* by which they mean an extension of the self towards, and even care for the other. It establishes listening as a fundamentally relational practice, where stories, tellers and listeners mutually affect and constitute each other. In this way listening is not passive but becomes an 'active pursuit of stories waiting to be told' (p. 25).

Stories can assist us to imagine alternate subjectivities or realities. They can distil an otherwise complicated theory or ideology into a tangible, understandable product. Haraway is a strong advocate for situated storytelling as a means of knowledge creation. Stories can help to fulfil the posthumanist possibility of being both a navigational and analytical tool:

> We need stories (and theories) that are just big enough to gather up the complexities and keep the edges open and greedy for surprising new and old connections.
>
> Haraway 2016, p. 101

Responsibility

Joan Tronto's (1993) second element in the political ethic of care is *responsibility,* by which she means that after a need is noticed, understood and apprehended (caring about/being attentive), there follows the responsibility that something should be done to provide for the need in question. Tronto (1993) differentiates between obligation which emanates from a sense of duty or formal/legal ties, and responsibility which is a response after recognising a need for care. Responsibility is frequently equated with accountability – both Haraway (2008, 2016) and Barad (2007) regard them as interchangeable. Barad (2012, pp. 46–7) sees responsibility or accountability as an ethico-onto-epistemological commitment to understand how different agential cuts matter in the reiterative intra-activity of worlding, that is, the entanglements of 'spacetimematterings'. Being accountable means seeing yourself as entangled and part of the world as well as being obligated, bound to and indebted to the Other (Barad 2012). Barad (2007) also relates responsibility to what matters and what is excluded from mattering. She emphasises that responsibility is not ours alone but is about entanglements with self and other – (not necessarily a human other) 'here and there, now and then' (p. 394). It is not something one chooses, but it precedes intentionality of consciousness:

> Ethics is therefore not about right response to a radically exterior/ized other, but about responsibility and accountability for the lively relationalities of becoming of which we are a part.
>
> Barad 2007, p. 393

Haraway (2008, 2016) reminds us that responsibility or accountability are never finished and also never solely located in dualistic relations but also multidirectional relationships which can include other species, recognising as well the asymmetry of these relationships. Taking responsibility means being accountable for the non-innocence in our intra-actions and the non-innocence of the agential cuts that are enacted. Haraway (2016) explains that responsibility is not about representing the other, rather a becoming-with in an ethical manner.

A responsible pedagogy

A responsible pedagogy would mean attending to ethico-onto-epistemological issues in our teaching which involves more than being accountable for what we and our students know. It involves how we get to know, what we do and help enact, what commitments we take on for what exists and our entangled relations of inheritance (Barad 2007). In other words, a responsible pedagogy showcases how we are actively learning-with, doing-with, making-with, and becoming-with each other tied together in sympoiesis as teachers and students, and matter. Rather than engaging with binaries like subjects/objects, teachers/students, we explore teaching as the relational phenomenon that is constituted through intra-actions leading to a becoming-with. This approach affirms difference generating new possibilities that move beyond traditional binary thinking.

When we speak of 'becoming-with', there is a mutual relationship in which teachers and students render each other capable. Such becomings are not about imitation, nor literal transformations (the student becoming like the teacher, for example), but rather the proliferation of multiple identities and ways of being in the world. We take this idea from Haraway's (2003; 2008) 'becoming worldly with' and Giugni (2011, p. 26) who building on Haraway's concept suggests that:

> Becoming worldly with' is a practice of 'grappling with' looking for and creating leakages; colouring outside the lines; pushing ourselves to be, think and do beyond what we consider knowable and comfortable.

A key practice of becoming-with is being accountable for the agential cut of how we enact our positionalities. Braidotti (2013) talks about the importance of locating oneself: 'the posthuman subjectivity I advocate is rather materialist and vitalist, embodied and embedded, firmly located somewhere' (p. 51). In order to 'develop critical tools to deal with the complexities and contradictions of our times' (p. 52) being accountable means that we are responsible for the positionalities that we enact and that also enact us, as discourses are both material and performative (Barad 2003). In our intra-actions, the outcome is not a separation of student (exterior object) and lecturer (subject) but a becoming-with in a way of staying with the trouble in terms of problematising conventional positionalities of race, class, gender, and the power differentials of other established categories. Choosing to focus on the performativity of our race, gender, class is key to being responsible. We are not suggesting that these positions are fixed subject positions but that we are aware of the agency of our gendered black, white, brown bodies, our specific accents, languages, class trappings and the discourses surrounding them as the intra-actions emerge within our teaching contexts. The agential separability (the way the phenomenon of teaching is agentially cut) should allow for lecturers to be learners, for students to be teachers as well as for both to enact new intra-active configurations. What we focus on in our teaching constitutes an agential cut that is enacted from and through our entanglements as part of the world. Thus the textbooks, teaching artefacts, languages, mediums and modes of teaching that we choose (or those that choose us) are critical for the type of agential separability that is elicited through our teaching. The affect and emotions that emerge in the phenomenon of teaching are also moments of becoming-with and constitute an important site of accountable intra-action in a responsible pedagogy.

Applying a responsible pedagogy to our own context

Our different contexts have invoked several ways of engaging with responsible pedagogies. Abdullah acknowledges that his responsibility to his students requires conscious accountability of mutual-becoming. By questioning his enactment of a socially just pedagogy, his sense of responsibility led to a self-critical stance in his effort to be accountable to his students:

> So again I only look at myself – so critical for me is looking at how what I'm doing perpetuates injustices. So the critical part would be my awareness of what I do that inadvertently without me knowing, perpetuates injustice, and that's the critical dimension: in thinking about your own involvement or your own role in the perpetuation of injustice.

This shows a connection with students and an acknowledgement of the non-innocence of Abdullah's social location, despite all good intentions. One of the challenges of rendering students capable within current higher education knowledge practices, is a lack of cognisance of students' needs (attentiveness) and a carelessness in pedagogical practices, leading to an irresponsible pedagogy. Abdullah makes himself available to assist students through his open door approach, so as to ensure that the asymmetrical power relations between him as a lecturer and students can be managed in a responsible and accountable manner. The idea is not just to assist but to see how he can further his becoming an attentive and responsible lecturer through these interactions. It is the intra-action between the students and himself that renders him a capable lecturer:

> I've always had an open policy to students, I've always tried to assist. There have been a few students that when they came to me and they said, "please help with this", and then I would make that effort. And there were times where I would make myself available at lunch time, and say that anybody with any problem can come.

In Veronica's interview she explained how her innovative human rights workshops around health issues of lesbian, gay, bisexual and transgender communities were initiated by her departmental response to the curricular gap. Students were attentive to the necessity for including difference in the curriculum, questioning the injustice of disregarding this key population group's healthcare needs. The healthcare of sexual and gender minorities is now the topic of compulsory participatory workshops with senior undergraduate medical students, run together with invited guests from the community. An open and collaborative approach enables the past to be entangled with the present to render future doctors more capable of addressing and responding appropriately, without judgement, to the needs of all, rather than marginalising a vulnerable minority group where difference can be detrimental to quality of care.

A responsible pedagogy is strongly linked with affect and the politics of emotions (Ahmed 2004). Daniela made use of this political view of emotions, that emerged during sharing and listening to stories, to enable her students to understand their socio-cultural and historico-political positioning. This is an example of how students can become-with their stories, peers and their teachers. Daniela explained:

> I want them to reflect back on the emotional responses they have both in writing and hearing their stories and when listening to other stories. So it's one way of showing that what's happening in the classroom is political and not just individual; the emotions that they experience ... it's not because they are the person they are, but because they're part of a bigger system and they have been socialised into a specific system. Some of the emotions that they feel, they might experience them because of the social group they belong to and not just because of them being who they are.

This excerpt indicates how the teacher can assist students to realise their own non-innocence in becoming-with each other in pedagogical spaces. While experiencing emotions, such as guilt, shame, pity, can be seen as 'moments of pedagogic affect' (Watkins 2015, p. 5), these situations prove difficult for her as a facilitator, as she continues to explain:

> For me that is my biggest challenge is to how to be with those students who act understandably defensively because they are being put immediately in a position of the oppressors or the ones who are guilty or who are painted guilty because of where they are coming from. So how to deal with that, how to make sure you don't lose these students from the onset but to try to be empathetic, understanding where they're coming from – and it's a reflecting back on my own defensiveness.

Stories, students and teachers are entangled in inherited pasts, presents and futures, all occupying a position of non-innocence. Time, space and matter constitute our becoming-with our responsibilities towards each other that are always open, multi-directional and never finished (Barad 2007). What is needed is an ongoing awareness of what matters in our entanglements:

> It matters what matters we use to think other matters with; it matters what stories we tell to tell other stories with; it matters what knots knot knots, what thoughts think thoughts, what descriptions describe descriptions, what ties tie ties. It matters what stories make worlds, what worlds make stories,
>
> Haraway 2016, p. 12

In conclusion – moving towards a pedagogy of response-ability

Both attentiveness and responsibility diffracted through posthumanist ideas constitute what we term a *pedagogy of response-ability*. We diffracted elements of Tronto's ethics of care with Barad and Haraway's writings on attentiveness and responsibility, in order to outline the generative superpositions (overlaps) and differences between these theorists.

Haraway (2016) refers to response-ability as the capability to respond, especially in relation to 'staying with the trouble of complex worlding' in relation to 'living and dying well together' (p. 29) cautioning us that '[c]ultivating response-ability requires much more from us. It requires the risk of being for some worlds rather than others and helping to compose those worlds with others' (p. 179).

For a response-able pedagogy, knowledge practices involve a becoming-with that is processual, intra-active through material-discursive practices. For Barad, '[k]nowing is a direct material engagement, a practice of intra-acting with the world as part of the world in its dynamic material configuring, its ongoing articulation' (Barad 2007, p. 379). A pedagogy of response-ability that takes knowing as a material practice means that teaching and learning are entangled. The teacher and learner become co-learners – rendering each other capable, constituting each other through their entanglement. The phenomenon of teaching where bodies, time, space and matter intra-act and render each other capable leads to a becoming-with.

We acknowledge the inherent risks as we each experiment with different encounters, attempting to involve ourselves in ethico-political spaces that have opened up in our teaching events. The emotional labour in working with unjust practices is challenging, within a context where humans and non-humans are treated as discrete unrelated entities. Still our teaching strategies ought to promote fearlessness. In writing together and apart we help each other become less fearful. Reconsidering our teaching and research practices, we have all felt the tensions in shifting from traditional individualistic approaches towards making relationships matter in a democratising manner. In our becoming-with students, stories, learning materials and socio-political events, we have needed to and continue to adjust our thinking and doing to patterns of relationality. As our thoughts move away from ourselves as discrete entities separated from those (human and non-human) around us, there is an on-going process of staying with the trouble.

Notes

1 Diffraction is a method of examining theories through each other and the effects of these interferences (Barad 2007).
2 Haraway's (2016, p. 2) figure of sf incorporates 'science fiction, speculative fabulation, string figures, speculative feminism, science fact and so far'.
3 Both Haraway and Barad use an ethics of 'worlding' to indicate interdependence – becoming-with and being part of a collective human and more-than-human world, calling into question the notion of the autonomous human subject.

References

Ahmed, S. (2004), *The Cultural Politics of Emotion*, Edinburgh: Edinburgh University Press.

Åsberg, C., K. Thiele and I. van der Tuin (2015), 'Speculative *Before* the Turn. Reintroducing Feminist Materialist Performativity', *Cultural Studies Review,* 21(2): 145–72.

Barad, K. (2007), *Meeting the Universe Halfway: Quantum Physics and the Entanglement of Matter and Meaning*, Durham: Duke University Press.

Barad, K. (2010), 'Quantum Entanglements and Hauntological Relations of Inheritance: Dis/continuities, Spacetime Enfoldings, and Justice-to-Come', *Derrida Today*, 3: 240–268.

Barad, K. (2014), 'On Touching – The Inhuman That Therefore I Am (V.1.1)', in S. Witzgall and K. Stakemeier, (eds), *Power of Material/ Politics of Materiality,* Berlin: diaphanes.

Bozalek, V. (2016), 'The Political Ethics of Care and Feminist Posthuman Ethics: Contributions to Social Work', in R. Hugman and J. Carter (eds), *Rethinking Values and Ethics in Social Work.* Basingstoke: Palgrave MacMillan, 80–96.

Despret, V. (2016), *What Would Animals Say if We Asked the Right Questions?,* Minneappolis: University of Minnesota Press.

Dolphijn, R., and I. van der Tuin (2012), *New Materialism: Interviews & Cartographies,* Ann Arbor, MI: New Humanities Press.

Frankish, T. (2009), *Women's Narratives of Intergenerational Trauma and Post-Apartheid Identity: The Said and Unsaid*, unpublished thesis, Durban: University of KwaZulu-Natal.

Giugni, M. (2011), '"Becoming Worldly With": An Encounter with the Early Years Learning Framework', *Contemporary Issues in Early Childhood,* 12(1): 1–27.

Haraway, D. (2008), *When Species Meet,* Minneapolis: University of Minnesota Press.

Haraway, D. (2016), *Staying with theTtrouble. Making Kin in the Chthulucene,* Durham and London: Duke University Press.

Juelskjær, M. and N. Schwennesen (2012), 'Intra-active Entanglements: An Interview with Karen Barad', *Kvinder, Koen og Forskning*, 21: 10–23.

Lenz Taguchi, Hillevi (2012), 'A Diffractive and Deleuzian Approach to Analysing Interview Data', *Feminist Theory* 13 (265): 265–281.

Low, B., C. Brushwood Rose and P.M. Salvio (2017), *Community-Based Media Pedagogies – Relational Practices of Listening in the Commons.* New York: Routledge.

Noddings, N. (2002), *Educating Moral People: A Caring Alternative to Character Education*, New York: Teachers College Press.

Ruddick, S. (1989), *Maternal Thinking: Towards a Politics of Peace*, New York: Ballantine.

Tronto, J. C. (1993), *Moral Boundaries: A Political Argument for an Ethic of Care*, New York: Routledge.

Tronto, J. C. (2013), *Caring Democracy Markets, Equality, and Justice*, New York: New York University Press.

Watkins, M. (2015), 'Gauging the Affective: Becoming Attuned to its Impact in Education', in M. Zembylas and P. Schutz (eds), *Methodological Advances in Research on Emotion in Education,* New York: Springer, 71–81.

Young, I. M. (1997), 'Asymmetrical Reciprocity: On Moral Respect, Wonder, and Enlarged Thought', *Constellations*, 3 (3): 340–363.

7

Me Lo Dijo Un Pajarito – Neurodiversity, Black Life and the University As We Know It

Erin Manning

She studies, starting in the middle. She reads, always from the outside-out. She speaks, stuttering from the edges of language. She fails, her work refusing to order itself to the measure she has been given.

She restarts, the work pulling at her again. She re-reads. She knows she should read something new. But those familiar words just have a taste she can't resist.

She studies, working from the edges. She reinvents, from the middle. The form stumps her. She forgets to cite. She forgets that there was a beginning, a place from which knowledge traced itself. She forgets to impress. She doesn't pass.

In a private exchange, she writes:

> And of course the question of ecological ways of knowing and producing may surface and we listen. i guess it is always a question of limit, scale and elasticity, a question of an ecosystem that would allow for unattended or decapitated expressivities to come forth. In Spanish there's an expression that i truly love: "me lo dijo un pajarito," a bird told me. My 8-year-old son talks with birds constantly since he was very little. me lo dijo un pajarito also moves with the possibility of a secret that you know without necessarily knowing in the common way of knowing, towards undercommon ways of cawing.

What are these undercommon ways of cawing, the sounds lost, left behind, not only unaddressed but unregistered, in the systems of power/knowledge we call academia? What cannot be heard? What cannot be listened to? And what are the stakes of the performance of knowledge that plays out in the name of the 'norm' that upholds what is too often generalised around the concept of 'quality' or 'rigour'?

Neurodiversity in the University

Creating the conditions for neurodiversity in the university is not about creating a space for difference, a space where difference sequesters itself. It is about attuning to the undercommon currents of creative dissonance and asymmetrical experience always already at work in, across and beyond the institution. It is about becoming attentive to the ways in which the production of knowledge in the register of the neurotypical has always been resisted and queered despite the fact that neurotypical forms of knowledge are rarely addressed or defined as such. It is about exploring a juncture, a cut I perceive in the here-now, a change I want to linger with, that puts the university at risk in the very same gesture that it puts neurodiversity at risk. It is about asking what happens when the turn toward neurodiversity begins to be felt in a way that neurotypicality is truly threatened.

In an article called 'Body/Power' Michel Foucault writes: 'one needs to study what kind of body the current society needs' (1972, p. 58). While the university is certainly not the only site of power/knowledge, I turn to the university for this account of 'what kind of body the current society needs' because it is a site of contestation where the exception often reigns in the name of alternative pedagogies and practices, a site where many of us, myself included, imagine other ways of working and sometimes are even able to activate them. I turn to the university because there is a troubling asymmetry at the heart of teaching and learning practices, on the one hand creating a path for new ways of thinking and making while on the other imposing forms of knowledge that do violence to the bodies they purport to address. I turn to the university because there is of necessity a discontinuity between the individual and collective practices of experimentation it houses and the neoliberalism that undergirds it. I turn to the university because it has been a site of resistance, and a site where new orientations toward study have been born: black studies, queer socialities, postcolonialism, disability studies. And I turn to the university because most days I am not at all certain that the site for these explorations and activations of power/knowledge is actually capable of the kind of complex work necessary for the decolonisation of knowledge, at least not as long as the centrality of the (white) (neurotypical) human as purveyor and guarantor of experience reigns supreme.

What has shifted in the university as regards neurodiversity is the steady entry into the bounds of its edifice not only of neurodiverse bodies, but of accounts of what neurodiversity brings. Those bodies that 'pass' have been there all along, 'functioning' at the limits of what constitutes the docile body they, we, have been taught to mimic. The other bodies, the ones classically excluded remain excluded for the most part, but there are exceptions, and these more visible exceptions are troubling what it means to be included in the edifice of learning. They are making themselves heard, teaching us how to bring facilitation into the classroom, reminding us of how inaccessible most of our practices of teaching are, how unaccommodated the non-docile body remains despite the many academic discourses that circulate supporting its presence.

With the writings and movements of these bodies, of our bodies, shared at their pace through the wild library of neurodiversity blogs on the internet, and published, more now than ever, in the academic presses have come new propositions for ways of learning, new questions about the relationality of facilitation expressed always with the confusion about how it is that we could figure pedagogy as being anything but a site facilitation. It is these interventions, as well as those of artists who write sideways into the academy, making art that refigures what expression can look like, that move the diagram of power/knowledge in the institution and mark this moment of recalibration. Of course the diagram is always mobile, and it is shifted by more tendencies than those I can name here – the point is not to reduce the undercommons of the university to these tendencies but to add them to all the others that, like termites, have been eating the walls and reshaping them to their needs. Perhaps one way to speak of this moment is precisely to speak of proliferation, of the inability to name (or even to hear) all that is at work, and all that is at stake.

What interests me are these termite-ridden walls and the questions they ask, urgently, about whether the sites of power/knowledge we build and sustain are really equal to those who inhabit them.

Spinoza speaks of the institution as a pact, reminding us that what we live in is also what we build, and what we take down (Balibar 2007). What is the pact the university demands? What bodies does it need to survive? What knowledges?

The asymmetries the university produces are reflected in the asymmetries of its 'we', asymmetries of duration and scale. Placing the power (or repression) in the individual won't begin to address the complexity of the bodyings that chew at the joints of its foundations. To speak of us, the 'we', as one, as identifiable, as measurable, would be to underestimate the creativity of our movements. It would make us human, all too human, when in fact our bodyings are transversal, collective before they are individual, more-than. It would also underestimate the power of capital that runs through each artery of the institution, connecting to speeds and durations also always more-than human. Any 'we' is always already composing at the interstices of these uneasy collaborations between different valences of the more-than.

Other approaches are necessary, probably approaches that move at the speed of termites, unbuilding the edifice from within in strategic duplicity with durations more-than human. Because trying to accost the system from another angle, trying to break the system from within its own modes of intelligibility, will only in the end reduce us to victims and perpetrators, to humans firmly enveloped in a dream of self-sufficiency. We must instead begin with the differential of the more-than human that composes us, with the tendencies that make us more-than ourselves, engaging the edifice of power/knowledge not frontally but with the very asymmetrical durations that (de)compose us. Connecting to power/knowledge this way may allow us to hear how else knowledge is being crafted on the undercommon edges where a caw can be heard, attuning to modes of knowing that exceed capture. From this perspective we can feel the dissonance between the rhythm of the work produced in the undercommons and the university's own glacial pace, committed, despite rhetoric to the contrary, to modes of knowing that are all too human. Despite the wealth of work that goes into attempting to alter the system from within, despite the extraordinary research that pushes back against the norms of knowledge production, despite the resistance on the part of artists to ally to industry, preferring instead to engage in a pragmatics of the useless that explores alternative modes of expression, alternative modes of existence, the problem remains: the university is a slow-moving machine. It is structurally incapable of changing at the speed of the thought that moves through it.

The university is beyond rebuilding. The building is already beyond repair. The outside is pushing in. Outside doesn't mean a space already created. Outside is the undercommons working it, eating it from within. There is no space preexisting that can replace the buildings in ruins. The undercommons must always be invented anew. It is a question of moving sideways, of attuning to the sideways movements already there, following their line of flight.

The urgency of these undercommons cannot be ignored. We are moving through them, but are we proliferating enough? Are we inventing at the speed, in the duration, of the movements of thought that move us to ask what else it can mean to know? Because when neurodiversity makes itself too keenly felt, when it refuses to adhere to norms of neurotypical knowledge production, the university as machine for existing power/knowledge resists, it must resist, and the more noise there is, the more the university will be at risk, and the more it will resist. The more *we* will resist. This is particularly the case when the student, she who studies but doesn't learn-to-measure, refuses to adhere to the labels that mark her as a liability for the pursuit of knowledge. She will not pass. She will not get credit. And this will matter because she is still paying, she is still in the system of debt and credit, and we have promised her that the system knows how to enfold her. We have admitted her. She will not be one of the few students who are allowed to flow through the membrane, the few who are given the opportunity to mark their difference, a difference that only works to keep the norm in place. Or if she gets through one membrane, she won't get through the next one, she won't get the job, or the tenure. Because we won't know how to recognise her difference. We won't have created a space where it can be sequestered. She will not have given us the tools to do so, to space her as one of the few who should receive an exception, as one of those who need to populate our otherwise white, neurotypical environment in order for it to have been inclusive.

Difference will always be accepted to a degree. As long as the norm is upheld it will always be good to have a few exceptions, especially when those who enter that space clearly mark themselves as different. But she is not one of those. She doesn't want to speak in the name of her difference. She doesn't want to teach you how to know her, how to write about her. She won't speak for all indigenous people, for all black people, for all queer people, for all autistics. She won't explain. She will resist citing you. She isn't interested in 'according to'. She won't be aligned, she won't be colonised. Not because she is a rebel. But precisely because she operates in another mode, in the mode of the more-than which listens to undercommon ways of cawing. From the perspective of this more-than always yet to be composed, to be speciated, she won't presume the symmetry rebellion presupposes. She won't presume neurotypicality.

Power/Knowledge

Power is never individual. The individual is, at the very most, the expression of its passage, not its operator. These teachings of Foucault's are often backgrounded in analyses of power that would still situate power within the bodies that wreak destruction or suffer its consequences. It is important, in thinking the systemic nature of power in the university to clarify how power operates, how it is at once ours and beyond a 'we' that preexists, how power is a mode of circulation more than it is a targeting practice. Power is what moves through the diagrams that co-compose us.

To work with the circulation of power, it is necessary to move beyond body to bodying, beyond the notion that there are preexisting individuals that are powered by a hierarchy that measures their movements. The university is not a field that operates through such cut-and-dried hierarchies. The university is a diagram of power through which 'we' are created and recreated as power/ knowledge bodyings. 'We' are the university, emboldened to become-bodies under circumstances we co-compose. Or, at the very minimum, we are a field of forces that makes it possible for those tendings-toward-bodies the university promotes to keep agglomerating. It is 'we' who make its thinking possible, even if only by remaining in its midst. And it is 'we' who pass or fail those for whom the qualities of bodying the university presupposes and creates are insufficient to survive, and to thrive in its framework.

Bodying as a verb reminds us that bodies are a field of forces through which individuations emerge and shift. How a body individuates depends on the circumstances of its surrounds, on the ecologies that compose it, here, now, on the histories that orient it, on the futurities that give it potential or unmoor it from the grounds of its participation in the world. These orientations toward difference are pragmatic and operative. How a body becomes the body it is, here, now, the body it is identified to be, also depends on what it means to be a body, here, now, on the stakes of the form-taking, on the limits of that form. Bodies are routinely obliterated at the very point where they individuate into this or that recognisable form. Much is at stake in the shape of individuation: there is no doubt that a continuous policing occurs that denies bodies the potential of their transitions, of their becomings, solidifying them from the outside into an identity that cannot be assimilated. I am thinking of the spastic body, of the disabled body, of the trans body, of the black body, of the lower-caste body, there are so many who populate these unassimilable categories. What is important, I think, is to recognize that these captures are occurring because of the threat of bodying. What is terrifying is the very potential at the heart of bodying, the potential for a body to become, to shift, to alter the conditions of life-living, life in the register of the more-than, life beyond a dichotomy of the human and the nonhuman. To ask what kind of body our society needs is to take the operations of power seriously and to inquire, each time anew, how this body, how this neurodiversity, shifts the field of experience, shifts the terms of power/knowledge.

Bodying is a process we all engage in. Usually, we become a body we already recognise, reproducing ourselves in the image we have come to associate as ours. This is particularly the case for those amongst us whose bodyings are least contested, those whose whiteness, whose neurotypicality already conforms to the mould of what a body should be. When Édouard Glissant incites us to 'consent not to be a single being', he is reminding us, I think, that the mould of that one form, that one body, should never suffice, that relations are what compose us, relations always in excess of the given, relations as the radically empirical more-than, that continuously refashions what it means to world (Glissant 2011, p. 5).

Bodying need not include an alignment with humanism, with existing modes of defining what it means to be human. This is something I learn from autistics who remind us about the more-than that animates the field of experience that is life-living. Through their work, each in their own way engages a reorienting of what matters in experience to include the constitutive field of the more-than in the edgings of the not-yet. Amelia Baggs's video *In My Language* (2007) perhaps still stands out as the most chilling account of how nonspeaking autistics are excluded from the realm of the human, their personhood extracted precisely because of the breadth of more-than human feeling their language, their living, includes. In her eight-minute video, in which the first four minutes are spent listening to and smelling and touching the objects around her, and the next four minutes are spent typing on a voice-activated computer, she says:

> It is only when I type something in your language that you refer to me as having communication. I smell things. I listen to things. I feel things. I taste things. I look at things. It is not enough to look and taste and smell and feel. I have to do those to the right things [. . .] or else people doubt that I am a thinking being, and since their definition of thought defines their definition of personhood so ridiculously much they doubt that I am a real person as well.

There are an infinity of gestures coming out of the neurodiversity community that repeat this experience that neurotypical folks have a much too limited idea of what constitutes experience, a perceptual dearth that doesn't allow for the vividness of the more-than of worlds in the making.

There is a certain resonance here with accounts from Black Studies around the concept of black life. Frank Wilderson writes: 'Though it might seem paradoxical, the bridge between blackness and antiblackness is "the unbridgeable gap between Black being and Human life"' (Wilderson 2010: 57 in Moten 2013: 749). Blackness, Fred Moten writes, 'must free itself from ontological expectation, must refuse subjection to ontology's sanction against the very idea of black subjectivity' (2013, p. 749).

I turn to these voices in Black Studies to ask whether there isn't an important bridge to be built between neurodiversity and black life, particularly around the question of how else experience could be articulated within the register of the more-than where the stakes are not to measure experience against the worn concept of humanity as defined in the West, but with the force of an ontogenesis that moves in rhythm with the emergent sociality of bodying. Because bodying and sociality cannot be disentangled.

Research-Creation

Foucault writes:

> It is a case of studying power at the point where its intention, if it has one, is completely invested in its real and effective practices. What is needed is a study of power in its external visage, at the point where it is in direct and immediate relationship with that which we can provisionally call its object, its target, its field of application, there – that is to say – where it installs itself and produces its real effects.
>
> 1972, p. 97

In *The Minor Gesture* (2016), I wrote about the way I see study, as Fred Moten and Stefano Harney define it, as aligned with a certain version of research-creation. This alignment involves seeing research-creation – the entry into the university of artistic practice at the doctoral level – as the potential destabiliser it is in relation to the ways in which the university tends to mobilise knowledge production. The shift toward research-creation in the university has taken place roughly over the past decade, unsettling the certainty of what counts as knowledge and what can be valued, or evaluated, as 'contributing' to the field. The problem, of course, is that the field of 'research-creation', if it is a field, is still under construction, testing its limits, wondering about its place, or even if it wants to take a place.

Research-creation, as SenseLab has argued over more than a decade of practice, can be an alignment to the ways in which study itself is a practice. It can be a mode of inquiry that asks what (other) forms learning can take. It can refuse to privilege the materiality of language over other materialities while at the same recognising that thinking is a creative practice in its own right. When practiced this way, research-creation creates the conditions to ask how the theory-practice split continues to give knowledge-production a certain linguistic overtone, understanding practice more as that which needs to be studied than as study itself.

When the artist refuses to produce an object as the object of her work, when the artist refuses to be the subject of the work, when the philosopher refuses to write at a distance, when the work becomes the practice, when the practice invents its own language, research-creation deeply threatens the power/knowledge that holds the academy in place. It was fine to have the artist in the academy as long as the artist behaved like an artist, as long as the object could be defined. As long as there was something to evaluate.

The bodyings crafted through such neurodiverse acts, the life that moves through the acts that resist the neurotypicality of knowledge production, create new diagrams for thinking. Power begins to circulate differently. Knowledge inflects to excite a rethinking, a reorienting of what study can be. Foucault writes:

> Power is employed and exercised through a net-like organization. And not only do individuals circulate between its threads; they are always in the position of simultaneously undergoing and exercising this power. They are not only its inert or consenting target; they are always also the elements of its articulation. In other words, individuals are the vehicles of power, not its points of application.
>
> 1972, p. 98

It's not simply that power is circulating differently, that new ways of knowing are finding temporary forms, that new forms of practice are shifting the process of coming to something we might call knowledge. It's that bodyings are created in the practicing, bodyings that trouble what it means to be a student, to be admitted as a student in the circuit of debt and credit that is the university as we know it. Deeply engaged, thinking wildly, touching the limits of thought, the becoming-body can finally stim as much as it needs to, connecting to the world's rhythms, its bodyings out of sync with the forces that would seek to capture it, outside the cycle of recognition that would identify it as the guarantor of university's system of debt and credit.

The Outside

Gilles Deleuze writes:

> Between power and knowledge there is a difference in nature or a heterogeneity; but there is also mutual presupposition and capture; and there is ultimately a primacy of the one over the other. First of all there is a difference in nature, since power does not pass through forms, but only through forces. Knowledge concerns formed matters (substances) and formalized functions, divided up segment by segment according to the two great formal conditions of seeing and speaking, light and language: it is therefore stratified, archivized, and endowed

with a relatively rigid segmentarity. Power, on the other hand, is diagrammatic: it mobilizes non-stratified matter and functions, and unfolds with a very flexible segmentarity. In fact, it passes not so much through forms as through particular points which on each occasion mark the application of a force, the action or reaction of a force in relation to others, that is to say an affect like 'a state of power that is always local and unstable.

1988, p. 73

If the asymmetry between power and knowledge concerns the relation of force to form, what happens to knowledge when it begins to resist the very idea of form as final mode of knowing? How is its force of form altered by the conditions of study that don't hold to the human as central to experience, that heed indigenous and black and neurodiverse and queer forms of knowing? What does knowledge look like when it has become unmoored from its capture as form?

Foucault speaks of 'a new type of relation, a dimension of thought that is irreducible to knowledge' (in Deleuze 1988, p. 74). This dimension of thought, this outside of recognizable knowledge is not new. It already exists – we hear it in the stories passed down through generations as told to us by indigenous scholars, we feel it in the care for material practices as shared to us by African American quilt-makers, we hear it in the break, as Moten says, 'where that shit breaks down'. Thought irreducible to practice moves outside the registers of categorisation, shifting the conditions of undercommon ways of cawing.

The outside is the name Deleuze and Foucault give to the circulation of forces at the heart of power's operations where thought remains irreducible to knowledge. The outside is not the exterior (as opposed to an interior). It is not spatial – it is intensive. The outside is what remains unthought in thought, what remains unfelt in feeling. It is what accompanies all emergent relationalities, what moves with all social life in the making:

> [T]he outside concerns force: if force is always in relation with other forces, forces necessarily pertain to an irreducible outside which no longer has a form, made up of nondecomposable distances where one force acts upon another or is acted upon by another.

1988: 86, *translation modified*

The outside is an intuitive concept for the more neurodiverse amongst us. It is what accompanies all experience in the making. What leaves those traces that still vibrate on the edges of what we call objects. It is the edgings into experience, the colourings of time, the echoes of futures on the cusp that interrupt that chunking neurotypicals continuously seek in their search for categories. It is the world that isn't yet quite there before the chunk, the world that accompanies without quite situating itself, a kind of continuous refrain that orients the not-quite of all form-takings. It is the intensities that so many don't seem to hear, those intensities that are continuously getting in the way of the human voice – that privileged site of human expression, the intensities that whisper to us that the world is lively and living beyond the space the human takes. The outside is not where most of our knowing is focused, though those of us who teach art have an affinity for it. We may speak in terms of hunches, of feeling, of affect, of tendency, of force – all of these synonyms for that which participates but cannot be circumscribed. This is not the knowledge we've been taught to recognise, not the knowledge of forms already captured. The outside is not the formed matter, the segmented, the archivable. It is the anarchic share of striated knowledge, the share of experience which resists scripting yet nonetheless affects what the script can do. Anarchival knowledge, neurodiverse knowledge, is not outside form so much as in the cleaving between form and force. It is what calls knowledge back to its edgings-into-experience. It is the diagram, the force of form, of knowledge where knowing meets unknowing.

When knowledge begins to escape stratification, when its form begins to blur, its anarchic share surfacing, its alignment to power also shifts. Power and knowledge begin to compose differently. It's not that knowledge is no longer irreducible to power (Foucault's point, after all, is that this irreducibility is what gives the potential for resistance), it's that the irreducibility begins to scintillate in ways that give knowledge the breadth, the force, to subvert the striations that usually constrain it.

Perhaps, at the point of scintillation, knowledge is no longer the right term. Study is a better term. Or research-creation. These are thicker concepts, I think, for the texture of what I am trying to gesture towards, when I speak of knowledges unknowing. But for now, I want to hold on to the possibility that the term itself, that knowledge could still be carried forth as that which has the capacity for doing the work differently, if only to emphasise the trouble neurodiversity brings to the academic institution, trouble that most often erupts around the question of who knows how to know.

Emergent Socialities

Neurodiversity, and particularly autism, is often referred to as the most asocial of modes of living. It is a sign of our neurotypical human-centredness that we only feel heard when we have eye-contact, when the body we are speaking to consents to be a single being, excluding its more-than human tendencies. So much meaning is given to the way attention is oriented that we rarely stop to think of the violence of those frontal modes of attention that force us to block out the scintillations of the world and its many qualities of attending. When the neurodiverse amongst us listen, they listen to those scintillations, they are moved by them, hearing the more-than that echoes across the threshold of the sensory. Sometimes this is just too much, but always it is there, moving amodally across the bodying activated by the relation. This relation is not only to me, to you. It is a relation to the world as it has come together just now, here. A relation to the field of experience making itself. Eye contact is ridiculous in this context, ridiculous because it misses so much. There is no emergent sociality in the pressure to pay attention in just this neurotypical way. Emergent sociality is a listening – with the array of potential socialities in our surrounds. Moved by the outside, it asks that sociality be invented anew each time, that the world, and worlding become the occasion for study.

When autistics are framed as arhetorical, it is usually around the concept of sociality. Melanie Yergeau writes:

> My flapping fingers and facial tics signify an anti-discourse of sorts: Where is my control? Where is my communicability? Would anyone choose a life of ticcing? How can an involuntary movement, an involuntary neurology, a state of being that is predicated on asociality – how can these things be rhetorical?
>
> 2017: 11

In the neurotypical model of sociality, the measure is always that of communication as direct exchange. I speak, you look and listen. Then you speak, connecting your thoughts to mine. When this doesn't happen, when the encounter doesn't read for the neurotypical as communicational, the response is depersonification, dehumanisation:

> Autism is frequently storied as an epic in asociality, in non-intention. It represents the edges and boundaries of humanity, a queerly crip kind of isolationism. We, the autistic, are a peopleless people. We embody not a counter-rhetoric, but an anti-rhetoric, a kind of being and moving that exists tragically at the folds of involuntary automation. Our bodyminds rotely go through the motions, cluelessly la dee da.
>
> 2017: 14

Cluelessly la dee da. Me lo dijo un pajarito.

The Free Indirect

Emergent sociality edges into experience as the force which unmoors expectations about the relationscapes that compose us. It speaks from the corners, from the ledges and edges and thresholds of experience still taking form. It flies off the bodying with sparks, it stims and tics and hollers. It melts down when the world is just too much to take, the tensions of the world speeding like lightning along the body's feeling-alwaysfeeling surfaces. The world is too much and yet it is lived, fully, again and again to a limit unconceivable for most neurotypically inclined. Neurodiversity invents life. Life-living.

The invention of socialities is a study in living, a living study. It speaks often in pronouns intermixed – it is not unusual to hear autistics speak of themselves in the third person. A cold coming on, Adam Wolfond writes (in a conversation with his mother, Estee Klar, on 19 March 2017):

> I think my body jumps because I am feeling sick. I think I have a cold in my boy nose. I am really wanting razor sharp always feeling body to be very calm and I want the body to wash away like the water you use. I want the water to always give me answers about how to stay quiet in my body. My body is always trying to stay calm. Talking as you do is away from the way my not very calm hated body talks. Hated is calming way of Adam and always questioning and asking people.

At once I and Adam and boy, Adam and the cold co-compose, water the teacher that may give the directions to ordering the body within neurotypical parameters. Because having, being a moving autistic body is dangerous in a neurotypical world. Not only will it get you sidelined (as unintelligent, as deviant) – if you happen to be autistic and black, it may also get you killed.

The stakes are high, the body must stay still, and words must come out in the order in which neurotypicals can hear them, can order them. Pronouns must be adjusted or we will be seen as stupid. This is something I've heard too often. And yet no language proceeds directly. This is what Deleuze and Guattari teach us in their chapter on linguistics in *1000 Plateaus*. 'Me lo dijo un pajarito' is how the linguistic utterance actually functions. Knowledge, as it moves through language, always comes sideways. Deleuze and Guattari write:

> Language is not content to go from a first party to a second party, from one who has seen to one who has not, but necessarily goes from a second party to a third party, neither of whom has seen.

> 1987: 77

Heard from the sidelines, what is it about language that makes us believe that it is direct, unmediated? It is the order-word that does this work, ferrying the free indirect into the semblance of direct communication. An often redundant structure of language, the order-word is what organises the potential disorientation of the free indirect quality of language, providing the utterance with a history of directions. 'An order always and already concerns prior orders, which is why ordering is redundancy [...]' (Deleuze and Guattari 1989: 75). Speaking in the free indirect, catching language in the making, the order-word is carried in the performance of what the need not even be said. It is not language that constrains knowledge, but the order-word that moves through it.

For Deleuze and Guattari, the order-word is the 'elementary unit of language' (1987: 76). Order-words keep the saying in check. And yet, textual disarray is continuously unmooring language, unfastening it of its order-words. The emergent sociality of textuality is just too complex. 'There is no individual enunciation. There is not even a subject of enunciation' (Deleuze and Guattari 79).

Order-words are less language than the condition for 'the superlinearity of expression' (1987: 85). They are only one of the ways language is moved from its field of potential to its pragmatic instantiation, here, now. We must not be cowed by them. But to make the turn toward the conceptual work of activating language's outside, we do have to train ourselves to hear undercommon ways of cawing. Because the neurotypical mode of listening always hears the human voice before the caw, as Krumins might say, and almost never hears the undercommon ways of cawing:

> It's not that I could hear better, although I could hear much higher pitches than most people, but I was aware of what I was hearing. Most people attend to voices above all else. I attend to everything in the same way with no discrimination, so that the caw of the crow in the tree is as clear and important as the voice of the person I'm walking with.
>
> 2003: 86–87

Moved beyond the register of the order-word, language begins to do something else. It begins to make heard the forces that populate it, the ways of knowing that curb it toward modes of sociality yet to be invented. When Baggs moves through her living room sounding the furniture and smelling the books in her video *In My Language*, when she turns on the tap and cuts the stream of water with her fingers, sounding all the while, when she taps the dresser and turns the knobs and scratches the computer case, language is moving (through) her. This is her point: that language moves and that its movements are lost to those of us who seek to hear only how language stops thought, how it signifies and orders expression. Baggs' language is never hers alone. It is the language that moves across sensibilities that exceed the range of the human voice, that speak not only in words but also in textures, and in the sounds that resonate with them.

Undercommon ways of cawing trouble order-words and the matrix of signification that keeps them intelligible. They do this all the time. What happens if we begin to listen?

More-Than Human

What is it about the stimmy, ticcy, or spastic body that threatens neurotypicality? What is it about it that so readily reads as unintelligent, unknowing? Is it its unabashed excess? Its uninhibited wealth of expression? Is it the fact that it makes felt the breadth of intensity signification can never quite capture?

We know that bodies get in the way of learning, of knowing, of speaking. Otherwise why would we have to sit in chairs all day, and stand still when we speak and stop to pay attention? Is that why neurodiversity is so threatening to neurotypicality's certainty about what it means to know? Because neurodiversity bodies language? Is that also what is so threatening about black life? That it moves? That it moves sound, language, life in ways as yet uncharted?

How does a 'Poethics of Blackness' (Denise Ferreira da Silva's term), connect to neurodiversity, to neurodiverse life? Gesturing toward decolonial ways of living, of writing, a poethics of blackness 'announce(s) a whole range of possibilities for knowing, doing, and existing', writes Ferreira da Silva (2014, p. 81). What kinds of emergent sociality are invented at this interstice?

Emergent sociality is an ecology of practices. Always more-than, always more-than human, emergent sociality moves at the speed of the unformed that courses through the formed. What we hear at the interstice: the anarchic share of experience that accompanies experience in the making.

Alexander Weheliye writes:

> Black life is that which must be constitutively abjected – and as such has represented the negative ontological ground for the Western order of things at least for the last five hundred years – but can never be included in the Western world order, especially the category of Man. Phrased differently, there can be no black life in the territory of Western, humanist Man, which is why the existence of black life disenchants Western humanism.
>
> 2014b, p. 5

A similar account moves through the writings around neurodiversity: 'Autistic bodies [...] these are bodies that not only defy social order, but fail to acknowledge social order's very existence. Autism, then, poses a kind of neuroqueer threat to normalcy, to society's very essence' (Yergeau 2017, p. 36). A more-than defies the concept of the human in both cases, a more-than that deeply unsettles the human as he is defined by the (white) discourses of neurotypicality. The human as the omnipresent category that holds dominion over knowledge in every walk of life.

Who speaks the order-word of the human. From whom do we hear it?

The more-than moves experience, its shape unsettled. It can't be counted. It can't be known as such. But it matters. It matters in that it qualifies, orients, thickens and textures experience in the making, reminding us that the human is a junction, an interstice toward a certain quality of shaping, of speciation.

This speciation is a diagram, a field of forces that activate a set of relations through which certain becomings occur. This diagram is a mode of survival as much as it is an orientation for the creation of new modes of existence. For the ways in which power and knowledge agitate on its vectors has effects as regards what else living can be when life is no longer organised by the neurotypical diagram that places Man in the centre of the panopticon.

In the Ruins

The university is in ruins, I heard. Me lo dijo un parajito.

The university is in ruins, she said. That colonial space that didn't allow my voice, that didn't hear my cry. He said.

It was just too human. Too full of subjects. Too disciplined. Too corporate. It couldn't survive.

Except the university is still there and she still has debt and no credit.

And we're still teaching, still hiring, still investing your debt. Still paying my mortgage. Still distributing my grants. Still organising my calendar. Still calling meetings.

I hear the cry. They don't pass. The work they do is not accepted as knowledge. 'I see no research here,' I am told. 'This doesn't look like work.' 'You are not supervising adequately.' 'You are not doing your job.'

I've paid my debt and now I have credit. And I'm afraid of losing it. Aren't we all?

But I can't stand it, I can't stand the measure of value. And so I study, I learn to study in the undercommons of the university.

I have never learned so much, never studied quite this way. I am a student.

I know some of us will get through. I am a professor, I made it through the gates, passed every single hurdle until I hit the highest ceiling. I thought it would protect us. I thought it would make it possible for me to squeeze you through the membrane. But they didn't let you through. We didn't let us through.

In the end, we are the termites. We eat away at the structure, residing in the holes we create. They are warm and we can nest. There is some comfort here. But at night, when we scurry around the hallways listening to the anarchive, I hear echoes of other modes of study, and I hear you hear them too.

References

Balibar, É. (2007), *Jus-Pactum-Lex: On the Constitution of the Subject in the Theologico-Political Treatise*, T. Montag (ed.), 187, Minneapolis: Minnesota University Press.

Deleuze, G. (2008), *Foucault*. Trans. Sean Hand. Minneapolis: Minnesota UP.

Ferreira Da Silva, D. (2014), 'Toward a Black Feminist Poethics', *The Black Scholar: Journal of Black Studies and Research*, (44): 2, 81–97.

Fitzgerald, A. (2015) Available online: Interview with Fred Moten. Part 1. *Literary Hub*, http://lithub.com/an-interview-with-fred-moten-pt-i/ (accessed 4 December 2017).

Foucault, M. (1972), *Power/Knowledge: Selected Interviews and Other Writings 1972–1977*. Trans. Colin Gordon, Leo Marshall, John Metham, Kate Stoper. New York: Pantheon Books.

Glissant, E. (2011), *Poetic Intention*. New York: Nightboat.

Hartman, S. (1994), 'The Territory Between Us: A Report on Black Women in the Academy: Defending Our Name: 1894–1994', *Callaloo*, 17(2): 439–449.

Israel, J. (ed.), (2007), *Spinoza: Theological-Political Treatise*. Cambridge: Cambridge University Press.

Kedar, I. (2012), *Ido in Autismland: Climbing Out of Autism's Silent Prison*. Self-Published.

Krumins, D. (2003), 'Coming Alive In A World Of Texture', in J. K. Miller (ed.), *Women From Another Planet*. Bloomington: 1st Books.

Moten, F. (2013), 'Blackness and Nothingness (Mysticism in the Flesh)', in *The South Atlantic Quarterly* 112(4): 737–780.

Moten, F. and S. Harney (2013), *The Undercommons*. Minor Compositions.

Weheliye, A. G. (2014), *Habeas Viscus: Racializing Assemblages, Biopolitics, and Black Feminist Theories of the Human*. Durham: Duke University Press.

Weheliye, A. G, (2014b), *Introduction, The Black Scholar: Journal of Black Studies and Research*, 44(2): 5–10.

Wilderson, F. B. (2010), *Red, White & Black: Cinema and the Structure of US Antagonisms*. Durham: Duke University Press.

Yergeau, M. (2017), *Authoring Autism: On Rhetoric and Neurological Queerness*. Durham: Duke University Press.

8

An Ethico-Onto-Epistemological Pedagogy of Qualitative Research: Knowing/Being/ Doing in the Neoliberal Academy

Candace R. Kuby and Rebecca C. Christ

"My cognitive fire hasn't been this awake in a long time and I'm loving it."
– Harriet, student in course

Awakening a cognitive fire. When we[1] read the above statement on a course evaluation, we were overcome with several emotions and curiosities. First, we felt humbled and surprised that her experiences in the introductory qualitative research (QR) course produced this awakening for Harriet (all student names are pseudonyms). We were curious as to what specifically Harriet might pinpoint as the catalyst for the awakening. We also wondered what this (affective) awakening produced for her then and what might come of it. Was this awakening unexpected to Harriet? To us?

But shouldn't all QR courses awaken students' cognitive fires? QR was conceived with radical possibilities to address social, educational, and economic disparities and challenge the notion that understanding can always be quantified and/or objectively removed from the researcher (St. Pierre 2011a). Unfortunately, this awakening is no easy task, especially in the face of the neoliberal academy that perpetuates an environment of content knowledge as commodity and knowledge-creation as part of a corporate model; conservative attacks on science and narrowing definitions of 'what counts' as research; students as consumers with a 'plug in a methodology and go' attitude; the 'publish or perish' mentality; and pressures to secure large, extramural funding within a model that values brute data and conventional humanist qualitative methodologies that resemble (post)positivism (Baez and Boyles 2009; Cheek 2005; Denzin and Giardina 2006; Lather 2006; St. Pierre 2011a; b). In this era of narrowly defined research outcomes, neoliberalism is at work.

Our first aim is to share our process of planning an introductory QR course[2] from an ethico-onto-epistemological approach, which we conceptualised as a way to counter neoliberalism in academia and provide a space for more socially just pedagogies. Ethico-onto-epistemology is a paradigmatic stance rooted in the belief that:

> Practices of knowing cannot fully be claimed as human practices, not simply because we use nonhuman elements in our practices but because knowing is a matter of part of the world making itself intelligible to another part ... We don't obtain knowledge by standing outside the world; we know because we are *of* the world.
>
> Barad 2007, p. 185, emphasis in original

Therefore, doing (ethico – relationships, ethics), being (onto – realities), and knowing (epistemology – knowledge, learning) are all entangled in a process of the world becoming, and in our case, of students becoming qualitative researchers. An ethico-onto-epistemology pedagogical approach is needed in order to open space(s) for graduate students to not only learn about QR, but to imagine and try-out possibilities of QR beyond what is privileged by the academy. We see this as ethical and justice-oriented as we believe the pedagogical spaces and decisions made about courses produce (certain types of) scholars. We believe it is a matter of ethics to be response-able to students and to the communities and places with which we research – to create more just relationships and ways of being (see Barad's chapter in Dolphijn & van der Tuin [2012] for discussion on response-ability). We wanted students to not only *know* (epistemology) disruptive[3] ways of engaging in QR, but also engage in the politics of inquiry related to *being* (ontology) and *doing* (axiology) socially just work.[4] As St. Pierre (2016) writes, 'research training too often gets in our way, prevents us from recognising the "new" that is always already there in the world, and shuts down futures that might be – an education-to-come we might desire' (pp. 2–3). We are hopeful that ethico-onto-epistemological pedagogies not only help students to experience a range of different paradigms, theories, and method(ologies), but to understand the politics of inquiry, possible consequences of decisions, and potential joys of engaging in inquiries that they can't let go of, suppress, or fit into the formulaic practices of doing QR. We want students to consider how/what material ← → discursive[5] entanglements produce scholarship, scholars, the academy, and the communities we work with as researchers.

Our second aim is for readers to experience – within the limits of language and (re)presentation – diffractive processes of analysis from teaching the QR course. Diffraction is, as Barad (2007) writes, '... marked by patterns of difference

... Of reading insights through one another in attending to and responding to the details and specificities of relations of difference and how they matter' (p. 71). We found that while diffractively working with data-theory-memories-syllabus-textbooks-students' feedback (and so forth), the unexpected became apparent to us – specifically why an ethico-onto-epistemology is needed in the teaching → ← learning of QR.[6] Therefore, we aim (or attempt) to be transparent in our diffractive analysis and share excerpts (i.e., video clip & written) of diffractions unfolding, emerging in the moment. And, in spirit with postqualitative[7] ways of inquiring, we want readers to not search for *meaning* per se, but to experience and consider what our diffractive processes and (re)presentations *produce* for/in/with you, for research on pedagogies in higher education.

This manuscript is not a roadmap or template for others to (re)produce an introductory QR class like the one we created (nor to replicate our methodological, diffractive journey). Our goal is to illuminate the multiple, complex, and contested ways of educating students with an ethico-onto-epistemological approach to become qualitative researchers. We do hope that others will (re)consider their current teaching practices and think about ways to embrace ethico-onto-epistemology. As Lenz Taguchi (2010) writes, this type of pedagogy 'is about allowing yourself to become anew with each event, and to be affirmative of learning as a state of transformation' (p. 94). Therefore, replication is not our goal – but fissuring, creating newness, ideas, transformation, becoming anew – in ways of teaching QR and ways of researching it. Our invitation is to encourage scholars, especially ones who theoretically and philosophically align themselves with critical posthumanism, new feminist materialisms, and affect theories to (continue to) consider how these are not just tools for doing their research, but how the theoretical concepts directly entangle with and produce socially just pedagogies. We hope our chapter illustrates, as inspiration, one way that an ethico-onto-epistemological pedagogy was enacted.

Teaching ← → Learning of Qualitative Research: Neoliberalism and The Material Turn

Teaching (and therefore, learning) is confronted by neoliberal constraints as faculty members feel the need to adequately prepare graduate students for what life is like in the academy. Graduate students, at least in the US context, (feel they) must learn how to write successful grant proposals, publish numerous publications in journals with the highest index ratings and impact factors, and do all of this quickly, as job acquisition and tenure/promotion seem to expect more in a short period of time. Therefore, graduate students are not immune to the current climate of neoliberalism in higher education, where producing 'good' QR means following the prescribed methods of data production (often called data collection), analysis, and publication (St. Pierre 2011b; 2014). As such, these graduate students are taught and mentored to fit into academia's neoliberal practices, where procedures have become naturalised, and ultimately, produce standardised knowledge(s) (Brown, Carducci, and Kuby 2014; St. Pierre 2016).

We resonate with Stark and Watson (1999) who discuss the difficulties of teaching QR within the technical and academic structures, which have tamed desire and 'removed reality from everyday experiences into a classroom conceived of and assessed by the maxims of modernity' (p. 719). Newman and McNamara (2016) write similarly about neoliberal managerialism which remains dominant in the academy and, thus, makes a focus on socially just ethico-onto-epistemological approaches to QR difficult to teach. These two sets of authors believe, as we do, that there are things that can be done pedagogically to disrupt the a/effects of disciplinary power, invoke desire and passion in teaching ← → learning QR, and intra-actively produce a more socially just world. We feel the need to (re)examine neoliberal tendencies in the teaching ← → learning of QR – a place to unsettle the current disposition toward standardised ways of thinking about and doing research (with/on humans). We are not advocating to rid QR courses of more human-centered, historical ways of inquiring (e.g., narrative inquiry, ethnography), as we think it is important for students to know about these possibilities (and perhaps engage with these approaches). However, we do want students to understand the paradigmatic assumptions and politics of inquiry associated with each and imagine ways of troubling and/or expanding these approaches as they think, read, analyse. Ethically and morally, we believe that teaching QR is critical in preparing scholars to engage in work for the betterment of society – a society entangled with humans and nonhumans. But it is also about the now – about the realities produced in classrooms and how those spaces and relationships produce identities of students (and instructors) and the research they undertake.

St. Pierre (2011a) boldly stated that the expected ways of doing QR have become boring and preoccupied with following proper procedures. While this is a broad generalisation and perhaps does not attend to the particulars that posthumanism invites us to consider, we understand her sentiments. Even if graduate students articulate a new topic or question for research, they often plug their ideas into a formulaic procedure pulled from a methods textbook, and the outcomes are often mundane. Many students (and sometimes faculty) still fear moving (i.e., the being/doing) beyond what is normal, appropriate, status quo in their disciplines. Candace often hears comments such as 'that methodology is really fascinating, and it would be useful in my research, but my dissertation committee won't support it' or 'wow, this theory resonates with me, but if I used it in a conference proposal it wouldn't be accepted.' Comments such as these indicate that while inventive, thinking-ways of doing QR are possible (i.e., students have knowledge about disruptive approaches), students often feel trapped to conform (i.e., the doing and being disruptive is difficult). We need scholarship that helps higher education instructors to imagine socially just ways of being/doing/knowing/teaching/thinking pedagogies for QR, especially given the material turn that is happening in the wider research community.

The material turn describes a movement that decenters anthropocentric and logocentric assumptions and practices. Instead of letting go of language and discourses, this movement builds upon them and also believes that the becoming of the world happens through entanglements of humans and nonhumans. We situate our inquiries (and teaching practices) in this movement. Readings on posthumanism and concepts like intra-action and ethico-onto-epistemology changed us. We now see/experience/know the world from this stance of intra-actively *becoming with the world*. If one believes realities, knowledges, and truths are produced intra-actively – we question, how does that belief shape one pedagogically? In the teaching of QR? To be clear, we did not assume our students would paradigmatically align with posthumanist theories; it was not our goal to 'convert' our students to this paradigm. However, we were curious how to pedagogically create a space where we (the instructors) were aware of and intentional in fostering spaces for students to know/be/do QR entangled, intra-actively in a material (neoliberal) world.

Intentional Planning: What We Sought To Do

Candace taught Qualitative Methods in Educational Research I in the Spring 2015 semester, and Becky collaborated as a research and teaching intern. We sought to create a ethico-onto-epistemological course that:

1. promoted critical thinking in students to **understand** (i.e., knowing) how paradigmatic, philosophical, and theoretical assumptions directly influence methodological decisions and actions,

2. helped students ***imagine*** (i.e., knowing) methodological possibilities beyond traditional methods of data production and analysis (i.e., traditionally defined as the 'Creswell 5' – case study, narrative, grounded theory, ethnography, and phenomenology), and

3. supported students in finding ways and spaces to ***live out*** (i.e., doing/being) disruptive practices within a neoliberal and conservative academic environment tied to politics of doctoral committees, graduate schools, grant activity, and publishing venues.

Overall, we attempted to create an introductory course that boldly promoted engaging in *thinking* – with philosophies, paradigms, and theories as a way *into* method(ologies) – which disrupts the status quo conceptualisations of QR (and teaching) at our university (and perhaps elsewhere). While we separated the aims above into three separate phrases for clarity, we see them enacted interconnectedly (i.e., knowing/being/doing is not separated). These aims were our intentional ways of trying to counter neoliberal tendencies in our teaching ← → learning and open spaces for students to know/be/do QR differently (Kuby, Aguayo, Holloway, Mulligan, Shear and Ward 2016). Neoliberalism enacts a mindset that teaching and learning are binaries, and perhaps that teachers are the holders and distributors of knowledge. However, within ethico-onto-epistemological perspectives, the teacher doesn't hold knowledge, but participates with students-materials-discourses in creating knowledges and ways of being/doing (in our case) QR. We aim to break-open the neoliberal perspective and demonstrate how neoliberalism as a force acts with/upon both teachers and students in learning how to navigate and change the current climate and practices of/within the academy.

Entangled Becomings: (Some of) What We Did and Why

An ethico-onto-epistemological pedagogy helped us to unsettle perhaps more normative conceptions of teaching ← → learning QR through assignments, readings, and course expectations. At our institution, it was common for introductory QR classes to focus on teaching the 'Creswell 5 – a methods-first approach to QR' (see Creswell 2012). We intentionally sought a theory(ies)- and paradigm(s)- first approach to the course and, therefore, disrupted expectations and pedagogies. We started the semester reading about paradigms, philosophical origins, and each student chose one theory to read deeply before we began conversations about method(ologies). The first major assignment in the course was a 'thinking with theory' paper where students read Jackson and Mazzei's (2012) writing on thinking with theories, read a theory of choice, developed a list of three to five theoretical concepts, and began to think about how they might put these concepts to work with data produced in the course (i.e., field notes and an interview transcript). In class, the students intra-acted with a range of art materials, digital technologies, and printed out copies of their 'thinking with theory' papers to produce new knowledge(s) about their theory. This working-with-glue-paper-materials-peers-and-so forth produced space(s) for newness to emerge by not only *knowing* their theory but also *being* and *doing* theories with other humans and nonhumans.

After reading several pieces on paradigms in QR, we also engaged in a mask activity (adapted from Dr. Barbara Dennis). In small groups, students became an 'expert' about one paradigm – they had to read and *know* key components about the paradigm's philosophical roots. However, the students also had to perform their paradigm with the mask. This *being/doing* paradigm – or paradigming – produced new knowledges about paradigms (see Kuby and Christ 2017). In addition to this course activity, we threaded discussions on paradigmatic assumptions through each conversation about method(ologies) during the remainder of the semester. For example, when discussing interviewing, we opened up conversational space(s) about how a feminist paradigmatic perspective shapes how one conducts an interview, the relationship with the participant(s), and the types of questions asked.

After these experiences of knowing/being/doing paradigms and theories, we read and discussed a range of methodological approaches. We intentionally juxtaposed a more traditional introductory text (Savin-Baden and Howell Major 2013) which has the 'Creswell 5' plus other approaches such arts based, collaborative, etc.) with a disruptive text (Brown, Carducci, and Kuby 2014) that is explicitly situated in the politics of doing QR in a neoliberal academy. The introduction of the Brown, Carducci, and Kuby (2014) book discusses the politics of inquiry at macro, meso, and micro levels with each chapter author(s) attending to these levels. We threaded conversations and questions related to these levels of the politics of inquiry throughout discussions on methodologies and the paradigmatic assumptions of each. This fostered space(s) for conversations related to the *doing* of inquiry and on *being* a qualitative researcher within the neoliberal academy.

Data Production/Theories/Methods:
Our (Processes of) Thinking

We identify with postqualitative ways of being/doing/knowing inquiry (St. Pierre 2011b; see also endnote 7). In doing so, we engaged with various philosophical readings and plugged them into our planning/teaching/learning/ thinking/data producing/analysing/writing (Jackson & Mazzei 2012). We bricolaged together poststructural and posthumanist theoretical concepts in order to

1. think differently about the teaching ← → learning of QR,
2. think differently about data[8] and attempt to overturn neoliberal tendencies in our research, and
3. demonstrate the practices in which we asked our students to engage (i.e., thinking with theories and materials).

Playing-with-Materials-Theories: Thinking/Analysing/Diffracting/ Creating the Video

In line with posthumanist ideas of intra-activity, we asked the students to play-with-materials – such as field notes, interview transcripts, theories, literature reviews, discarded library books, construction paper, scissors, glue, tissue paper, and so forth, as a way to produce newness and to produce newness differently (St. Pierre, 2014). We too felt we needed to play-with-materials to better understand *how* we were educating students. We videoed ourselves as we engaged in thinking/analysing/diffracting with materials from teaching and theoretical concepts as described below from Deleuze and Guattari (1980/1987), Barad (2007; 2008; 2013), and Lenz Taguchi (2010):

- A node of a **rhizome**, like a bulb or tuber, can fissure and flourish in numerous directions. The concept of rhizomes helps us think about moments where instructors and students fissured expected practices.
- Porous and nomadic spaces are **smooth** while rigid and sedentary spaces are **striated**. The concepts of smooth and striated spaces help us to see how curricular decisions produced spaces of innovation (smooth) even within expected (striated) spaces of teaching QR.
- **Assemblages of desire** are relations, processes, bodily affects, connections, productions, flows and intensities. Learning takes place in the in-between-ness or flows of students/teachers/materials/time/space.

- Students and instructors were in fluid and intersecting relationships of **becoming** qualitative inquirers. The concept of becoming helps us see the ever-changing nature of teaching/learning QR as well as newness produced between teachers/students/materials/time/space.
- **Intra-activity** focuses on the force and production between human and nonhuman. Intra-activity helps us decenter the human and look at how texts, assignments, discourses, classroom environment, space(s), time, and materials worked together to produce new understandings and practices.

We used these concepts not only for analysis of data, but they also informed our teaching ← → learning over the semester. By putting to work these ideas (see Kuby and Gutshall Rucker 2016; Kuby, Aguayo, Holloway, Mulligan, Shear and Ward 2016; Kuby and Christ 2017), we were living out socially just pedagogy. For example, we embraced a rhizomatic pedagogy, where students were asked to make changes in how they wanted to use class time after Candace had posted a class agenda. Or, by inviting students to play and think with materials, we provided a space to intra-act to produce new knowledges and realities differently.

According to Barad (2007), the larger purpose of diffraction is to produce 'a new way of thinking about the nature of difference, and of space, time, matter, causality, and agency . . . in order to study the entangled effects differences make' (p. 73). Mazzei (2014) articulates that a 'diffractive reading of data through multiple theoretical insights moves qualitative analysis away from habitual normative readings (e.g., coding) toward a diffractive reading that spreads thought and meaning in unpredictable and productive emergences' (p. 742). We, too, were interested in the difference, the entangled a/effects of difference in teaching the course disruptively from neoliberal expectations and goals.

Below you will experience two images and the opportunity to view a video and/or an excerpt of a (re)presentation from our diffractions. Figure 8.1 is an image of our thinking with theory and diffracting analysis session in progress. We thought with the theoretical concepts described above as we intra-acted with data such as our memories and experiences from the course, copies of the syllabus and course calendar, copies of the textbook covers and table of contents, the IRB (University Institutional Review Board for Research Studies) consent forms and recruitment script, planning notes before the class begun, art materials, and our beliefs on neoliberalism. Figure 8.2 is an image of the final artifact from our thinking/analysing/diffracting with theory session. As shown in Figures 8.1 and 8.2, there is a newspaper with the heading 'Disruptors: The

Future of . . .' and an image of robotic pilot hands with the words 'Planes without Pilots'. A student shared the newspaper in class, and we did not realise how it would entangle with us in this analysis session to produce newness (a rhizomatic fissure).

This diffractive analysis session happened within the last few weeks of the semester. While we have a lot of data produced from the course, because of consent and IRB restrictions until grades were turned in, we only had our own conversations and planning notes to use as data for this session, which was about one and a half hours long. We created a script based on thinking with theories to accompany the video and through voice-over, layered questions and important concepts onto the video. We sped up the video speed for a shorter clip which we initially used for a conference presentation (Kuby & Aguayo, 2015) (view the video here: https://youtu.be/ZAAbI7TUrz4).

Continuing to Think/Analyse/Create: Additional Diffractive Analysis

After the conference presentation, we (re)entered the video/script, data produced in the course, theoretical readings, and the end of semester course evaluations to engage in additional diffractive analysis. We wanted to diffractively enter, fold, re-enter, and be-with theoretical ideas and data from the QR course (as well as what was produced from the first thinking/analysing/diffracting session) in order to study the a/effects of the entanglement of people, space, time, and materials in hopes of producing unpredictable newness. What was produced in this QR course (and for whom)? What emerged? How might diffractive readings a/effect our practices as QR instructors? As Barad (2007) reminds us, 'diffraction is an ethico-onto-epistemological matter' (p. 381), and the world is materialised differently through different practices. How might the teaching of QR materialise differently through our experiences as we diffractively read/encounter theories, philosophies, and data? And while we can't speak to this yet, we wonder if/how the students will engage in research differently after this course (and why this ethically matters).

Cutting Together Apart: (Re)Presenting

The process of taking the original video/script of thinking/analysing/ diffracting and then (re)entering diffractively to continue thinking/writing this manuscript produced a feeling of 'cutting together apart' a concept that Barad discusses; she invites readers to take out their 'quantum physics scissors' (Barad 2013, p. 30), which we see connected to her concept of the agential cut. This is in contrast to the Cartesian cut that divides subject and object. Instead, Barad's (2007) notion of the agential cut claims 'relata do not preexist relations; rather, relata-within-phenomena emerge through specific intra-actions' (p. 334). Therefore, we are not standing outside of the entanglement of the QR course (students, readings, assignments, etc.), but rather we are intra-actively entangled in the becoming of the course (i.e., cutting together apart). We cut together apart the teaching ← → learning from the original video/analysis session and additional diffractive engagements as we continued to think with theories, data, and literature on teaching (see https://drive.google.com/file/d/0B6K2236UqP9yaVdDWEZGZEh2bzA/view?usp=sharing for an excerpt (re)presentation). This diffractive (re)presentation is a sampling of our written (re)presentation of our thinking/diffracting process. The main text is a transcript from the videoed session as referenced above and the text boxes are additional theoretical ideas we are thinking-with. The document acts as a sample (re)presentation of layering our various thinking/analysing/diffracting sessions; it gives a glimpse into the ideas and inquiries created from reading theories, data from the course, memories, feelings, a newspaper, art supplies, and … and … and … through/with one another. There isn't one right way to experience this (re)presentation, and we don't see our writing as finalities but rather thinkings, insights, and provocations still on the move.

We struggled with how to 'represent the edginess of data – the very event that resists representation' (Springgay and Zaliwska 2015, p. 140). However, we find inspiration in Springgay and Zaliwska's (2015) statement, 'This [viewing data as open assemblages] challenges us not only to do research differently, but also to represent and articulate our research differently' (p. 140). Thus, we acknowledge that the (re)presentations (see Figures 8.1 and 8.2, the video clip, and written (re)presentation) might feel rhizomatic – meaning quotes and statements don't always linearly connect, but shoot off in various directions – this is intentional. In any case, we encourage you to experience the video clip shared above as you read the written (re)presentation and see what newness emerges. For us, the diffractions happened in the doing/being/knowing that is 'captured' on the video; the written (re)presentation (found from the weblink above) is a small piece of that.

Figure 8.1 Playing-with-Materials-Theories: Thinking/Analysing/Diffracting/ Creating the Video.

Figure 8.2 Artifact from Thinking/Analysing/Diffracting/Creating.

An Ethico-Onto-Epistemological Pedagogy: What It (Can) Produce(d)

It was through the processes of playing-with-materials diffractively that new insights and knowledges about teaching QR from an ethico-onto-epistemological perspective emerged. Creating an ethico-onto-epistemological pedagogy was not about adding art materials to a graduate class, choosing a disruptive textbook for the sake of disrupting, or even privileging theories over methods. However, these choices stem from a paradigmatic belief that we come to *know* from *being* and *doing* in the world. Therefore, if we wanted to produce emerging scholars that not only *knew* about ways to examine and respond to neoliberalism in the academy and imagine socially just research practices, we had to also create space(s) for them to wrestle with (and try out) ways of *being* and *doing* inventive, disruptive, and/or non-traditional QR – and the politics of these engagements.

Course readings and assignments produce; they can produce and perpetuate the status quo, or they can open up new ways of knowing/being/doing QR. Having students read Jackson and Mazzei's scholarship (2012) early in the semester produced a tenor, discourse, ways of being/doing/knowing QR. Juxtaposing two books (Savin-Baden and Howell Major, 2013 and Brown, Carducci, and Kuby, 2014) produced tensions and possibilities for students. Giving students time and space to play-with-materials produced permission, vulnerabilities, and newness of ideas and ways of being/doing in the neoliberal academy. As the second aim of this chapter was to invite readers to experience a diffractive methodology, we hope that our video clip, images, and excerpt from our analysis/thinking/diffracting demonstrate the messy, unpredictable, fruitful, and vulnerable work of thinking-with-theories-and-materials. While the aim is not to replicate, we do hope that graduate students and faculty members are inspired to take risks, create, invent, and produce newness. As Deleuze and Guattari (1991/1994) remind us, 'to think is to experiment' (p. 111). Olsson (2009) considers research as a wild empiricism which 'would in this sense mean to collectively invent rather than discover at a distance. It would imply fully recognising that when doing research, one is also inventing and adding things to the world' (p. 97). Research as experimentation, inventiveness – not discovering at a distance, criticising, and reducing practice. These are radical shifts in thinking about what research is and for what purpose. If research is an encounter between theory and practice then research must be created in the moment, much like what we did thinking with data-theory-art materials-spaces-time-each other. Research then is about producing newness and becoming.

Finally, as Barad writes, ethics is deeply rooted in posthumanist concepts. 'Just as the human subject is not the locus of knowing, neither is it the locus of ethicality ... Ethics is therefore not about right response to a radically exterior/ized other, but about responsibility and accountability for the lively relationalities of becoming of which we are a part' (Barad, 2007, p. 393). It is our response-ability to rethink how we teach QR because we are a part of the becoming of QR and because our pedagogy produces (certain types of) scholars. If we want scholars who will question, take action in their scholarship to disrupt neoliberalism, and experiment philosophically, theoretically, and methodologically, we must embrace and put to work ethico-onto-epistemological ways of teaching ← → learning. Neoliberalism is not solely an abstract idea; it is manifested in a material world through actions and practices related to grant funding, publication venues and expectations, tenure and promotion guidelines, and so forth. In other words, we are all entangled in the materialism[9] of neoliberalism. Typically, QR courses focus on the *learning* of QR (knowledge production and consumption) and tangentially on the *doing* of QR (writing research, seeking grants) perhaps at the expense of *being* – ethically (in a material turn sense) – qualitative researchers in the neoliberal academy. The ethics and politics of this work matter. It is our response-ability as faculty members to create space(s) for ethico-onto-epistemological pedagogies to come to matter. How can we not only awaken our students' cognitive fires, as Harriet shared, but also (co)produce space(s) for students to try-out possibilities and be(come) disruptive, socially just (philosophical, theoretical) inquirers?

Notes

1 Candace is a faculty member, and Becky was a doctoral student/researcher/teaching intern for the course.
2 The introductory QR class had 18 graduate students from the College of Education at various points in their programs and representing a range of disciplines (e.g., science education, art education, literacy education, counseling, sports psychology, and information sciences) as well as two international visiting faculty members. We planned for the course during the preceding summer and fall, and during the semester, we met for an hour weekly to discuss class meetings and plan together.
3 'Disruptive' is a word that is sometimes used to describe research practices that fall outside of the normative ways of knowing/being/doing QR because they challenge taken-for-granted assumptions held/enacted by traditional practices (see also Brown, Carducci, and Kuby 2014).
4 With this first aim in mind, we see this chapter as a broad overview to how we intentionally created the course. At the time of initial analysis/writing, we did not have permission to use data from the course (e.g., assignments, recorded class conversations, etc.) since it was still in session. Our institutional review board process stated that Candace could not be aware of who consented to the study until

after grades were submitted. Therefore, we signal readers to several other manuscripts that were written after the course that go deeper into specific assignments and/or experiences of students in the course. We understand that the chapter could be read as lacking 'students' voices,' and we want to be clear that the focus of the chapter is more about us as instructors diffractively thinking about what we planned and more broadly about what the course produced for us (and students).

5   We use hyphens, slashes, and double arrows to attempt to *write with theories* – to demonstrate intra-action, entanglement, and becoming within the limits of (re)presentation.

6   Teaching and learning are mutually constitutive; therefore, we resist binaries of teacher/student and teaching/learning (see Kuby, Aguayo, Holloway, Mulligan, Shear and Ward 2016; Kuby and Christ 2017).

7   As Koro-Ljungberg, Carlson, Tesar, and Anderson (2015) write, "'Post' refers to the different ontological, epistemological, and ethical conditions under which contemporary qualitative research operates' (p. 617). To us, postqualitative inquiry is about putting under erasure, in a Derridian sense, the normative, taken-for-granted assumptions of how to do (be, know) qualitative research(ers). Therefore, postqualitative inquiry is about inquiry 'post' (or after) conventional humanist qualitative inquiry as well as inquiry that puts to work 'post' (foundational) theories (St. Pierre 2011b).

8   We view data broadly, as St. Pierre (1997; 2014) describes transgressive data such memory data, emotional data, dream data, sensual data, and response data; therefore, data are not limited to traditional forms such as field notes, transcripts from interviews or focus groups, and the like.

9   Or how neoliberalism is manifested through publication and funding expectations, tenure and promotion practices and policies, and so forth.

References

Baez, B. and D. Boyles (2009), *The Politics of Inquiry: Education Research and the 'Culture of Science.'* Albany, NY: State University of New York Press.

Barad, K. (2007), *Meeting the Universe Halfway: Quantum Physics and the Entanglement of Matter and Meaning.* Durham, NC: Duke University Press.

Barad, K. (2008), 'Posthumanist Performativity: Toward an Understanding of How Matter Comes to Matter', in S. Alaimo and S. Hekman, *Material Feminisms,* Bloomington, IN: Indiana University Press, 120–156.

Barad, K. (2013), 'Ma(r)king Time: Material Entanglements and Re-memberings: Cutting Together-Apart', in P. R. Carlile, D. Nicolini, A. Langley and H. Tsoukas (eds),

How Matter Matters: Objects, Artifacts, and Materiality in Organization Studies. Oxford, UK: Oxford University Press, 16–31.

Brown, R.N., R. Carducci and C.R. Kuby (eds), (2014), *Disrupting Qualitative Inquiry: Tensions and Possibilities in Educational Research*. New York: Peter Lang.

Cheek, J. (2005), 'The Practice and Politics of Funded Qualitative Research', in N.K. Denzin and Y.S. Lincoln (eds), *Handbook of Qualitative Research*, Thousand Oaks, CA: Sage Publications, 387–409.

Creswell, J. W. (2012), *Qualitative Inquiry and Research Design: Choosing Among Five Approaches* (3rd edition). Thousand Oaks, CA: Sage Publications.

Deleuze, G. and F. Guattari (1980/1987), *A Thousand Plateaus: Capitalism and Schizophrenia*. (B. Massumi, Trans.) Minneapolis, MN: University of Minnesota Press.

Deleuze, G. and F. Guattari (1991/1994), *What is Philosophy?* (H. Tomlinson and G. Burchell, Trans.). New York: Columbia University Press.

Denzin, N.K., and M.D. Giardina (eds), (2006), *Qualitative Inquiry and the Conservative Challenge*. Walnut Creek, CA: Left Coast Press.

Dolphijn, R. and I. van der Tuin (2012), *New Materialism: Interviews and Cartographies*. Ann Arbor, MI: Open Humanities Press.

Jackson, A.Y. and L.A. Mazzei (2012), *Thinking with Theory in Qualitative Research: Viewing Data Across Multiple Perspectives*. New York, NY: Routledge.

Koro-Ljungberg, M., D. Carlson, M. Tesar and K. Anderson (2015), 'Methodology *brut*: Philosophy, Ecstatic Thinking, and Some Other (Unfinished) Things', *Qualitative Inquiry*, 21(7): 612–619.

Kuby, C.R. and R.C. Aguayo (2015), 'Disrupting the Introductory Qualitative Research Course: Teaching and Mentoring Graduate Students to Resist Neo-Liberal Politics and Practices', in G.S. Cannella (Chair), *Critical Qualitative Research Initiative in Higher Education: Studies in Progress*. Paper in symposium session at the International Congress of Qualitative Inquiry, Champaign-Urbana, Illinois.

Kuby, C.R. and R.C. Christ (2017), 'Productive Aporias and Inten(t/s)ionalities of Paradigming Spacetimematterings in an Introductory Qualitative Research Course', *Qualitative Inquiry*. Article first published online: https://doi.org/ 10.1177/1077800416684870

Kuby, C.R. and T. Gutshall Rucker (2016), *Go Be a Writer!: Expanding the Curricular Boundaries of Literacy Learning with Children*. New York: Teachers College Press.

Kuby, C.R., R.C. Aguayo, N. Holloway, J.A. Mulligan, S.B. Shear and A. Ward (2016), 'Teaching, Troubling, Transgressing: Thinking with Theory in a Post-Qualitative Inquiry Course', *Qualitative Inquiry*, 22(2): 140–148.

Lather, P. (2006), 'Paradigm Proliferation as a Good Thing to Think With: Teaching Research in Education as a Wild Profusion', *International Journal of Qualitative Studies in Education,* 19(1): 35–57.

Lenz Taguchi, H. (2010), *Going Beyond the Theory/Practice Divide in Early Childhood Education: Introducing an Intra-Active Pedagogy*. New York: Routledge.

Mazzei, L.A. (2014), 'Beyond an easy sense: A diffractive analysis', *Qualitative Inquiry*, 20(6): 742–746.

Newman, A. and Y. McNamara (2016), 'Teaching Qualitative Research and Participatory Practices in Neoliberal Times', *Qualitative Social Work*, 15(3): 428–443.

Olsson, L. M. (2009), *Movement and Experimentation in Young Children's Learning: Deleuze and Guattari in Early Childhood Education*. New York: Routledge.

Savin-Baden, M and C. Howell Major (2013), *Qualitative Research: The Essential Guide to Theory and Practice*. New York: Routledge.

Springgay, S. and Z. Zaliwska (2015), 'Diagrams and Cuts: A Materialist Approach to Research-Creation', *Cultural Studies ← → Critical Methodologies*, 15(2): 136–144.

Stark, S. and K. Watson (1999), 'Passionate Pleas for "Passion Please": Teaching for Qualitative Research', *Qualitative Health Research*, 9(6): 719–730.

St. Pierre, E.A. (1997), 'Methodology in the Fold and the Irruption of Transgressive Data', *International Journal of Qualitative Studies in Education*, 10(2): 175–189.

St. Pierre, E. A. (2011a), *Philosophically Informed Research.* Paper presented at the Annual Meeting of the American Educational Research Association, New Orleans, LA.

St. Pierre, E. A. (2011b), 'Post Qualitative Research: The Critique and the Coming After', in N. K. Denzin and Y. S. Lincoln (eds), *The Sage Handbook of Qualitative Research,* Thousand Oaks, CA: SAGE, 611–625.

St. Pierre, E. A. (2014), *Poststructural Theories of Language and the Limits of Coding.* Paper presented at the Annual Meeting of the American Educational Research Association, Philadelphia, PA.

St. Pierre, E. A. (2016), 'Untraining Educational Researchers', *Research in Education.* 1–6. DOI: 10.1177/0034523716664581.

Part Three

Locating Social Justice Pedagogies in Diverse Contexts

9

Finding Child Beyond 'Child': A Posthuman Orientation to Foundation Phase Teacher Education in South Africa

Karin Murris and Kathryn Muller

Decolonisation, coloniality and child

In recent years, student activism at South African universities has inspired salient debates about social justice in higher education and has provoked an impetus for reconceptualising and reconfiguring higher education and its pedagogical practices. Current political actions initiated by university students across the country, and with global impact on other universities, have given urgency to what it means to decolonise 'coloniality'[1] in an educational institution. However, these political actions tend to focus on *human identity*, without moving beyond anthropocentric frames of human meaning-making with adults as social change agents (Murris 2016a). No room is made epistemologically and ontologically for children, the more-than-human world and multispecies relationality; the exclusive focus is on '"Third World" peoples, women and queer folks' (Allen and Jobson 2016, p. 129).

In an interesting overview of the 'decolonising generation' in the African diaspora, including Africa itself, anthropologists Allen and Jobson (2016, p. 130) agree with the need to regard knowledge construction as temporal, therefore each generation has to construct anew an imagination of its future, including the meaning of decolonisation. It is significant that decolonisation as an open, ongoing project, currently does not include children themselves, nor age discrimination. They are still invisible and excluded from the decolonising agenda; neither is it recognised that they are victims of oppressive pedagogical practices that position them as inferior, lesser human beings, nor are they taken seriously as agents of change. In the case of black African child, an even lesser degree of humanity has been attributed by virtue of not only being black, but also being child – a double, or even triple blow when child is also female.

Child subjectivity is constructed within a web of knowledge claims, drawn mostly from western versions of histories, institutions, economies, politics and practices, and are riddled with distinctions, neo-liberal norms and yardsticks by which children's progress and development is measured and found wanting (Dahlberg and Moss 2005; Viruru 2005). There are remarkable parallels between colonialism and cognitive theories of child development e/merging at the same time in Europe (Nieuwenhuys 2013, p. 5). There is an intricate historical connection between child and 'savage', both so-called of Nature and in need of Culture (Murris 2016b). Importantly though, the introduction of childism as a form of colonisation is not on the back of settler colonialism, typically conceived of in terms of race, resources extraction and land occupation. As Rollo (2016: 2; our emphasis) puts it poignantly: 'The idea of a telos of progress from animal child to human adult is both a *historical and conceptual antecedent* of the idea of European civilisation, prefiguring its stories about maturation and progress from cultural ignorance to enlightenment'. Entangled connections between imperialism and the institutionalisation of childhood have been made (Nandy 1987; Burman 2008; Cannella and Viruru 2004). Thus, the terms 'coloniser' and 'colonised' take on a *double meaning* in the context of childhood (Cannella and Viruru 2004: 87).

Enlightenment notions of progress and reason have colonised education through its curriculum construction that positions children in need of recapitulating the development of the species: like Indigenous people, children are seen as simple, concrete, immature thinkers who need age-appropriated interventions in order to mature into autonomous 'fully-human' beings. This injustice is not just social, but also *ontoepistemic*. The subjectivity implicit in most educational theories and practices is the white, grown up and autonomous, male, able-bodied, heterosexual subject of humanism (Braidotti 2013). The signifier 'child' relies on the transcendental signifier 'I' of humanism (Murris 2016b). Although human exceptionalism is indeed of major concern in relationships between humans and animals, humans and the material world, humans and nature, how child is positioned as knower in pedagogical relations often tends to be forgotten in liberatory humanist and even some posthumanist education. Decolonising educationalists can perpetuate colonising child:adult relationships in their desire to teach the truths in which they are installed, thereby reducing children to knowledge consumers, rather than knowledge producers – a social, ontological *and* epistemic injustice (Murris 2016b, Ch 10). Children are not listened to because of their very *being* a child and therefore unable to make claims to knowledge, because it is assumed that they are (still) developing, (still) innocent, (still) fragile, (still) immature, (still) irrational and so forth. As Kathryn concludes in her final assignment below, child is only rendered capable when we move away from focusing on child as a *being* (with a stable personality, characteristics and essence), and instead focus on child as an embodied and embedded *becoming*. Throughout the history of western thought, education has been regarded as the formation of childhood (Kohan 2015; Stables 2008). Thus, the need to decolonise and disrupt current childhood discourses does not apply to only previously colonised countries – age discrimination concerns *all* children.

The complex connection between postcolonialism and childism is the background of a teacher education programme described and illustrated in this chapter. Here, childism refers to the denigration and subordination of children and childhood based on a hierarchical relationship between adult and child (with age as the category of exclusion). The objective is to show how, against the odds, a higher education curriculum can prepare students for the implementation of posthuman pedagogies in their future classrooms. Post-age and post-developmental pedagogical relationships are made possible through a reconfiguration of subjectivity as in/determinate and ageless (Haynes and Murris 2017). We report on how an innovative childhood studies course purposively written into a new teacher education Post-Graduate Certificate in Education (PGCE) Foundation phase[2] programmes can disrupt the anthropocentric gaze – a gaze that not only puts certain humanimals in terms of race, gender and class, but also of a particular age, above other bodies (including the material world) and deterritorialises the metaphorical and psychological language that has become so naturalised in early childhood, primary and teacher education worldwide.

Age performativity and justice-to-come

Like elsewhere (File 2012, pp. 34–38), the South African school curriculum positions adults in charge of meaning and knowledge, and authorises them to set the rules of criticality based upon rigid correspondences between a person's age – the *performative agency* of number – and their views, status, behaviours or abilities. Age categories, numbers and other quantifications (e.g. statistics) materialise ageist pedagogical relationships and cause ontoepistemic and social injustice because of the ethical hierarchy and biological taxonomy on which it is grounded.

By moving away from humanist relationality in education with its colonising focus on representational practices and its power producing binaries (child/

adult, body/mind, nature/culture, human/nonhuman animals, animate/ inanimate, organic/nonorganic, developed/undeveloped etc.) opportunities are created for decolonising intra-active pedagogies.

In teacher education, students also need to have embodied lived experiences of such pedagogies themselves in order to enact these pedagogies in their own professional practice. We exemplify this through Kathryn's striking final assessment as a student of the childhood course that is part of the PGCE programme. Her art installation – supported by a link to a video she made from spliced YouTube clips and unified by a voiceover – materialises a reconfiguration of child and childhood(s). Passages from Kathryn's essay have been interspersed in a different font. Also, some key images have been included, not with a purpose to clarify, illustrate or somehow support the discursive, but to affect the readerviewer by *showing* how student teachers can become activists for a 'justice-to-come' (Barad 2012, p. 81) through a programme that creates an imaginary for what might be possible – to find child beyond 'child'. For queer theorist and quantum physicist Karen Barad, justice is about 'proceeding responsibly', which involves the impossible task of allowing the response of the 'between' she says she is trying to gesture toward. Barad (2012, p. 81) explains:

> (Doing justice is a profound yearning, a crucially important if inevitably unachievable activity, an always already inadequate attempt to respond to the ethical cry of the world.) Or, rather, perhaps I can put it this way: It is the very question of justice-to-come, not the search for a final answer or final solution to that question, that motivates me. The point is to live the questions and to help them flourish.

This decolonising move is therefore not about *truths about a just future* as perceived by the educator to be taught (transmitted) to the learner, but to continue to ask the awkward questions (including what it means to decolonise). Importantly, it also means to allow children to ask the questions that *matter* in class. This decolonising pedagogical move reconfigures children as knowledge co-creators and as such includes them in the becoming of their own futures (both immediate and long term). At the same time, treating children differently, as able, competent, capable, etc., and including the more-than-human in knowledge construction also involves a reconfiguration of the normative human Subject (read; adult). Allowing child 'in' inescapably requires a reconfiguration of the knowing Subject and what it means to be human.

Decolonising childhood discourses requires a radical openness to in/ determinacy, with an ethics located in the posthuman *methodology* (e.g.

diffraction) used by educators for both teaching and research which generates new knowledge. Posthuman teaching and research involves being 'attentive to, and responsive/responsible to the specificity of material entanglements in their agential becoming' (Barad 2007, p. 91). The implications for ethics are significant in a relational ontology and the diffractive methodology which unsettles the separateness of being, knowing and responding. The link between posthumanism and the call for decolonising the curriculum is that the binary of human/nonhuman animals is based on certain engrained habits of thought about knowledge and intelligence and is 'inherently oppressive and violent' (Lennard and Wolfe 2017, n.p). For Barad it is impossible to separate or isolate practices of knowing and being: 'they are mutually implicated' (Barad 2007: 185). However, this does not mean that making specific worldly configurations are made up 'ex nihilo, or out of language, beliefs, or ideas, but, as Barad (2007, p. 91) explains 'in the sense of materially engaging as part of the world in giving it specific material form' ('worlding'). Knowledge is constructed through 'direct material engagement with' and not by 'standing at a distance and representing' the world (Barad 2007, p. 49). One must *perform* in order to see, for example, 'you learn to see through a microscope by doing not seeing' (Barad 2007: 51). Barad's diffractive reading of quantum physics and queer theory offers *empirical* evidence that '[k]nowing, thinking, measuring, theorizing, and observing are *material practices of intra-acting within and as part of the world*' (2007, p. 90; our italics). Her notion of performativity also disrupts the power producing child/adult binary. Like gender and species performativity (Pedersen 2016), age performativity 'otherises' through repeated material-discursive practices, consolidated through intra-actions over time. For justice-to-come, that is not predetermined and includes children's ideas in shaping how we will live together, contesting this habitual and institutionalised othering of child is urgent. The material-discursive story in this chapter is about one such adventure and academic experiment.

Posthuman Teacher Education in South Africa

In 2012, Karin was employed to design and convene a PGCE Foundation Phase. This project was funded by the European Union to support higher education institutions to improve the quality of Foundation phase teaching (Grade R[3] – Grade 3). There were, and still are, serious concerns about the continued poor performance of South African primary and secondary learners on national and international benchmark tests. To design an innovative decolonising posthuman curriculum was challenging for various, entangled reasons: the hegemonic developmental orientation of childhood education in higher education institutions, student teachers' own expectations of what a good education is based on their own experiences of schooling, and third, the government's solutions to the educational 'crisis' by introducing a new revised national curriculum: The Curriculum and Assessment Policy Statement [CAPS]. Since CAPS, teachers are under pressure to work with standardised national workbooks in combination with the Annual National Assessments (ANAs) (DBE 2011, p. 5), including highly prescribed, specified, sequenced and paced guidance regarding the content that should be taught in schools with scripted lessons and worksheets in an attempt to cover for the claimed lack of teacher content and pedagogic content knowledge (Taylor and Taylor 2013). These interventions by the government reinforced the already existing focus in teacher education on strengthening the teaching of school subjects in their programmes, mathematics and literacy. Less value is attached to the subject 'life skills' in the Foundation phase and includes a mixed bag of, for example, the natural and social sciences, the creative arts and physical exercise. Although life skills is regarded as one subject in schools as well as universities, they tend to be taught separately – pedagogy is associated with the subject (the 'content') that is taught and assumes child: adult and human/more-than-human relationships. But pedagogy cannot be only content driven as the relationship between self and other and every notion of childhood is inscribed. Although multimodality has gained traction, especially through the inclusion of visual texts, materials and embodied meaning-making practices, the important epistemological shift does not necessarily involve an *ontological* shift in subjectivity that is necessary for more socially just child: adult relationships. The adult remains firmly in charge of what counts as meaning and truth. Moreover, meaning making remains an anthropocentric affair with a separation of the knower (mind) from the known (body) and knowledge (epistemology) from being (ontology) as argued above.

The Enlightenment focus on rationality, combined with the geopolitical issues of global colonisation has shaped curriculum construction and how humans see their place in the world (Viruru 2005, pp. 15–16). The current curriculum is an expression of evolved and deeply engrained educational practices and power relations – not only in South Africa. Dominant is the I.R.E.[4] (Initiation Response Evaluation) framework, a pedagogical approach that assumes knowledge as a 'body', mapped by disciplinary experts and the world re-presented through reading, writing, drawing and colouring-in exercises. Curriculum materials in the form of prefabricated worksheets and prescriptive, often moralising, texts assume children learn best 'about', for example, nature in a disembodied manner through 2D paper and pen exercises without being in touch (literally) with the real world. Devoid of wonder, imagination or opportunities for experimentation, learners, as well as teachers, miss out in worlding (see above).

Instead, the official and hidden curriculum of schools socialises learners (and student teachers) into particular discriminatory animal: human and child: adult relations. Segregated and enclosed spaces for children, adults, animals and plants are regulated though various inside/outside binaries that include and exclude, keeping the 'other' at a distance. Schools, zoos, aquariums, botanical gardens, etc., are colonising material-discursive spaces. These spaces assume non-egalitarian power relations between adult and child, humans and animals, and humans and plants. Although not referring to age discrimination, we can find inspiration in the transdisciplinary philosophies of Donna Haraway and Karen Barad for intra-generational pedagogical practices with humans of all ages 'rendering each other capable' – a 'becoming-with' that also includes matter and nonhuman animals (Haraway 2016).

[5]*Here I suddenly see a way to return to the idea of Child, a way to let Child into this space. The key word (truly in the manner of one that unlocks) is 'with', a grammatical preposition denoting a relation between one object/subject and another. 'With' doesn't stand alone, however, it is accompanied by two other concepts, 'being' and 'becoming' so that instead of seeing the child, or the teacher, or the table or chair or sand or water or book or idea as simply being, they are seen as 'being-with' one another. Standing proudly in the present tense, these beings intra-act with one another and 'being-with' becomes an acknowledgement of mutual influence. This is part of the essence of posthumanism and the material turn – a recognition of the mutual influence of all matter on its surroundings. Furthermore, instead of seeing 'becoming' as an isolated process undertaken separately by individuals, there is the idea of 'becoming-with'. From here, instead of trying to distinguish the processes of child becoming adult; student becoming teacher; tree becoming paper; paint becoming picture, an entanglement of all these material-discursive existences ensues and they are all 'becoming-with' one another.*

Posthumanism and child as 'fellow traveller'

Critical posthumanism has inspired a reconfiguring of relationships with the more-than-human in teacher education, focusing on reconfiguring animal/ human relationships in schools, the material world, the environment and the relationship between theory and practice (Lenz Taguchi 2010; Pacini-Ketchabaw and Nxumalo 2014; Pedersen 2016; Taylor 2014). This important feminist scholarly work has inspired Karin's promiscuous PGCE curriculum of 'subject' and 'Subject' boundary crossing. The other courses 'literacy', 'mathematics' and 'life skills' are as integrated as the pragmatics of university life allow for, with an emphasis on storytelling, narrativity, philosophy with children and the creative arts as guiding principles for teaching and learning (Murris and Verbeek 2014). The age-less Subject of this curriculum is 'a prosthetic entity, a distributed, dispersed "assemblage" constituted by many elements, some of them physical and material and biological, some of them not . . . it exists nowhere as a totality' (Wolfe interviewed by Lennard 2017, n.p.). Education in the posthuman age abandons the patriarchal Cartesian project and urges everyone to live without bodily boundaries and to queer humanist binaries. The ontological shift in subjectivity means that in a sense 'adult has become child . . . a being who is incomplete, always on-the-way, who is never finished developing' (Kennedy 2006, p.10). The implication of understanding subjects as always-in-process for educational relationality is that child becomes a 'fellow traveller' rather than being treated as a 'future-worker-consumer-citizen' (Kennedy 2006, p. 11). Posthumanism encourages educators philosophically and practically to engage with more robust and complex accounts of the relationality involved in pedagogical encounters:

> *Posthumanism is a perception and philosophy that seeks to understand non-human matter and material beyond the reductive and simplistic idea of what that matter or material can do for humans. In other words, it is deliberately and consciously non-exploitative.*
>
> *In terms of conventional schooling this highly ethical stance poses some problems. The main one is that the idea of exploiting materials (be it other human beings, animals, buildings, plants, books or all manner of other matter) for the purpose of educating 'the Child' is hardwired into our very idea of what education is. Child is at the centre, everything else is simply instrumental to their being child and becoming adult.*

The philosophical shift in subjectivity poses profound challenges in teacher education as student teachers need strong systems of support and mentoring through carefully designed pre-service education. Primarily designed as a quick preparation for becoming a teacher, how does one teacher educate posthumanly in the PGCE and does it work?

> *I have found that ideas of posthumanism have sunk deeply into places where verbal language cannot go or be retrieved. I think of the activities we did of 'being' with*

paper, rock, beach debris. Perhaps understanding this theory is also a matter of learning to 'be' with it and to let it be with me.

Childhood studies in the historical period of the 'Great Dithering'

The ethical concern is that posthumanism is a conscious and deliberate attempt to move away from humanistic, human-centred ways of looking at the world, as it is clear that human self-involvement and self-interest is very bad for the planet and even for humans themselves.

In many ways, the student teachers of this one-year qualification find themselves torn in several different directions. They have been socialised into hegemonic discourses about child and childhood(s) through their own experiences and memories of being child, sibling or sometimes a parent. However, the posthuman pedagogical orientation taught and enacted in their childhood studies course does not resonate with the pedagogies they are taught elsewhere at university, neither in their prior undergraduate degrees (e.g. psychology, social work), nor as part of their becoming a teacher through the PGCE. Moreover, during Teaching Practice (one-third of their degree), students often witness abusive child:adult relations, such as corporal punishment or verbal humiliation. Finally, students often voice their political concern about the highly abstract, densely written posthuman literature with no or little reference to age discrimination or practical guidance.

Despite the persistence of material entanglement and the sense that entanglement is unavoidable, there is something about the language of posthumanism that triggers a sense of detachment, of disconnect between words and the world. In trying to get closer, I end up feeling further away. Perhaps it is due to the intensity of analytical description that seems to be required, in order to inscribe every element of every encounter as fully agentic; to 'correct' perceived injustices done to the non-human by the human. Analysis like this, often highly technical and detailed, becomes so focused on describing the surrounding matter that evidence of the speaker or writer's own agency and responsibility is overshadowed or even erased; an over-correction perhaps, or is it an evasion? It feels ironic that to express posthumanism, we rely so heavily on human language and description, to acknowledge and give credence to intra-actions in our surroundings. Is it not perhaps humanistic after all, to want to inscribe agency into everything, and then tell each other about it, in words?

Then again, perhaps the reliance on language is temporary or at any rate introductory.

Given all these isolating contextual factors, how can a childhood studies course contribute to the decolonisation of a teacher education curriculum?

In order to move beyond colonising ontological relationality 'in-between' humans of a certain age, race, gender or class (and where they intra-sect) and 'between' human and more-than-humans, students need to take up an activist position seeking material and social transformation. Moving beyond notions of individual flourishing to 'multi-species flourishing' is required for collaborative intra-generational action during the 'Great Dithering' – Donna Haraway's term for the 'historical' period in which our bodyminds are 'currently' situated (between 2000–2050). She explains (Haraway 2016, pp. 144–145):

> The Great Dithering was a time of ineffective and widespread anxiety about environmental destruction, unmistakable evidence of accelerating mass extinctions, violent climate change, social disintegration, widening wars, ongoing human population increase ... and vast migrations of human and nonhuman refugees without refuge.

To make a difference *now*, while we still can, requires a reconceptualisation and rethinking of teacher education programmes. To include the boundary-crossing childhood studies course is one such innovative step for justice-to-come – and not only *social* justice. On the surface this sounds contradictory. How as teacher educators and student teachers make a difference now, when justice is in the future? What justice is cannot be prescribed. It requires imaginative, forever on-going, intra-generational work.

As an intricate part of the methods courses, childhood studies has equal credits to the traditional subjects: literacy, mathematics and life skills, and informs their pedagogies. Moreover, transdisciplinary field trips draw on these disciplines and create integrated curriculum experiences. Innovative forms of assessments and field trips express a posthuman relational ontology and queer humanist binaries. For example, each year students visit the aquarium in Cape Town. The students help create the e/mergent curriculum intra-actively, so each year the content varies. In 2015, preparing for this event included various experiential workshops. In one workshop, we started by watching an extract of a lecture by Jane Bennett on *Vibrant Matter* on YouTube, after which an art educator engaged the students in having 'conversations' with materials: a being-with wood and a being-with paper, first individually (Figure 9.1) and then collaboratively they created a sculpture out of paper and then wood (Figure 9.2). Visually, Figure 9.1 powerfully expresses the juxtaposition between the *use* of paper (on top of the table) and having an *encounter* with paper *as* paper (under

Figure 9.1 Being-with-paper.

Figure 9.2 A group sculpture – being-with-wood.

the table). These activities were followed up by a group 'sculpture' created by students' own moving bodies.

They were then blindfolded and in pairs explored each other's hands, taking time to pay attention to the intricate details and differences between their hands. The students' bodies were gently moved around the room by the teacher educators and still blindfolded they had to find each other's partners, by touching and exploring the hands of their peers. Plenary discussions and small groups writing in their diffractive journals[6] online followed this event, with students making connections between their experiences and how schools tend to use materials and other bodies in the room (e.g. corporal punishment). Another workshop involved encounters with various materials associated with an aquarium (e.g. sand, shells and stones). The students intra-acted with these materials through their mobile phones, overhead projectors and specially made light-boxes, while the politically engaged documentary *Oceans* (2009; directors Jacques Perrin and Jacques Cluzaud) was screened on the Interactive White Board (Figure 9.3).

Figure 9.3 Intra-actively working together: human and more-than-human.

During the field trip to the aquarium, students critically engage with the space as a colonising one, not just the animal bodies captured in it (after all, they are there for the sole purpose of human use), but also the children. In particular, we observe how the children intra-act with the nonhuman animals and how the teachers in turn intra-act with the children. The venue is always busy with school children on school outings. Kathryn and another student were particularly struck by the intra-action between penguins and a group of young children running behind their enclosure. It was this event that inspired Kathryn's art installation, which is the main assessment of the childhood studies course. She presented this at an exhibition at the end of the year, with the other students who also showcased their year's work in childhood studies as well as literacy and life skills (Figure 9.4).

Figure 9.4 Kathryn's art installation at the final exhibition.

Posthumanism requires an unprecedented and somewhat unlikely shift; it asks 'what would happen if the child was not at the centre of our idea of Child and Childhood, and Education?' What would education look like if the materials of education and childhood were not exploited, but invited or even incidental to the learning that unfolded, between Child and Other?

These questions bring me to the video clip of penguins that I filmed at the aquarium. At the time of filming I was drawn to the penguins because of their uncanny, collective stillness. This surreal stillness, which makes the video-frame seem like a photograph, is interrupted suddenly by a burst of movement as a group of pre-schoolers rustle and bustle their way in and out of the frame, behind the penguin enclosure. I did not notice the children at the time of filming this video, the contrast of their liveliness to the penguin's stillness only became apparent to me when re-watching the footage.

Thinking about this encounter, in relation to the ethical stance of posthumanism made me wonder about how animals in zoos and aquariums are constructed, by parents, teachers and educational programmes, as 'learning opportunities' for children. Of course, education is not the only reason that zoos and aquariums exist – the creatures found there are understood to be kept in captivity for their own good, or at least for the greater good of conservation. But the role of education is central to this project too; children are, after all, the future. . .aren't they?

I became curious to find other footage of children at zoos or aquariums, interacting with animals. I was particularly struck by moments when children seemed to interact with animals on a level beyond what any book or grown-up could tell them. In each of these clips, the intra-actions between animal, child, water, ground and glass are physically close, even intimate; and the results that are created are surely explosions of poetic, entangled life.

The course outline stipulates that the assessment '*includes an installation (e.g. a construction, series of photographs, collage) expressing your own changing ideas about child and childhood this year with a short written explanation in the form of an essay indicating the reasons for these shifts and a rationale for the installation (max 1500 words)*'. In Kathryn's case, the external examiner was invited to watch her video made from spliced YouTube clips and unified by a voiceover. We also invite you to read her essay and to join the examiner on an imaginative journey *with* the examiner and follow her to the laptop positioned under the table (Figure 9.5) and then to watch the DvD https://www.youtube.com/watch?v=aub04QlpdLI.

In order to do this, in your imagination, you must kneel and crawl like a child at a much less comfortable level than you are used to, moving awkwardly from the light into the dark. You will encounter little notes attached to things, such as the table, the torch, the curtain (Figure 9.6), the pillow, the earphones.

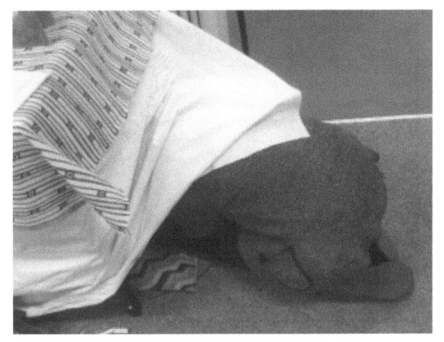

Figure 9.5 The external examiner assessing the art installation.

I am firm and flat, 75cm high. My upper surface is commonly used, as it is here, to hold other objects, smaller than me (such a variety I cannot begin to recount!). But underneath this busy upper surface, I am a different space altogether. I am. . .a den, a nook, a cranny of darkness. A low space, a neglected space.

*

I am cold to the touch; heavy and metallic; mostly cylindrical, but for some even ridges and textures across my surface. At one end of my body, there is a button and at the other end, a bulb. By applying pressure to the button, perhaps with the thumb of the hand that holds it, a switch is activated that sends electricity into the bulb of the torch, causing it to light up. Yes, I am a source of light. . . Another dose of pressure switches off the circuit; cuts of the electricity and with it the light from the bulb. Yes, I am a source of non-light too.

*

I am a curtain. I have enveloped this space in darkness. I am the entrance. If I let you in, know that with you comes the light, the weight of your knees, the fury of your head against my fabric shield. Be careful, clumsy human.

*

I am soft, full of airy stuffing and encased neatly in a pocket of woven thread, fabricated. Your knees sink into my surface, squashing all the fine fibres of my insides against one another, cushioning your knee against the hard-scratchy ground. Don't mind me.

*

I have soft and hard parts, designed to fit oh-so-ergonomically against two human ears. A tangle of chord connects me to a power supply, which produces waves of electronic sounds. These are sent along the wires to the cushions around your ears. Inside these cushions are my two diaphragms. They vibrate on the impact of the sound waves, and amplify the sound into human ears. On your head, they are snug, aren't they? They swallow the sound of your world and offer you another. Get down here, human, please come in . . .

*

These notes are a narrative device to emphasise, perhaps overemphasise, as Jane Bennett (2010, p. xvi) puts it 'the agentic contributions of nonhuman forces . . . in an attempt to counter the narcissism of humans in charge of the world'.

This anthropomorphising serves to not only trouble the organic/inorganic binary, but also the child/adult binary, as animism tends to be associated with primitive forms of human development (read: 'child' or 'savage'). Kathryn starts her assignment as follows:

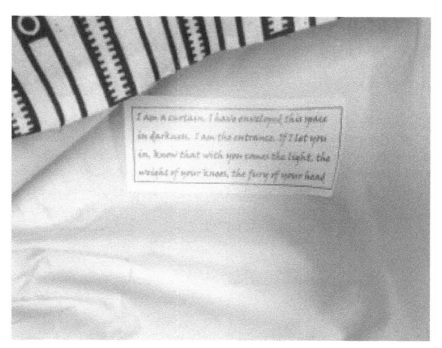

Figure 9.6 I am a curtain . . .

Here, at the onset of my installation the agency of different materials that make up my installation are encountered by viewers, both in the dark and the light. I ask them to consider the boundaries and body of the torch, the block-out fabric, sponge, headphones and the relation of these to their own bodies. I ask the reader to consider them not as inert, inactive matter but as matter with material-discursive agency (Lenz Taguchi 2010, p. 40).

The challenge that arises from this initiative is how to bring the idea of Child into play with this 'acknowledgement' of material agency; especially when there are no actual children around and ideas are all we have.

So, let's be clear, there is no child here, not one. But, children do exist. They occupy space and time and memory. 'Child', as an entity, intra-acts with its world, making impressions and being impressed upon, not unlike how we as students, researchers and teachers have intra-acted with materials in this course (or with this installation, for example). Child, we conclude, is part of the world of agentic matter; it is inter-dependent, enmeshed and entangled.

In the absence of 'actual' Child (by no means any easier to pin down) ideas of Child and Childhood must somehow be fashioned from other materials, symbolised and represented; evoked through other medium, like a streetlamp that passes for the moon.

It is this decolonising move(ment) that the childhood studies course aims to provoke beyond the signifier 'child' into a pedagogical space of epistemic uncertainty and ontological in/determinacy. The inclusion of visual texts, materials and embodied meaning-making practices, as well as the field trips have been central in making an *ontological* shift in subjectivity that is necessary for more socially just child: adult relationships. As Kathryn concludes, posthuman pedagogy involves a moving away from putting the human (child) at the centre:

If you want to find Child, what I have learnt is that you have to look elsewhere. You have to look at either side of Child, above and below, before and after. If you keep your eyes and mind pinned to the Child alone, you are likely to miss out on it altogether.

Acknowledgement

We would like to thank all the 2015 PGCE Foundation phase students for our inspiring collaborative work together and kind permission to use images as part of the university's ethics clearance procedure.

Funding

This work is based on research supported by the National Research Foundation of South Africa [Grant number 98992].

Notes

1 Coloniality remains when colonial administrations have left, but continue to determine long-standing everyday hierarchical patterns of power and 'superiority is premised on the degree of humanity attributed to the identities in question' (Maldonado-Torres 2007, p. 244).
2 The Foundation Phase in South Africa refers to children aged 5–9 years old.
3 Grade R is the pre-school age group 5–6 year olds and the first year of compulsory Foundation Phase schooling in South Africa.
4 The basic structure of the IRE framework has the following sequence: Teachers *initiate* by asking a question, a learner *responds* by giving an answer and the teacher *evaluates* the answer (e.g. by saying 'well done').
5 This is the first of a series on passages from Kathryn's essay, interspersed in the text and available as a complete essay on the link where Kathryn reads it out aloud in the background.
6 In groups of three the students keep a weekly journal on a Google document in which they diffract with each other and make sense together of the Childhood Studies sessions. The groups have been set up electronically in such a way that the teacher educator can see who participates and how often, and also diffracts with the students. For more information, see Murris (2016b)

References

Allen, J.S. and R.C. Jobson (2016), 'The Decolonizing Generation: (Race and) Theory in Anthropology since the Eigthies', *Current Anthropology*, 57(2): 129–148.
Barad, K. (2007), *Meeting the Universe Halfway: Quantum Physics and the Entanglement of Matter and Meaning*, Durham: Duke University Press.
Barad, K. (2012), 'Intra-Actions: An Interview with Karen Barad by Adam Kleinman', *Mousse*, #34 June: 76–81.
Barad, K. (2014), 'Diffracting Diffraction: Cutting Together-Apart', *Parallax*, 20(3): 168–187.
Bennett, J. (2010), *Vibrant Matter: A Political Ecology of Things*, Durham: Duke University Press.

Braidotti, R. (2013), *The Posthuman*, Cambridge: Polity Press.

Burman, E. (2008), *Developments: Child, Image, Nation*, London and New York: Routledge.

Cannella, G. S. and R. Viruru (2004), *Childhood and Postcolonization: Power, Education, and Contemporary Practice*, New York: RoutledgeFalmer.

Dahlberg, G. and P. Moss (2005), *Ethics and Politics in Early Childhood Education*, London: Routledge.

Department of Basic Education (DBE) (2011), *Curriculum and Assessment Policy Statement* (CAPS).

File, N. (2012), 'The Relationship Between Child Development and Early Childhood Curriculum', in N. File, J. Mueler and D. Basler Wisneski (eds), *Curriculum in Early Childhood Education: Re-examined, Rediscovered, Renewed*, New York: Routledge, 29–42.

Haraway, D.J. (2016), *Staying with the Trouble: Making Kin in the Chthulucene*, Durham: Duke University Press.

Haynes, J. and K. Murris (2017), 'Intra-Generational Education: Imagining a Post-Age Pedagogy', *Educational Philosophy and Theory*, available online: http://dx.doi.org/10.1080/14681366.2017.128668.

Kennedy, D. (2006), *The Well of Being, Childhood, Subjectivity and Education*, New York: State University of New York Press.

Kohan, W. (2015), *Childhood, Education and Philosophy: New Ideas for an Old Relationship*, New York: Routledge.

Lennard, N. and C. Wolfe (2017), 'Is Humanism Really Humane?', *The New York Times*. THE STONE 9 January. Available online: https://www.nytimes.com/column/the-stone (accessed 10 January 2017).

Lenz Taguchi, H. (2010), *Going Beyond the Theory/Practice Divide in Early Childhood Education*, London: Routledge Contesting Early Childhood Series.

Maldonado-Torres, N. (2007), 'On the Coloniality of Being', *Cultural Studies*, 21(2): 240–270.

Mignolo, W.D. (2007), 'Coloniality and Modernity/Rationality', *Cultural Studies*, 21(2–3): 155–167.

Murris, K. (2016a), '#Rhodes Must Fall: A Posthumanist Orientation to Decolonising Higher Education Institutions', *South African Journal of Higher Education*, 30(3): 274–294.

Murris, K. (2016b), *The Posthuman Child: Educational Transformation through Philosophy with Picturebooks*, London: Routledge Contesting Early Childhood Series

Murris, K. and C. Verbeek (2014), 'A Foundation for Foundation Phase Teacher Education: Making Wise Educational Judgements', *South African Journal of Childhood Education*, 4(2): 1–17.

Nieuwenhuys, O. (2013), 'Theorizing Childhood(s): Why We Need Postcolonial Perspectives', *Childhood*, 20(1): 3–8.

Pacini-Ketchabaw, V. and F. Nxumalo (2014), 'Posthumanist Imaginaries for Decolonizing Early Childhood Praxis', in M.N. Bloch, B.B. Swadener and G.S. Cannella (eds), *Reconceptualizing Early Childhood Care & Education. A Reader*, New York: Peter Lang, 131–142.

Pedersen, H. (2016), *Animals in Schools: Processes and Strategies in Human-Animal Education*, West Lafayette: Purdue University Press.

Stables, A. (2008), *Childhood and the Philosophy of Education: An Anti-Aristotelian Perspective*, London: Continuum Studies in Educational Research.

Taylor, A. (2014), 'Situated and Entangled Childhoods: Imagining and Materializing Children's Common World Relations', in *Reconceptualizing Early Childhood Care and Education: Critical Questions, New Imaginaries and Social Activism*. London: Peter Lang, 121–130.

Taylor, N. and S. Taylor. (2013), 'Teacher Knowledge and Professional Habitus', in N. Taylor, S. Van Der Berg and T. Mabogoane (eds), *What Makes Schools Effective? Report of the National Schools Effectiveness Study*, 202–230. Cape Town: Pearson.

Viruru, R. (2005), 'The Impact of Postcolonial Theory on Early Childhood Education'. Available online: http://joe.ukzn.ac.za/Libraries/No_35_2005/The_impact_of_postcolonial_theory_on_early_childhood_education.sflb.ashx (accessed 1 June 2015).

10

Embodied Pedagogies: Performative Activism and Transgressive Pedagogies in the Sexual and Gender Justice Project in Higher Education in Contemporary South Africa

Tamara Shefer

Introduction

The last few years in South African higher education has been characterised by student protests as referred to and explored by a number of chapters in this volume. While students' challenges to continued exclusionary practices and injustices in the university and its curriculum are by no means new in the country's history, such activism has reinvigorated these efforts and captured the imagination of many beyond the 'ivory tower'. In this chapter, I examine how certain moments, actions and events that have been directed at gender and sexual justice dialogue with critical posthumanist and new feminist materialist thinking, both with respect to decolonising the curriculum and also in relation to larger struggles against intersectional gender injustice and the violence that accompanies this. In this chapter I focus on a number of current examples of embodied gender and sexual justice activism to think about how we might engage materiality in disrupting the colonial and patriarchal heritages of inequality and exclusion in higher education. The chapter argues the importance of acknowledging such moments as forms of posthumanist activism in that they bring to consciousness the binarisms inherent in a humanist academy. I also suggest the value of recognising and bolstering such disruptive moments and events through inviting creativity and performativity into the classroom.

While South African universities have been engaged in a long project of 'transformation' in higher education, the last two years has witnessed an intensification of calls by students, staff and workers to 'decolonise' South African higher education. Such moves are encapsulated in #Rhodesmustfall, #feesmustfall and #fallism and other related activisms, and have shifted higher education into a renewed urgency to re-think such efforts (Mbembe 2015a; 2015b; Badat 2016; Jacobs 2016). Students' activism has in particular foregrounded the significance of the material and symbolic realm and how the geographies, spaces and territorial contexts of higher education, evident in architectures, classrooms and curriculums, are implicated in discomforting, unsafe and marginalising experiences for many.

Higher education in South Africa remains characterised by multiple forms of discursive, social and material difference and inequalities, which shape exclusionary and unequal practices both inside and outside the academy (for example, Badat 2010; Badat and Sayed, 2014; Bozalek and Boughey 2012; Department of Education 2008; Jaggesar and Msibi 2015; Msibi 2013). In the South African context of higher education, exclusionary practices have also been powerfully entangled with raced and classed inequalities which shape certain erasures, often directly excluding certain peoples and bodies from a sense of belonging and safety in higher educational contexts (see for example, Bhana 2014; Bradbury and Kiguwa 2012; Clowes, et al., in press; Ngabaza, et al. 2014; Shefer, Strebel, Ngabaza snd Clowes 2017; Vincent 2008).

South African higher education has had a long engagement in challenging inequality and injustices in the academy. A proliferation of efforts over the last few decades have been directed at ensuring historically excluded students' access to university both materially and intellectually (see Morrow 2009; Muller 2014 for notion of epistemological access), and social justice pedagogical projects (for example Bozalek and Carolissen 2013; Bozalek et al. 2010; Leibowitz et al. 2012; Gachago et al. 2013; 2014). Yet, student protests across the country flag the lack of progress as well as the complexity of the project of social justice in higher education and South African society more generally.

Notwithstanding the emphasis on change and justice in higher education in South Africa, much of these efforts have been driven by an inadvertent humanist and western endeavour which focuses on promoting individual scholars within the normative orthodoxies of the (post)colonial academy. There has been little acknowledgement that scholarship in South Africa (and globally) is characterised by centuries of a humanist project pivoting about a Cartesian dualism, privileging consciousness, cognition and rationality, and 'marked by disembodiment, egocentricity and ocularcentricity' (Jung 1996, p. 3). New feminist materialism's critique of the humanist project of control over other species and the planet,[1] has contributed to a deeper understanding of how these histories and presents shape hegemonic practices of scholarship, exaggerated by contemporary neoliberal imperatives and the commodification of education.

Dominant forms of knowledge production, notwithstanding decades of critique such as foundational Foucauldian analysis of governmentality and bio-power, continue to privilege the pursuit of 'neutral', scientific knowledge towards the reproduction of rational, disciplined subjects and knowledge that predominantly serves ruling social interests. The materiality of everyday embodied life, including the bodily, material and affective experiences of those who participate in academic life as teachers or learners, have been largely excluded from such endeavours, predominantly finding their place as 'objects' of research and regulation. Decades of feminist scholarship, built upon and taken forward in current theoretical work within the frameworks of posthumanism and new feminist materialism, have foregrounded the exclusion and marginalisation of the body and women's knowledges, evident at multiple levels in spaces of higher education. Indeed, on the basis of being 'embodied others', those 'who are not allowed *not* to have a body', those embodied in female, Black and other subjugated bodies have endured centuries of exclusionary practices, constructed as 'inevitably disqualifying and polluting bias in any discussion of consequence' (Haraway 1988, p. 575).

The exclusion of the body and the erasure of embodiment within the cartesian binarism of mind/body, is arguably poignantly implicated in students' educational journeys at universities. Thus, while much emphasis in social justice education is placed on entry, representation and the curriculum, little attention has been placed on the materiality of everyday life on campus and in classrooms, and how such materialities matter and are implicated in multiple forms of exclusion. Yet bodies continue to intrude, transgressing the erasures of body and affect and disturbing normativities and power inequalities that are interwoven into the shape and form of universities in South Africa as they are elsewhere.

In this chapter, responding to the call to rethink 'the fundamental concepts that support such binary thinking' and to recognise 'the agential possibilities and responsibilities for reconfiguring the material-social relations of the world' (Barad 2007, p. 35), I explore a number of activist and performative events that have been a part of the contemporary student decolonisation movement in South Africa to think about the disruption and disturbance of 'business as usual' in the patriarchal, colonial and neoliberal project of the academy. Three inspiring occasions of performative activism of feminist and queer activists are shared here as providing powerful pedagogical interventions through the deployment of particular bodies in particular spaces. I argue the importance of acknowledging and intra-acting (Barad, 2007) with such 'disturbances' within a critical posthumanist social justice pedagogical project.

Young women disrupting the colonial project of higher education: the ascendancy of African femininity in the case of the fall of Rhodes

Since the start of current student protests in South African higher education in early 2015, young Black women have been particularly active in leading sexual and gender justice struggles in the decolonial movement (Gouws 2016, 2017). While feminist discourse has notably been historically rejected as a white, middle class and colonial import in South Africa (Dosekun 2007; Gouws 2016; Shefer, Potgieter and Strebel 1999), a clear feminist and queer agenda was evident in student activism calls for intersectionality in the decolonial agenda, as will be elaborated in the cases studies that follow.

On 9 April 2015, a statue of Cecil John Rhodes, the most infamous colonial figure in South Africa was removed from its prominent place on the campus of the University of Cape Town (UCT) after some weeks of protest calling for its removal from the university. While the physical removal of the statue was taking place, a well photographed installation by Sethembile Msezane, a Masters graduate at UCT's fine art school was performed in parallel.[2] Msezane stood on a plinth near the Rhodes statue for the entire time, a few hours, that the statue was being removed. She was dressed as a Zimbabwe bird, representing soapstone statues that were removed from the ruins of Great Zimbabwe during the colonial period and that were sold to powerful settler men like Rhodes (see Huffman 1985; Hubbard 2009). Rhodes purchased one of these art works, ironically known as the 'Cecil Rhodes' Bird', and the piece is still housed in his former home in Groote Schuur estate in Cape Town (Hubbard 1990). Msezane's performative activism is a powerful material-discursive disruptive moment in reminding the viewers of the multiple layers of colonial theft and violences. Further, the installation gestures to a disruption of the imperialist, humanist civilising project that drove (still drives) the pursuit of dominant academic knowledge. In this decolonial moment of the ascendancy of African femininity, of the taking flight at the very moment that the statue of the male, northern settler topples down, there is not only a symbolic reclaiming of that which was stolen, but also a disruption of colonial and patriarchal power in the academy and elsewhere.

The entanglement of patriarchy with colonisation, long theorised by postcolonial feminists is powerfully represented here. As Rosemarie Buikema (2017 p. 147)[3] argues, Msezane's performance 'thus inserts both academy and art into an activist performance, creating an image which forever links the de-colonisation movement's critique of imperialism and patriarchy in an innovative and thought-provoking way'. Msezane (2017) herself is very clear that her artwork is about addressing intersectional inequalities and redressing erasures and marginalisations that are the legacy of apartheid, colonisation and patriarchy. As she articulates this in her artist statement at her recent exhibition:

> Having been confronted with monuments erected to celebrate British colonialism and Afrikaner nationalism, I revisit contested sites of memory in my performances and choose African women as re-imagined protagonists … For this reason, performance has been key, in my practice to re-locating the presence of the black female body … Collectively these works narrate resistance and self-assertion in response to dominant ideologies in the public space.
>
> Msezane 2017, n.p

Deploying the imagery of a stolen artwork that represents an animal[4] is perhaps significant not only for 'correcting' the colonial plunder, but also in that the installation speaks to an entanglement of 'subalternity' (Spivak 1988) – colonised 'subjects', femininity, non-human beings (the Great Zimbabwe Bird) and the non-sentient being (a statue). The entanglement is subjugated within a humanist, 'civilising project' with universities like the University of Cape Town, at the helm of the associated intellectual endeavour. Strategically intra-acting with the moment at which the statue of a white northern patriarchal colonialist was removed, Msezane draws attention to intersectional inequalities and abuses of the past. She performs the ascendance of an African woman in the form of a Zimbabwe bird stolen from Great Zimbabwe, historically a place of power and strength. Not only is a symbolic challenge to patriarchal (post)colonisation and the university as vehicle articulated, but so too is a symbolic disruption of the civilising and violent humanist scholarly project achieved.

Troubling the erasure of bodies

Queer activism and an emphasis on LGBTIQ+ struggles have undoubtedly been an integral part of student activism over the last few years. While clearly not uncontested, the argument that sexual and gender justice and intersectionality in general is entangled in the decolonial struggle has been powerfully articulated within the larger framework of student protests (Gouws 2017). Key in taking forward sexual and gender justice concerns has been a strident voice from queer and feminist activists, notably a group located primarily at UCT, the Trans Collective (#transfeministcollective),[5] who have taken up the exclusion of non-normative sexualities and genders and placed these struggles firmly on the decolonial agenda:

> An intersectional approach to our blackness takes into account that we are not only defined by our blackness, but that some of us are also defined by our gender, our sexuality, our able-bodiedness, our mental health, and our class, among other things. We all have certain oppressions and certain privileges and this must inform our organising so that we do not silence groups among us, and so that no one should have to choose between their struggles. Our movement endeavours to make this a reality in our struggle for decolonisation. (https://www.facebook.com/transfeministcollective/posts/113220963351248, accessed 18 June 2016).

The centrality of embodiment, both in narrative discourse and in the forms of activism taken up, has been key to this group's activism, arguably serving to trouble the continued erasure of bodies, and particularly those of marginalised groups, in the academy.

In March 2016, the Trans Collective presented a powerful embodied intervention when they disrupted a photo exhibition held at UCT to commemorate a year of student activism. Protesting in partial undress, yet painted with narratives in red paint, this group of activists also painted slogans in matching red paint[6] over some of the exhibited photographs to flag what they experienced as an erasure of their contributions to the larger student movement and a lack of serious commitment to an intersectional struggle. Protesters further lay in front of the entrance to the exhibition as a performative illustration of their sense of being both marginalised in the movement and yet exploited for strategic political purposes, arguing that: 'It is disingenuous to include trans people in a public gallery when you have made no effort to include them in the private. ... We have reached the peak of our disillusionment with RMF's trans exclusion and erasure.' (Wagner, 2016).

This powerful moment of articulating a sense of dispensibility and subjugation, succeeded in facilitating extreme discomfort, since all who attended would have to figuratively 'walk over them' to enter, and therefore unavoidably acknowledge their impassioned call and embodied presence. Important to this performative activism was the use of semi-clothed and non-conforming bodies inserted into a space of higher education still located in an intellectual project in which bodies are invisible. The Trans Collective, in this moment of inserting their bodies that resist regulatory and normative dress and gender, and in a manner and place (laid at entry to the venue) that cannot be ignored, into an event and space 'sanitised' by scholarly association, are multiply transgressive. The deployment of a semi-clothed body in this context, made vulnerable at multiple levels (such as the lack of material and symbolic protection in the form of clothes; positioned in a prostrate position, vulnerable to being stood on; exposure of bodies that are 'othered' in gender and raced binaried hegemonies), represents a powerful subversion of the heteronormative, patriarchal, colonialist and humanist project of the university and the larger social world. Further, the performativity of lying down at the door to the exhibition, so that all who enter are forced to step over their bodies symbolises, in graphic terms, the sense of 'being walked over', of being both brutalised and invisibilised, not only in terms of the exhibition itself but within a larger hetero-patriarchal society in which non-normative desires, bodies and practices remain 'othered' and subject to symbolic and physical violence.

Unruly bodies against sexual violence

A final set of activism to consider here is a strong current of protests against sexual violence, which signify a powerful intersectional understanding of sexual violence as embedded in histories and continuities of patriarchal colonisation (Gouws 2016, 2017). Over the last few years there have been several protests across the country at universities that challenge high rates of violence, viewed as endemic in South African societies (Gqola, 2015), and also shown to be a major challenge at universities with high rates of gender-based violence and women's lives regulated by fear of sexual violence (for example, Bennett et al. 2007; Collins 2014; Hames 2009; Dosekun 2013).

One key example within the student protests has been a wave of activism at various universities against sexual violence. In April 2016, Rhodes University students protested, formed human chains, and marched in the streets of the small city around the University (see Macleod and Barker, 2016, for a more detailed overview). Students called on university management to revisit policies that they argued fail to protect rape victims. This followed the presentation of a list of alleged rapists, 'the RU reference list' to university authorities who had failed to respond in any meaningful way but rather drew on legal discourse to protect the accused. A majority of Black women[7] students led the protests, again foregrounding their embodiment and deploying partial nakedness through exposing their breasts and writing texts such as 'revolt', 'still not asking for it', calling into question the shame of the victim, victim-blaming and sexist rape myths that are widespread in South African popular contexts (Shewarega Hussen, in press). As Gouws (2016, 2017) points out, these struggles were important in bringing an intersectional project to sexual violence activism, in flagging the coloniality and racism of sexual violence. The narratives employed in the protests also extended, as did the actions of the trans collective, an intersectional vocabulary to the larger decolonial movement in higher education and further afield:

> The actions of women students in the #endrapeculture campaign, on a symbolic level, articulate how the intersectionality of race, gender and sexuality positions black African women as sexual subjects in relation to men but also in relation to white women and white men – something that an intersectional African feminist identity expresses.
>
> Gouws 2016, n.p.

Naked protest, while of course not uncontested, has a long history internationally and locally (see for example, Meintjes 2007), and across contexts and histories, 'strategically employed as a mode of social and political action' (Lunceford 2012, p. ix) and with 'embodied performance as a critique of the social system we live in (Sutton 2007, p. 141). As with the protests of the Trans Collective, these activists, deployed the semi-naked body strategically, articulating both vulnerability and agency and 'claiming space' in the university and the larger city space to destabilise higher educations' binaristic attempts to keep its intellectual project apart from embodied and material experience. It is a powerful reminder that what happens on university campuses is also about what happens to bodies, not only intellectual pursuit. Moreover, the use of the uncovered body, asserted with pride, strength and agency, gestures to the ways in which naked bodies have been part of historical subjugations and violences, implicated in slavery, genocides, sexual violence and everyday humiliations, and by implication the way in which these are bound up with the kinds of authority and power invested in the university. In addition, within the university displaying undressed bodies, in particular bodies that historically 'don't belong' (Black, female, transgender) disturbs and disrupts the sanitised logic of an academy founded on a mind-body divide which excludes body and affect/other logics/ sensibilities.

Thinking performative activism with social justice pedagogical imperatives

What do these powerful forms of performative activism that speak to intersectional gender and sexual justice mean for higher education and critical social justice pedagogies? Bozalek and Zembylas (2016 p. 195), representing a growing scholarship engaging with reading pedagogical practice through critical posthumanism and new feminist materialism, make a passionate call for this project:

> Currently in higher education where gross inequalities continue to affect pedagogical practices in South Africa and other geopolitical contexts, there is a need to consider new theories which call into question commonplace humanist assumptions, so prevalent in the imaginings of socially just higher education pedagogies.
>
> Bozalek and Zembylas 2016, p. 195

In sharing these three examples, I have tried to surface the way in which these forms of inspiring performative activism resonate with posthumanist, new materialist, and affective thinking that question the ontologies, epistemologies and methodologies normative to the academy and that emerge from and serve to reinstate histories and presents of power and violence against 'other' humans, non-humans and the planet. The resonance is perhaps most powerfully evident in the way in which bodies and materiality are made visible in these powerful moments of challenge. In particular, a posthumanist, feminist materialist reading allows for appreciation of how such moments of political transgression speak not only to racial, gender and sexual binarisms on which violences are founded, but also to the enmeshments of such binarisms with the humanist project of control over nature in which all subjugated, peoples, non-human species and what is constructed as non-living are othered, excluded and violable.

Student protests have raised issues that remind South Africa of a lack of progress as well as flagging some key challenges for higher education that speak powerfully to new directions for pedagogical and scholarly energies. To elaborate, first, is the reminder that the entire project of higher education, as evident in global Southern contexts, is one conceived and developed as a colonialist project that has a history of authority, surveillance and regulation in ensuring hegemonic practices of privilege and power in larger social contexts. Arguably, the forms and mechanisms of the academy in South Africa, further energised by neoliberal imperatives of internationalisation and competition, remain entangled in this 'civilising' project, bolstering global and local inequalities, albeit paying lip-service to projects of social justice and equality.

Second, student protests prompt acknowledgement that, no matter what vocabulary we adopt, the social justice project in higher education is necessarily decolonial and intersectional and speaks to the entanglement of inequalities and social identities that link with multiple binaries embedded in (post)colonial histories and present, most obviously the contemporary hegemony of hetero-patriarchal, neoliberal capitalism. Third, the academic project here as elsewhere is a humanist project invested in perpetuating the power of particular groups of people, representing particular forms of geopolitical, material and social power, over 'others', the planet and non-human species; indeed, always choosing 'the side of the powerful, the winners, the victors' (Wels 2015, p. 243).

These understandings point to a radical rethink of how we 'do' our everyday scholarship in universities and this is by no means a new project. There is a growing body of work that begins to share some of these valuable and creative ways of pedagogical intra-action and post-qualitative research. Key to this project is to think about how to undo the normative pedagogical and research practices that privilege the 'expert' and 'other' students and research 'subjects' within an authoritative/authoritarian framework, hinging around competition and epistemological (and material/discursive) violence. Such thinking is not novel: bell hooks (1994 p. 7–9), over twenty years ago called for transgressive teaching, arguing that it requires 'movement beyond accepted boundaries' to creativity, enjoyment and excitement, which she unpacks as hinging around destabilising the authority of the teacher and subverting 'an absolute set agenda governing teaching practice'. Further, a large body of scholarship by feminist researchers has questioned the normative privilege of the researcher and the way in which knowledge production is invested in reproducing hegemonic discourses and practices in any particular field. Yet, dominant pedagogical and research practices, for the most part continue to model the binarism of 'expert' and those people, other species and the planet that are the 'subject' of our disciplinary projects.

Importantly, the performative activisms shared here are themselves powerful pedagogical interventions in their affective and intellectual impact which disturbs and discomforts, both at a material individual and ideological, symbolic level. As argued by social justice pedagogy scholars, a pedagogy of discomfort and affect is to be embraced rather than avoided for its pedagogical possibilities (for example, Boler and Zembylas 2003; Zembylas 2013a; 2013b). Zembylas (2013c p. 110) argues '... discomforting emotions – which occur as the very result of attempting to address the 'difficult' issues of living with the 'enemy-other' – serve as the springboard to uncover and undo the mechanisms with which hegemonic values and beliefs about others continue to operate in daily habits, routines, and unconscious feelings. The effect of the occasions elaborated here on those intra-acting with them is evident at an affective, bodily and cognitive level. Social justice pedagogies, inspired by the critiques of current posthumanist and new materialist thinking, may draw fruitfully on these disruptive moments, moments that challenge the erasure of bodies, affect and materiality in the neoliberal, individualist, civilising project that is hegemonic (and gaining stronger foothold) in higher education in South Africa and globally. Articulating our pedagogy as politics and political actions as pedagogy will also challenge the reified divide between scholarly practices and the public domain and provide space for transgressive knowledges. As argued by Chantelle Gray van Heerden (2016 p. 341) in her thinking through current South African decolonial struggles:

> ...by interrogating form and content in educational spaces, such as higher education, and joining forces with grassroots movements and students we can, together, minimise such complicity towards effectuating socially just pedagogies. A feminist praxis that combines the contributions made by critical posthumanist/ new materialist feminisms and prefigurative anarchist pedagogical practices, I argue, smooths the striated space of the State apparatus through deterritorialisations that set in motion radical and nomadic becomingswoman.

The performative, artistic and activist examples shared here indeed speak to such deterritorialisations that transgress and destabilise hegemonies of the academy, the state and the everyday, allowing for new imaginaries for social justice and ways of making knowledge.

Conclusion

> The university needs what she bears but cannot bear what she brings. And on top of all that, she disappears. She disappears into the underground, the downlow lowdown maroon community of the university, into *the undercommons of enlightenment*, where the work gets done, where the work gets subverted, where the revolution is still black, still strong.
>
> Harney and Moten 2013, p. 26[8]

In this sharing of three different intersecting moments of performative activism, I have attempted to explore the value of 'the material turn'[9] and posthumanist insight for destabilising the mind-body binarism endemic to and naturalised in higher education. I have argued how these moments and actions disturb the invisibilisation of the bodily, affective and material, both within learning and teaching as well as in material and geographical contexts, and in particular through the implication that certain bodies and their 'excesses' have no place, not only materially but within the academic project itself. Alldred and Fox (2017, p. 16) in a paper similarly reflecting on young people's activism through the deployment of bodies, argue that we should avoid setting up the binarism of power and resistance but rather see both as 'dual fluxes that permeate all assemblages, a shifting balance that is never finally settled'.

> They elaborate: Defining a certain affect as an assertion of power or an effort at resistance is less important than assessing the capacities that these affects produce. Rather than presenting certain events as examples of coercive or disciplinary power, and others as instances of resistance, the task of a materialist sociology is to bring its micropolitical concepts and tools to bear upon the daily actions and encounters between people, things and social formations. We can ask of any affect: does it close down capacities or open them up?' These examples of young women transgressing, resisting and disrupting everyday humanist academies and by extension the larger social world, and the powerful affects of discomfort, shame, inspiration, and many other invocations, arguably open up capacities; they broaden critique and understanding and make available alternative imaginaries within and outside of the university.

I have reiterated the argument here that it is opportune, even essential, to drastically rethink our project as those involved in knowledge production and pedagogical practices in the academy. Moreover, I suggest these inspiring performances offer insight into new imagineries, not only in relation to sexual and gender justice, but also in thinking about different practices and performances of scholarship. Some of what we, as those entangled with the academy, can do is to seek creative, inspiring and productive ways of challenging and making unimaginable hegemonic, often oppressive and violent practices in higher education. Especially significant is the opening up of possibilities for reimagining bodies, affect, materiality in the hallowed halls of a sanitised and civilising academy where so many feel unsafe, excluded, and even violated. This also means being sensitive to and opening up spaces for a pedagogy of relationality that is located in an ethics of care. This requires the foregrounding an ontology of relationality, recognition, interconnectiveness, belonging and safety both materially and symbolically, that values and draws upon embodied and situated knowledges (Haraway 1988).

Arguably, the performances and activism shared here poignantly remind us that bodies and materiality matter. Further, as I have tried to illustrate, such embodied intra-actions also, in Barad's (2015 p. 382) words, in reflecting on Susan Stryker's performative piece 'My words to Victor Frankenstein above the village of Chamounix: Performing transgender rage',[10] allow for 'harnessing energy and power to transform despair and suffering into empowering rage, self-affirmation, theoretical inventiveness, political action, and the energising vitality of materiality in its animating possibilities'. The examples shared here represent such harnessing of energies in the current South African context and further afield, which further emphasise the value of supporting, facilitating and drawing on such occurrences in pedagogical spaces.

Finally, rethinking critical social justice pedagogies in the light of the performative art and activism shared here, and diffracted through posthumanist and new feminist materialist (re)thinking, also means as Haraway (2016, p. 1) reminds us, to *not only* stay with the trouble, but to actively 'make trouble, to stir up potent response to devastating events'. while also creating safe spaces 'to settle troubled waters and rebuild quiet places' (Haraway 2016, p. 1). The latter should include spaces such as feminist, social justice pedagogical ones, which draw on creativity, agency and energy to work with entangled 'troubles' and open up new imaginaries. Occasions that 'make trouble' such as the examples of inspiring art, performance and activism shared here are rich resources for this project.

Acknowledgements

My appreciation to Viv Bozalek and Michalinos Zembylas for the sub-title on this chapter and other valuable intra-action with my thinking. I also am grateful to the reviewers for constructive engagement with the chapter.

Notes

1 While new materialisms arguably build on postcolonial theory, it is noted that new feminist materialisms and posthumanism are not unitary bodies of work but complex and multiple and also contested, including a skepticism of the 'new' of new materialism. Ahmed (2008, p. 36) for example, critiques the 'foundational gesture' of the abiologism of feminist theory, arguing that 'when we describe what it is that we

do, when we consider how it is that we arrive at the grounds we inhabit, we need to appreciate the feminist work that comes before us, in all its complexity'.

2   See https://www.theguardian.com/artanddesign/2015/may/15/sethembile-msezane-cecil-rhodes-statue-cape-town-south-africa for more detailed description and http://www.sethembile-msezane.com/projects/ for more of Msezane's work (accessed 4 December 2017).

3   This quote appears in Buikema's new book in Dutch, shortly to be translated, and in English in a conference in 2016.

4   Also of interest, authors report the Shona representation of birds as messengers, and eagles (thought to be the model for the Zimbabwe bird sculptures) in particular, as bringing messages from the ancestors and God and mediated between God and humans (Hubbert, 2009, Huffman, 1985).

5   See https://www.facebook.com/transfeministcollective/posts/113220963351248 (accessed 18 June 2016).

6   Thanks to Chantelle Gray van Heerden for this insight and the reader is referred to her chapter in this edition for a Deleuzian and Guattarian inicisive analysis of how this particular intervention serves as an example of a 'return to the materiality of the body – the naked body, the animality of the body', which she argues serves as defacialisation, in layperson's terms a challenge to continued privileging and power of particular 'faces' in the academy and elsewhere.

7   Gouws (2016) points to the significance that Black women with a clear feminist agenda are leading these protests, considering the historical negative construction of feminism as white, middle class and 'unAfrican'.

8   Erin Manning's chapter in this volume engages closely with Black Studies scholarship and I acknowledge, has guided me gratefully to this particular text.

9   I use this term with caution, acknowledging the importance of avoiding a canonisation of the 'new feminist material turn' (see Juelskjær and Schwennesen, 2012, in interview with Karen Barad).

10 This performance was originally performed in 1993, available on Youtube, https://www.youtube.com/watch?v=JlDKruTCsSY (accessed 4 December 2017).

References

Badat, S. (2010), *The Challenges of Transformation In Higher Education And Training Institutions In South Africa*. Development Bank of Southern Africa, 8.

Badat, S. and Y. Sayed (2014), 'Post–1994 South African Education: The Challenge of Social Justice'. *The ANNALS of the American Academy of Political and Social Science.* http://ann.sagepub.com/content/652/1/127 (accessed 4 December 2017).

Badat, S. (2016), 'Deciphering the Meanings, and Explaining the South African Higher Education Student Protests of 2015–2016'. Available Online: https://mellon.org/resources/shared-experiences-blog/south-africa-protests/ (accessed 30 June 2016).

Barad, K. (2007), *Meeting The Universe Halfway: Quantum Physics and the Entanglement of Matter and Meaning*. Durham: Duke University Press.

Barad, K. (2015), 'TransMaterialities: Trans*/Matter/Realities and Queer Political Imaginings', *GLQ: A Journal of Lesbian and Gay Studies*, 21(2–3): 387–422.

Bennett, J., A. Gouws, A. Kritzinger, M. Hames and C. Tidimane (2007), '"Gender is Over": Researching the Implementation of Sexual Harassment Policies in Southern African Higher Education', *Feminist Africa*, 8: 83–104.

Bhana, D. (2014), 'Race Matters and the Emergence of Class: Views from Selected South African University Students', *South African Journal of Higher Education*, 28: 355–367.

Boler, M. and M. Zembylas (2003), 'Discomforting Truths: The Emotional Terrain of Understanding Difference', in P. Trifonas (ed.), *Pedagogies of Difference: Rethinking Education for Social Justice*. New York: Routledge, 110–136.

Bozalek, V. and C. Boughey (2012), '(Mis)framing Higher Education in South Africa', *Social Policy and Administration*, 46(6): 688–703.

Bozalek, V. and R. Carolissen (2012), 'The Potential of Critical Feminist Citizenship Frameworks for Citizenship and Social Justice in Higher Education', *Perspectives in Education*, 30:9–18.

Bozalek, V., R. Carolissen, L. Nicolls, B. Leibowitz, L. Swartz and P. Rohleder (2010), 'Engaging with Difference in Higher Education Through Collaborative Inter-Institutional Pedagogical Practices', *South African Journal of Higher Education*, 24:1023–1037.

Bradbury, J. and P. Kiguwa (2012), 'Thinking Women's Worlds', *Feminist Africa*, 17:28–47.

Buikema, R. (2016), 'Academy, Art and Activism', Paper presented at RINGS (International Research Association of Institutions of Advanced Gender Studies) Conference 2016: The geopolitics of gender studies, Cornerstone Institute, Cape Town, 16–18 November 2016.

Buikema, R. (2017), *Revoltes in de Cultuurkritiek*. Amsterdam: Amsterrdam University Press.

Collins, A. (2014), 'Faceless Bureaucracy?: The Challenges of Gender-Based Violence and Practices of Care in Higher Education', in V. Reddy, S. Meyer, T. Shefer and T. Meyiwa (eds), *Care In Context: Transnational Gender Perspectives*, Cape Town: HSRC, 282–304.

Department of Education. (2008), *Report of the Ministerial Committee on Transformation and Social Cohesion and the Elimination of Discrimination in Public Higher Education Institutions*. Pretoria, South Africa: Government Printers.

Dosekun, S. (2007), 'Defending Feminism in Africa', *Postamble*, 3(1): 41–47.

Gachago, D., F. Cronje, E. Ivala, J. Condy and A. Chigona (2014), 'Using Digital Counterstories as Multimodal Pedagogy Among South African Pre-Service Student

Educators to Produce Stories of Resistance', *Electronic Journal of E-Learning*, 12: 29–42.

Gachago, D., E. Ivala, J. Condy and A. Chigona (2013), 'Journeys Across Difference: Pre-Service Teacher Education Students' Perceptions of a Pedagogy of Discomfort in a Digital Storytelling Project in South Africa', *Critical Studies in Teaching and Learning*, 1:22–52. doi:10.14426/cristal.v1i1.4

Gouws, A. (2016), 'Young Women in the "Decolonizing Project" in South Africa: From Subaltern to Intersectional Feminism', Paper presented at the Nordic Africa Days Conference 2016, Uppsala, 23–25 September.

Gouws, A. (2017), 'Feminist intersectionality and the matrix of domination of South Africa, Agenda, 31(1), 19–27, http://dx.doi.org/10.1080/10130950.2017.1338871

Gray van Heerden, C. (2016), 'Entering the Relation of Movement and Rest: Considering the State Apparatus, Becoming-Woman and Anarchism in Socially Just Pedagogies', *South African Journal of Higher Education*, 30(3): 329–345. Available Online: http://dx.doi.org/10.20853/30-3-648

Haraway, D. (1988), 'Situated Knowledges: The Science Question in Feminism and the Privilege of Partial Perspective', *Feminist Studies*, 14(3):575–599.

Haraway, D.J. (2016), *Staying with the Trouble: Making Kin in the Chthulucene*. Durham: Duke University Press.

Hames, M. (2009), '"Let us Burn the House Down!" Violence Against Women in the Higher Education Environment', *Agenda*, 23(80): 42–46.

Hubbard, P. (2009), 'The Zimbabwe Birds: Interpretation and Symbolism', *Honeyguide*, 55(2):109–116.

Huffman, T.N. (1987), *Symbols in Stone: Unravelling the Mystery of Great Zimbabwe.* Witwatersrand University Press, Johannesburg.

Jacobs, S. (2016), 'Student Protests and Post-Apartheid South Africa's Negative Moment', *American Political Science Association: Africa Workshops* 3, 2, April. 6–8.

Jagessar, V. and T. Msibi (2015), '"It's Not That Bad": Homophobia in the Residences of a University in KwaZulu-Natal, Durban, South Africa', *Agenda*, 29(1): 63–73.

Juelskjær, M. ans N. Schwennesen (2012), 'Intra-Active Entanglements – An Interview with Karen Barad', *Kvinder, Køn & Forskning*, 10(1–2): 10–24.

Leibowitz, B., L. Swartz, V. Bozalek, R. Carolissen, L. Nicholls and P. Rohleder (eds), (2012), *Community, Self and Identity: Educating South African Students for Citizenship*. Cape Town, South Africa: HSRC Press.

Lunceford, B. (2012), *Naked Politics: Nudity, Political Action, and the Rhetoric of the Body*. Maryland: Lexington Books.

Macleod, C. and K. Barker (2016), 'Angry Student Protests Have Put Rape back on South Africa's Agenda', *The Conversation*, 26 April. Available online: http://theconversation. com/angry-student-protests-have-put-rape-back-on-south-africas-agenda-58362 (accessed 18 April 2017).

Mbembe, A. (2015a), 'Decolonizing Knowledge and the Question of the Archive', *WiSER Wits Institute for Social and Economic Research* (website), May 1, 2016. Available

online: http://wiser.wits.ac.za/system/files/Achille%20Mbembe%20-%20
Decolonizing%20Knowledge%20and%20the%20Question%20of%20the%20Archive.
pdf (accessed 4 December 2017).

Mbembe, A. (2015b), 'Achille Mbembe on The State of South African Political Life'.
Available online: http://africasacountry.com/2015/09/achille-mbembe-on-the-state-
of-south-african-politics/ (accessed 22 September 2015).

Meintjes, S. (2007), 'Naked Women's Protest, July 1990: "We won't Fuck for Houses"', in
N. Gasa (ed.), *Women in South African History*, Cape Town: HSRC Press, 347–367.

Morrow, W. (2009), *Bounds of Democracy: Epistemological Access in Higher Education*,
Pretoria: Human Sciences Research Council.

Msezane, S. (2017), 'Artist Statement, Kwasuka Sukela: Re-Imagined Bodies of a (South
African) 1990s Born Woman', Masters of Arts (Fine Arts) Exhibition, University of
Cape Town.

Msibi, T. (2013), 'Queering the Transformation of Higher Education in South Africa',
Perspectives in Education. 31(2): 65–73.

Muller, J. (2014), 'Every Picture Tells a Story: Epistemological Access and Knowledge',
Education as Change, 18(2): 255–269, doi: 10.1080/16823206.2014.932256

Ngabaza, S., E. Bojarczuk, M. Masuku and R. Roelfse (2015). 'Empowering Young People
in Advocacy for Transformation: A Photovoice Exploration of Safe and Unsafe
Spaces on a University Campus'. *African Safety Promotion Journal* 13(1): 30–48.

Shefer, T., C. Potgieter and A. Strebel (1999), 'Teaching Gender in Psychology at a South
African University', *Feminism and Psychology*, 9(2): 127–133.

Shefer, T., A. Strebel, S. Ngabaza and L. Clowes (2017), 'Student Accounts of Space and
Safety at a South African University: Implications for Social Identities and Diversity',
South African Journal of Psychology, doi: 10.1177/0081246317701887.

Shewarega Hussen, T. (in press), 'ICTs, Social Media and Feminist Activism:
#RapeMustFall, #NakedProtest, and #RUReferenceList Movement in South Africa',
in T. Shefer, J. Hearn, K. Ratele and F. Boonzaier (ed.), *Engaging Youth in Activism,
Research and Pedagogical Praxis: Transnational and Intersectional Perspectives on
Gender, Sex, and Race*. New York and London: Routledge.

Spivak, G. (1988), 'Can the Subaltern Speak?', in C. Nelson and L. Grossberg (eds), *Marxism
and the Interpretation of Culture* Urbana, IL: University of Illinois Press, 271–313.

Sutton, B. (2007), 'Naked Politics: Nudity, Political Action, and the Rhetoric of the Body',
Journal of International Women's Studies, 8(3): 139–148.

Vincent, L. (2008), 'The Limitations of Interracial Contact: Stories from Young South
Africans', *Ethnic and Racial Studies*, 31, 1426–1451.

Wagner, L. (2016), 'Naked Trans Protesters: Rhodes Must Fall must fall', *Times Live*,
11 March. Available online: http://www.timeslive.co.za/thetimes/2016/03/11/
Naked-trans-protesters-Rhodes-Must-Fall-must-fall (accessed 27 May 2016).

Wels, H. (2015), '"Animals Like Us": Revisiting Organizational Ethnography and
Research', *Journal of Organizational Ethnography*, 4(3): 242–259. Available online:
http://dx.doi.org/10.1108/JOE–12–2014–0039 (accessed 4 December 2017).

Zembylas, M. (2013a). 'Critical Pedagogy and Emotion: Working Through Troubled Knowledge in Posttraumatic Societies'. *Critical Studies in Education*, 54(2): 176–189.

Zembylas, M. (2013b). Revisiting the Gramscian Legacy on Counter-Hegemony, The Subaltern and Affectivity: Towards an "Emotional Pedagogy" of Activism in Higher Education'. *CriSTaL*, 1(1): 1–21.

11

Narrative Vases as Markers of Subjectivity, Agency and Voice: Engaging Feminist Pedagogies Within the Context of #feesmustfall

Nike Romano

This chapter explores an art history pedagogical response to the South African #feesmustfall movement's call to decolonise the university and develop an African epistemological curriculum. While stakeholders in South African higher education grapple with the notion of decolonisation, it is not immediately clear what form decolonisation of the curriculum and pedagogy will take. For the purposes of this chapter however, decolonisation is understood as an open-ended process in which art history pedagogies that transform teaching and learning history of art and design praxes are explored with a view to building social justice. Located in the extended curriculum programme (ECP) of the Faculty of Informatics and Design at the Cape Peninsula University of Technology (CPUT), this enquiry focuses on a pedagogic intervention in the Design Foundation art history course that I convene. Structured around the teaching and learning of Ancient Greek vase painting, the chapter explores pedagogical strategies that seek to develop learner agency and voice through students' embodied encounters with artefacts. Drawing on Karen Barad's (2007) posthumanist theory of agential realism – that theorises diffraction as a process that embodies disruption as its being – the research utilises diffractive methodology to explore the intra-action[1] between western art history through students' lived experience.

Concomitant with the call to 'decolonise the mind' is the demand for the creation of new knowledges that interrupt Eurocentric cultural dominance within the academy. To this end, the relationship between personal narrative (both written and visual) and student empowerment is central to students becoming conscious of themselves as situated knowers who produce new knowledges that challenge Eurocentric hegemony (Haraway 1988).

In keeping with the relationality of empirical research, the chapter draws on students' narratives, reflections and insights, as well as my own voice, as testament to the role that students and educators play in co-creating knowledge. Consequently, learner agency, meaning-making and knowledge-construction are understood as mutually implicated in an ongoing process of becoming with/ through encounters with others. Having undergone no formal teacher training, my learning emerges out of the intra-action (Barad 2007) between my practices as visual artist and teacher. Characterised as learning through embodied engagement – both in the classroom and studio – I seek to uncover, recover and discover new forms of understanding that co-emerges through my encounters with the students, processes, materials and materiality.[2] Within this frame, the performative function of artworks as co-creators of knowledge and the process of art-making have ontological effects on my subjectivity as becoming teacher (Bolt 2004, pp. 9, 173).

I begin by discussing the challenges to art history pedagogies that have arisen out of the decolonisation of the academy debates. Thereafter I locate the enquiry within feminist theories of subjectivity and difference, that include situated knowledges (Haraway 1988), matrixial theory (Ettinger 1992) and posthumanist agential realism (Barad 2007), so as to explore how ongoing thresholds of interconnection, co-existence and becoming offer new ethical possibilities for design praxis in a differentiated world.[3] Finally, I provide background to the Design Foundation course before elaborating on the pedagogical intervention itself.

Issues of inclusion, inequality and assimilation are key to understanding the call to decolonise South African universities where many black students feel pressured to assimilate into the dominant culture of white privilege. As a result, they feel alienated, invisible and disempowered within the social and academic environment. It follows, therefore, that higher educators' respond to the above issues by developing pedagogies that support students' need for visibility and belonging within the academy. Building an African epistemological art history curriculum is concomitant with a critique of the normative Eurocentric gaze that perpetuates unequal power relations whilst reinforcing African inferiority. In *Ways of Seeing*, John Berger's (1985) critical engagement with looking and seeing reveals how western art history is re-presented retrospectively by the ruling class to justify history through the lens of privilege, inequality and exclusion. Arguing that the reciprocal nature of vision is more fundamental than that of spoken dialogue, Berger refers to early childhood development and notes that preverbal infants are aware of being seen and that 'the eye of the other combines with our own eye to make it fully credible that we are part of the visible world' (Berger 1985: 9). This observation is helpful in understanding the effect that in/visibility has on students' sense of agency, because in/visibility is key to one's sense of self.

The Eurocentric gaze has multiple effects that simultaneously exclude indigenous cultural production whilst foregrounding western cultural production as a dominant and normative practice. This inequality is further exacerbated by the predominant representation of the black body in positions of subservience, humiliation and violence within the canon (Enwezor 1997).[4] Likewise, the relative absence of an African Art History discourse within the canon intensifies an absence of agency and recognition of the majority of students' histories that have been systematically excluded and remain invisible to them. Bearing in mind these concerns, the enquiry turns to the transformative potential of a diffractive gaze whereby students' subjective engagement with artefacts redresses Eurocentric hegemony.

In the context of increasingly polarised local and global politics, the onus falls on educators and students to critique unequal power relations by addressing and navigating difference(s) in the classroom and thereby model compassionate behaviours that promote social justice. To this end, I refer to feminist theories that move beyond the dominant Cartesian logic of binary 'othering' to explore the notion of both/and conceptions of difference(s) and share a common understanding of subjectivity as partial, co-affecting and co-emerging. I begin by discussing Haraway's (1998) theory of situated knowledges, thereafter I examine Ettinger's (1992) matrixial theory and, finally, I engage with Barad's (2007) posthumanist agential realism.

Situated knowledges

Following Donna Haraway's (1988) theory of situated knowledges challenges to Eurocentric positivist notions of knowledge as universal, objective and value free, the teaching intervention recognises students as situated knowers who actively construct knowledge through their lived experience. Similarly, hierarchical power relations that characterise teachers as 'knowers' and students as 'learners' are disrupted as learners and educators co-create more socially just pedagogies that redress structural inequalities within institutions of higher education and society at large (Giroux 1998). In this regard, Sayers' (2011. p. 409) identification of the tensions between the discourse of the 'expert' and the discourse of 'local negotiation' in relation to visual art is helpful in understanding how teachers and learners can co-create critical pedagogical strategies that make visible students' non-dominant identities and knowledges within the canon of art history. In addition to transforming power relations within the classroom, situated knowledges also unsettles the Eurocentric gaze as the marginalised or 'not yet recognised' become visible within the discourse (Barrett, 2007: 4).

Matrixial trans-subjectivity

Co-emerging out of her practices as visual artist, psychoanalyst, and philosopher, Bracha Ettinger's (1992) matrixial theory of trans-subjectivity resonates with arts-based pedagogies – such as embodied practices of learning-through-making and becoming-with materials and materiality. Ettinger critiques dominant phallic notions of subjectivity that are founded on discrete boundaries and splits, and offers an alternative understanding of subjectivity that embraces sexual difference as its core (Pollock 2009). Imagined as an invisible web that co-exists within and alongside the phallic framework, Ettinger theorises human's prenatal/prematernal relationship – that simulatneously generates and defines human becoming – as partial, reciprocal, asymmetrical and co-emerging. Understood as such, matrixial subjectivity both embodies and generates difference[s] within a compassionate, inter-dependent and non-hierarchical web, thus foregrounding humans' inherent primary capacity for recognising, understanding and tolerating difference(s).

Concerned with the possibilities for accessing and processing trauma through aesthetic encounters, Ettinger moves beyond art's representational role and coins the term *artworking* so as to foreground the agential role of art as a symbolic 'transport station' – whereby trauma can be processed in a matrixial time-space that 'links the time of too-early to the time of too-late and plants them in the world's time' (Ettinger 2005a, p. 694). Furthermore, the matrixial gaze – which is understood as embodied and felt through all the senses as well as 'other unconscious dimensions of the psyche' (Ettinger 2005b, p. 710; 2008, p. 61) – offers a possibility of a copoetic[5] compassionate encounter-event between the artist, the artwork and viewer. Such an exchange depends on a compassionate response-ability as wit[h]ness to the unknown other in this aesthetic encounter (2009. p. 10). In her article entitled *Aesthetic Wit(h)nessing in the Era Trauma* (2010), Griselda Pollock attends to the ethical implications of wit(h)nessing when she writes:

...We cannot but share the pain or trauma, i.e. the events of the other. We cannot but bear it, transport it, and potentially create a future precisely by such sharing, by recognizing co-humanity rather than anxiously policing the boundaries of difference which are the hallmark of the phallic model.

Pollock 2012, p. 837

Agential Realism

Karen Barad's posthumanist theory of agential realism offers insight into the ethical possibilities and responsibility that teachers have in shaping the future for humans, non-humans and the material environment in the production of knowledge (Dolphijn and van der Tuin 2012, p. 69). Modelled on a quantum understanding of the process of diffraction, agential realism reveals how the ethico-onto-epistemological is activated through diffractive entanglements with others (2007, p. 132). Barad offers insights into how matter comes into relationship with knowing through material-discursive practices, and emphasises humans' position as part of, rather than separate from the world. As a methodology, diffraction highlights how knowledge is co-produced through entanglements of encounters between artefacts, art-making, teaching and learning practices, and materiality and confirms how matter and becoming are both integral to, and the result of, the production of knowledge.

Background to the Design Foundation Course

The Design Foundation course aims to develop students becoming through their engagement with history of art and design praxes. Rather than adopt a positivist methodology of teaching art history along a chronological timeline, relevant themes that resonate with student's lived experience are traced in multi-directions that traverse space and time. Coming from varied race and class backgrounds, many students encounter barriers to learning on entering the academy, where they learn in their second, sometimes third language. Likewise, whilst some students study visual art and design at high school, most attend schools that do not offer these subjects, and can feel they have little to contribute to class discussion. These feelings of exclusion highlight the role that cultural capital plays in entrenching unequal power relations (Bordieu 2011), as those who are unfamiliar with the canon of art history believe they have nothing of value to contribute to the learning community.[6] These feelings provide a useful starting point for this enquiry that explores various strategies that encourage students to participate equally.

Blair argues that agency is contingent on one's sense of self and the potential for one's transformative growth. Furthermore, she maintains that it is through using one's voice and listening to the voices of others that learners begin to feel part of the learning community (2009, p. 180). However, participation in the learning environment requires courage as learners run the risk of appearing to be incompetent in front of their peers and teachers. It follows therefore, that in order to feel safe, students are recognised and valued by their teachers and peers (Blair 2009, p. 181) and need to ensure that pedagogical encounters embrace mutual tolerance, compassion and respect. I now turn to the case study to examine how learner generated content can empower students' agency and voice, and highlight how learner informed processes such as self-reflection and assessment can position learners as co-creators of pedagogy and knowledge.

Case study: Design your own Greek vase

Ceramic pot making is a cultural practice that has a long and established tradition in Africa.[7] It made sense therefore, to foreground students' familiarity with this art form whilst they learned about the history of ancient Greek vase painting. I hoped, following Stewart (2007. p. 130), that new knowledge that disrupts the hegemony of western art history, would emerge out of the intra-action between 'art, teaching and life'. The inherent paradox of working within the paradigm of western art history whilst trying to dismantle Eurocentric cultural dominance is in keeping with critical feminist concerns of understanding difference(s) differently (Thiele 2014b, p. 10). Simlarly, Haraway's (2016, p. 20) notion of staying with the trouble – that advocates the recuperation of non-innocent and ambivalent pasts that are continuously present in ongoing patterns of differentiation – is helpful because, it encapsulates student's transformative entanglements with the very objects that embody the contradictions of South Africa's colonial legacy. The intention of the pedagogical intervention is one that works affirmatively with these differences in order to move beyond the phallocentric understanding of binary difference that is limited to either/or, towards an understanding of difference as an ongoing differentiation in which new commonalities are imagined (Thiele 2014a, p. 202).

After being introduced to the formal and stylistic characteristics of ancient Greek vase painting, students learned the various functions of the vases – as containers, as grave markers and importantly, as the ground on which visual narratives were depicted. The latter function provided the impetus for the assignment, which is discussed below.

Entitled *Design your own Greek Vase*, the assignment was structured in two parts. To begin, students wrote a story about an important life event that they then translated into visual form onto the silhouette of an ancient Greek vase. The aims of the first part of the assignment were complex and manifold. History of art and design teaching and learning practices at ECP level foreground the complexities arising out of the relationship between visual and spoken/written language. In addition to developing reading and writing skills, students need to learn to decode and critically engage with a visually dominated world. For example, I have observed that while students might understand concepts, they may have difficulty explaining what they understand these concepts to mean. The notion of 'voice' is understood as both spoken and visual, therefore voice and visibility are central to pedagogical praxis. The vase project created an opportunity for students to practice both reading images and writing about them. The assignment also explored the ongoing diffractive intra-actions between the scripto/visual, as a potential space in which students could articulate concepts through drawing, that they had difficulty verbalising. By drawing from personal experience, students engaged narratives that mattered to them and came to understand how their being is inextricably linked to their learning. Furthermore, by narrating in the first person, students overcame their resistance to writing and their confidence grew as they felt seen and heard. Students began to grasp that writing is a transformative ontological process of coming to know oneself, rather than the procedural practice they engaged in mainstream pedagogies (Yagelski 2012, pp. 188–90).

> Sometimes when I write I feel like I'm connecting to someone or something that won't judge me but let me state what I want to state without offering any advice or lecturing me cause ... writing has helped me to realize what was going on in my head.
>
> student reflection

Students' embodied intra-action with the ancient vases foregrounds the transformative role of a moderate hermeneutic approach that supports their exploration of subjectivity and meaning (Sayers 2015, p. 134; 2011, p. 411). This theme is further elaborated by Spector (2015, p. 448) who recognises the potential of diffractive pedagogies that by-pass the reproduction of knowledge, and in so doing prioritise the co-creation of something new. This approach collapses the theory/practice divide though the engagement with material discursive practices that are mutually implicated in and through the production of knowledge (Barad 2007, p. 136).

The emphasis on personal narrative redressed issues of inequality arising out of blanket inclusivity as students' values and frames of reference challenge normative cultural tastes and pervasive ideologies that reinforce feelings of

Figure 11.1 Story entitled *The story of a village boy.*

alienation (Sayers 2015, p. 144). Furthermore, the intra-action of the ancient artefacts through students' narratives produced ongoing interferences that made visible the relative absence of recorded indigenous artistic production. Through foregrounding these absences, students' re-presented their subjectivity in relation to the past. The subjective interpretation of Greek stylistic characteristics allowed for new knowledges to be produced and therefore bypassed the reproduction of knowledge that reinforces oppressive discourses and power relations (Hempel-Jorgensen 2015, p. 539). The following excerpt reveals how such a diffractive encounter empowered a student who grew up in rural poverty, as he reflects on himself as a 'young African who believes in culture and ancestors'.

> Everything that I mentioned on my story it's about the struggle that I was facing in my childhood, growing up under my grandmother's warm care so I thought that will be wise if I use my story on decorating my vase so that I can celebrate my past with my grandmother who was involved to my life.
>
> I believe that what is on my vase it's all about me, as a village boy who was struggling in life and I showed the activities that I used to do back then which we still do in our village now but in a better way than before. As I also include the way we're living back then, like we were using traditional huts for shelter and our field we were ploughing to get food for the families, that's the culture of Africans and I'm proud of being an African child because I'm a young African who believe in culture and on ancestors. I couldn't able to put everything that I mention to my story, instead of that I managed to use the important scenes that can make a viewer to be interested and can be easy to compare my story with the story that I decorated on the vase.
>
> Living on our villages in that time it was a good life to us although we were struggling to get modern life and to get a better education but we enjoy to live that life because we had no other option and we knew that god knew why he chose to give us that life. But I enjoyed to be in that environment of being suffering to live because it makes you to experience the challenges of life and it is also give you the courage of how to fight to live a better life and I think now I'm still on the mission of fighting to live a better life than before but I don't want to lie, I see the changes now than the life I was living on it back then.

The hermeneutic approach is a useful indicator for assessment because I can ascertain from their drawings whether students have understood key concepts that may have been difficult to explain in words. Furthermore, the emphasis on interpretation rather than mimicry diminishes the fear of being judged as right or wrong, as students are assessed as equivalent and unique individuals. By the same token, rather than being pitted against one another, students are assessed in relation to their own progress, as the following reflection reveals.

> I did enjoy writing my own story, because it is the best way for our lecturer to see and get the right perspective our own ways we could paint the vases.
>
> student reflection

Ettinger's notion of wit[h]nessing informed a compassionate response to those students who shared traumatic stories, and where necessary, some students were referred for additional support. In these instances, the artworks performed the function of containers through which students mediated their internal and external worlds by recording and processing their emotions through the embodied writing/drawing of their stories.[8]

> It felt like a load had been taken off my shoulder, and now I feel so relieved and free. It's like I've been wanting to tell my story but I wasn't ready but I'm glad I did now I can carry on with my life.
>
> student feedback

Below is an excerpt of the above student's reflexive writing where he lists the various ways in which his vase design embodies the story of his best friend's tragic murder whilst celebrating his birthday in a tavern in Khayelitsha.[9] I have included this example because it is symptomatic of the kind of violent trauma that many of our students face on a daily basis.

Figure 11.2 Story entitled *Expect the unexpected in life.*

The Greek vase that I drew or designed which portrayed a story about my friend who died last year unexpectedly. All the decorations and colours that are there have their own purpose that I used them for.

I will start about the decorations that I have used explaining how they reflect the story. As we know that life have its own ups and downs which means sometimes it is bad and good, happy today and not tomorrow. That is what I have seen when I look at that thick line on Keys decorations it goes up and down and that is what is on the story.

Now it is about the Tongues decorations when I look around the tongue shape there on the negative space on that red I see a 'U shape' like. That which stand for unexpected when you link it to the story. I did not expect what happened to my friend especially on that day it was really unexpected. I am getting on Rays decorations when I look at that decoration I see triangles that are very close to each other. The way that they are close to each other reminds me the friendship that we had with my friend. We were very close like those triangles that they form one thing. I am referring that to us as we were close as if there was nothing that can do us apart as friends.

I am still talking about those triangles although they are close like that they are in different sizes they are not equal. In the middle they are big and at the end and at the beginning of the decoration they are small. All that inequality of them remind me the way that his funeral was big and full of unequal people in terms of age, youth and old people which are same as those unequal triangles.

The last thing about the decoration on the handles both of them there are dots that are black and if you add them on both handles they will be 21. Which is how old he was when he died and also on his 21st birthday.

Black colour it is about being in a darkness whereby you feel like world the whole world is against you referring to me, his family, friends and the whole community as whole, we were all in that situation of darkness.

In addition to assigning symbolic meaning to his design and highlighting the expressive possibilities generated through the intra-action between the scripto-visual, the student also reflected on his somatic responses to the trauma:

I think in drawing to analyze the story that is in the vase, I see the pictures about what is happening in the story, it is easier than the words … at the same time it was healing me inside just because its like sharing it by writing it so I used to think about it a lot but since I wrote about it, its kind of healing me inside.

Gibbs' (2015, p. 223) enquiries into the affect on researchers (in this case students and educator) by traumatic histories being researched resonate with current debates around decoloniality. In this regard, the vases' agential role foregrounds as the traditional hierarchy of teacher/knower and student/learner is transformed. As I grapple with my position of privilege as a white middle-class woman, who has benefitted under the system of Apartheid and the current regime, I understand the need for researchers to analyse their relationship to the past and to research subjects in order to redress unequal relationships and positions of privilege. I learn from the students' knowledges through my encounter with their artworks, and my role as wit[h]ness to their experiences continues to affect my own becoming as teacher. In this light, Spector's (2010) writings on relational ontology are helpful in understanding how being with, and for others, underpins an ethical engagement with the world which should be the core of socially just pedagogies.

The second part of the assignment is self-evaluative. Students assess whether their vases reflect Ancient Greek stylistic characteristics and appraise the success of their translations between their written and visual and thereby learn how images 'speak' in ways that words cannot and conversely, what words 'reveal' that images cannot. Students were invited to offer feedback on the project and ethical clearance was given by those who were comfortable to share their stories in this research. The task of self-evaluation and critical enquiry marks the transformation of students as objects of research to becoming-with-research subjects each (Gibbs 2016, p. 224) thus positioning them as co-producers and generators of new knowledges and pedagogies that impact on the curriculum (Barrett 2007, p. 5).

In keeping with Bolt's (2007, p. 30) findings that we come to know the world theoretically after we have come to understand it through handling the process of learning through making, afforded the time/space for students to 'figure out' knowledge for themselves. The making process also activated entanglements between the students, the artefacts, and the ancient makers, thus affecting students ontological understanding of themselves as becoming-designers and thereby reaffirming how subjectivity is not pre-constituted. Similarly, agency is not discretely held in the student nor in their vase, rather it co-emerges through the entanglements between themselves, the ancient artists, and the ancient vases (Barad 2007, p. 178).

> Every time I look at my vase now, knowing that I created the story, I sort of like try and think about the people who are making their Greek vases so they were trying to tell their stories through their vase, the whole vase through . . .
>
> student reflection

By foregrounding the contemporary through the ancient, new interpretations and understandings of both past and present co-emerged, thereby disrupting western positivistic notions of progress and superiority.

It made me try and relate with the artists that were creating those ancient Greek vases and since I was now in the same position as them I had to try and make sure that each painting on that vase has a meaning that creates the story in an easy way that is understandable by the reader/observer.

student reflection

The assignment also highlighted the link between the process of drawing and the ontological process of the 'drawing out' of voice. In this regard, Catherine de Zegher's (2010, pp. 118–9) reflections on Ettinger's praxis resonate as she conceptualises the process of drawing out and sharing of stories as a core moral responsibility to the world. de Zegher writes, 'Art is congruent with our acting in the world: art draws from life as much as life draws from art. It enables attention to what surrounds us and for some understanding of our life' (2010, pp. 118–9). Similarly, in keeping with Barad's notion of agential cuts as 'diffractive readings [that] bring inventive provocations [and] are good to think with'[10] (Dolphijn and van der Tuin 2012, p. 50), the intra-action between the written and visual generated a multitude of possibilities that would not have occurred had students simply written or drawn their stories.

My journey of becoming a designer was not easy, I had to prove everyone wrong. Being left by your father at the age of 1 . . . really affected me a lot, and watching my mother struggling to raise me, she had to go and sell apples for us to eat, sometimes she would only sell 2 apples and that means no food for us for the night . . . I think that's what groomed me and made me to be who I am right now.

student narrative

In addition to becoming conscious of themselves as writers/artists, students gained understanding of the limits and possibilities of both written and visual language. Through distinguishing and embracing these differences, students developed a sense of 'ownership of knowledge' and its production, as interpreted through their internalised lived experience (Hempel-Jorgensen 2015, p. 541). Students also recognised their agency as storytellers with important messages to convey as the following excerpt by a typically reserved student reveals. Concerned with gender-based violence, the student writes:

The story line I have chosen is based on an experience I feel very close to. On the vase there is a woman on the floor and a man standing in front of her and another fighting him. My story is basically about woman abuse and a man standing up to the perpetrator by protecting her... what John did was unacceptable and does not deserve a second chance. You have no idea how strongly I feel about this, and think more should be done for awareness.

student narrative

Figure 11.3 Story entitled *My journey in becoming a designer.*

Figure 11.4 Untitled story about gender-based violence.

Conclusion

The case study describes and analyses an art history pedagogical response to the #feesmustfall protests' demand to decolonise the academy. Concerned with the call to 'decolonise the mind', the research explores how personal narrative challenges Eurocentric cultural dominance and validates students' lived experiences and local knowledges through encounters with ancient artefacts that embody the ambivalences of our colonial history (Haraway 1988, p. 2016). Furthermore, through processes of self-assessment and reflection, the research interrogates how students co-transform pedagogical (and wider social) relationships and practices, and reveals how their becoming is both central to and dependent on the co-creation of new pedagogies (Hempel-Jorgensen 2015). Barad's agential realist approach shows how locally produced meanings can emerge out of encounters with artworks in and across space and time. By the same token, the diffractive gaze makes visible the mutually transformative ontological and epistemological encounters between the ancient makers, the students and their respective vases.

The diffraction of the matrixial through agential realism broadens the understanding of the performative role of artworking. Whereas for Barad (2012), agency is 'an enactment, a matter of possibilities for reconfiguring entanglements',[11] Ettinger (2005) theorises art's ontological possibilities whereby artists, viewers and artworks have a 'response-ability' to the other. By the same token, the entanglement between Ettinger's notion of art as the 'transport station of trauma' and Barad's material-discursive intra-actions collapse the temporal and the spatial, thereby creating a space-time in which iterations of the past entangle with the present, thereby affecting outcomes for the future.

Finally, the diffraction of the theories of situated knowleges (Haraway 1988), matrixial trans-subjectivity (Ettinger 1996) and agential realism (Barad 2007) through one another generates an important conversation between inhuman and posthuman understandings of ethics that impact on both the present and the future, and thereby expand ethico-onto-epistemological possiblities of co-emergence and compassion in our increasingly polarised world (Thiele 2014a).

Notes

1   Intra-action is a key concept of Agential Realism that are understood 'agential cuts that do not produce absolute separations, but cut together apart (one move)' (Barad,

2014:168). Barad's disticinction between intra-action – that signifies the 'the mutual constitution of entangled agencies – and interaction – that is premised on discrete singular agencies – is critical in understanding how agencies emerge through their intra-action' (Barad, 2007:33).

2 Barbara Bolt's understanding of materiality as the operation of the energy of the matter in an artwork is useful to this enquiry. For further elucidation on the productive materiality of artworks and their power to produce ontological effects through material and somatic processes. (See Bolt: 2004.)

3 For further reading on how Barad, Haraway and Ettinger's imaginings of difference(s) and diffraction resonate with one another see Kathrin Thiele's article entitled Ethos of Diffraction: New Paradigms for a (Post)humanist Ethics. (See Thiele: 2014.)

4 The aforementioned observation is corroborated by students during class discussions, who confirm that these stereotypes continue to traumatise them.

5 Copoesis is understood as a transformational potentiality that evolves along aesthetic and ethical unconscious paths and produces a particular kind of knowledge. (See Ettinger. 2005b.)

6 These observations resonate with Hempel-Jorgensen's account of UK-based secondary school learners from disadvantaged backgrounds who display low self-esteem, feel they come from deficit and do not belong in the school environment. (See Hempel-Jorgensen, 2015.)

7 Fired clay represents one of the oldest artistic practices and techniques in the history of African material culture. Evidence of its production dates from the eighth millennium BCE (See Berns, 1989: 32.)

8 For more reading on art as a transitional space, see Winnicot (1971).

9 Khayelitsha is a large displaced urban settlement on the edges of the Cape Town Metropolitan area.

10 This resonates with Pollock's proposal that language itself has remembered, or unconsciously registered, in the double sense of the term matrix, that the maternal is both a generating structure that brings forth new life while symbolically representing imaginative and intellectual potentiality (Pollock 2009: 13).

11 Karen Barad interviewed in Dolphijn and Van der Tuin, 2012: 54.

References

Barad, K. (2007), *Meeting the Universe Halfway: Quantum Physics and the Entanglement of Matter and Meaning*, Durham & London: Duke University Press.

Barad, K. (2014), 'Diffracting Diffraction: Cutting Together-Apart', *Parallax*, 20(3): 168–187.

Berns, Marla C. (1989), 'Ceramic Arts in Africa', *African Arts*, 22(2): 32–102.

Blair, D. (2009), 'Learner Agency: To Understand and To Be Understood', *British Journal of Music Education*, 26(2): 173–187. DOI: 10.1017/S0265051709008420, Published online: 3 June 2009

Bolt, B. (2007a), *Art Beyond Representation: The Performative Power of the Image*, New York: I B Taurus & Co Ltd.

Bolt, B. (2007b), 'The Magic is in the Handling', in E. Barrett and B Bolt (eds), *Practice as Research: Approaches to Creative Arts Enquiry*, 27–34 New York: I.B.Tauris & Co Ltd.

Bourdieu, P. (2011), 'The Forms of Capital', in I. Szeman, and T. Kaposy (eds), *Cultural Theory: An Anthology*, 81–93. Chichester: Wiley-Blackwell.

de Zegher, C. (2010), 'Drawing Out Voice and Webwork', in B. Ettinger, C. de Zegher, G. Pollock, R. Huhn, and R. Verhaeghe (eds), *Art as Compassion: Bracha L. Ettinger*. Brussels: ASA Publishers.

Dolphijn, R and I. van der Tuin (2012), *New Materialism: Interviews & Cartographies*, Open Humanities Press.

Enwezor, O. (1997), 'Reframing the Black Subject: Ideology and Fantasy in Contemporary South African Representation', *Third Text*, 11(40): 21–40.

Ettinger, B. (1992), 'Matrix and Metramorphosis', *Differences*, 4(3): 170–208.

Ettinger, B. (2005a), 'Art, Memory, Resistance', *Ephemera*, 5(x): 690–702.

Ettinger, B. (2005b), 'Copoiesis', *Framework X Ephemera*, 5(x): 703–713.

Ettinger, B. (2006), 'Matrixial Trans-Subjectivity', *Theory, Culture and Society*, 23(2–3): 218–222.

Ettinger, B. (2009), 'Fragilization and Resistance', *Studies in the Maternal*, 1(2): 1–31.

Ettinger, B. and G. Pollock (2008), 'Fascinance and the Girl-To-M/Other Matrixial Feminine Difference', *Psychoanalysis and The Image: Trans-Disciplinary Perspectives* 60.

Gibbs, A. (2015), 'Writing as Method: Attunement, Resonance and Rhythm', in B. Knudsen and C Stage (eds), *Affective Methodologies*, 222–236. Basingstoke: Palgrave Macmillan.

Haraway, D. (1988), 'Situated Knowledges: The Science Question in Feminism and the Privilege of Partial Perspective', *Feminist Studies*, 14(3): 575–99.

Haraway, D. (2016), *Staying with The Trouble: Making Kin in the Cthulucene*, Durham & London: Duke University Press.

Hempel-Jorgensen, A. (2015), 'Learner Agency and Social Justice: What Can Creative Pedagogy Contribute to Socially Just Pedagogies?', *Pedagogy, Culture and Society*, 23(4): 531–554.

Pollock, G. (2009), 'Mother Trouble: The Maternal-Feminine in Phallic and Feminist Theory in Relation to Bracha Ettinger's Elaboration of Matrixial Ethics/Aesthetics', *Studies in the Maternal*, 1(1): 1–31.

Pollock, G. (2010), 'Aesthetic Wit(h)nessing in the Era of Trauma', *EurAmerica*, 40(4): 829–886

Sayers, E. (2011), 'Investigating the Impact of Contrasting Paradigms of Knowledge on the Emancipatory Aims of Gallery Programmes for Young People', *iJADE*, 30(3): 409–422.

Sayers, E. (2015), 'From Art Appreciation to Pedagogies of Dissent: Critical Pedagogy and Equality in the Gallery', in A. Hickey-Moody and T. Page (eds), *Arts, Pedagogy and Cultural Resistance: New Materialisms*, 133–152. London: Rowman & Littlefield.

Spector, K. (2015), 'Meeting Pedagogical Encounters Halfway', *Journal of Adolescent & Adult Literacy*, 58(6): 447–450.

Stewart, R. (2007), 'Creating New Stories for Praxis: Navigations, Narrations and Neonarritives', in E. Barrett and B. Bolt (eds), *Practice as Research: Approaches to Creative Arts Enquiry*, 123–134. New York: I.B.Tauris & Co Ltd.

Thiele, K. (2014a), 'Ethos of Diffraction: New Paradigms For a (Post)Humanist Ethics', in *Parallax*, 20(3): 202–216.

Thiele, K. (2014b), 'Pushing Dualisms and Differences: From "Equality Versus Difference" to "Non-Mimetic Sharing" and "Staying with the Trouble"', *Women: A Cultural Review*, 25(1): 9–26.

Winnicot, D. (1971), *Playing and Reality*. London: Tavistock Publications.

Yagelski, R. 2012. 'Writing as Praxis', *English Education*, 44(2): 188–90.

12

Thebuwa and a Pedagogy of Social Justice: Diffracting Multimodality Through Posthumanism

Denise Newfield

Pedagogy is a provocation of semiosis

Roger Simon

Diffraction has to do with the way waves combine when they overlap and the apparent bending and spreading of waves when they encounter an obstruction

Karen Barad

The experience of student protests in South Africa . . . has obliged society at large to reflect on whether academic institutions can be turned into spaces of radical hospitality

Achille Mbembe

This chapter is based on the diffraction of two theoretical waves, multimodality (Kress 1997, 2010; Jewitt 2014: Stein 2008) and posthumanism (Barad 2007; Braidotti 2011, 2013; Dolphijn and van der Tuin 2012), in relation to data from South Africa, hereafter referred to as the Thebuwa case study. 'Thebuwa' (which means 'To speak') was a secondary school pedagogical poetry project undertaken in the pursuit of a socially just education for black students during the first decade of South Africa's democracy, founded in 1994. The chapter uses 'multimodality' as a blanket term to refer to the framework of multimodal social semiotics, a form of semiotics which situates sign-making in the social and emphasises the multiple modes and materials used. 'Posthumanism' is used as a blanket term for posthumanist movements and theories including feminist new materialisms and their entangled progenitors, in relation to their common interest in socially just curricula and pedagogies. These two waves, each propelled by a visionary force, are brought together in the chapter in a diffractive relationship, as an apparatus to re-investigate data from a secondary school classroom in Soweto. The aim is to see whether and in what way issues, principles and practices that pertain to socially just pedagogies for present-day South Africa may be extracted from the case study. The assumption is that Thebuwa has something to offer a social justice approach to South African higher education today, given that South African education at all levels continues to manifest symptoms of the problematic history of separate and unequal educational systems for different racial groups. In the diffractive approach, insights will be read through one another, will 'interfere' with one another (Barad 2007; Haraway 1997), in an affirmative spirit rather than for the purposes of critique. The diffractive interference aims at productive synergies and new directions through the 'tensions' of different ideas (Kuby and Christ 2017, p. 6) and in the 'resonances between old and new readings and re-readings' (Dolphijn and van der Tuin 2012, p. 13). The chapter will explore whether and in what ways the transformed wave ensuing from the diffraction of the two theoretical waves can contribute to understandings of the entangled phenomenon under discussion – the teaching and learning of poetry in a Soweto classroom at a particular moment in history – as well suggest ideas for a pedagogy for social justice in South Africa at the present time.

The chapter begins with an overview of the historical, pedagogic and scholarly context of the data, with a focus on its social justice orientation. After explaining the diffractive approach, the data is described from a multimodal perspective. It is then re-examined from a posthumanist perspective. Finally, an attempt is made to sum up what Thebuwa offers to a socially just pedagogy in South African higher education at the present time.

The case study and its context

The case study of Thebuwa is part of a body of progressive, anti-establishment practice and research in the field of multimodality undertaken by a group of South African educators from the 1980s onwards, during thirty years of momentous historical change (for example, Andrew 2014; Archer 2006; Archer and Newfield 2014a, 2014b; Brenner and Andrew 2006; Harrop-Allin 2014; Newfield and Stein 2000, 2006; Newfield 2009, 2011a and 2011b, 2013; Newfield and Maungedzo 2006; Simpson 2014; Stein 2003, 2008; Stein and Newfield 2002, 2006; Walton 2014). During apartheid, this work challenged the inequalities and prescriptions of the schooling system, against which young people protested in the Soweto uprising of 1976. Since 1994, this social justice project has been aligned with South Africa's rewritten, post-apartheid constitution, which for the first time in South African history enshrines the rights of all people in South Africa and affirms the democratic values of human dignity, equality and freedom for all (Constitution of the Republic of SA 1996:6). It has pursued social justice through considering the ways in which semiotic practices in classrooms can lead to inclusivity, access, equality and redress, thus chipping away at the pedagogic legacies – the many wounds – of apartheid. Since 2016, however, strident and sometimes violent campaigns have been underway in higher education, expressing student dissatisfaction with the slow pace of transformation. Students are demanding free education for the poor and decolonised curricula that are hospitable and relevant to them rather than westernised and alienating.

In the hope of contributing to the social justice project of transforming higher education, this chapter seeks new directions for curricula and pedagogies through diffracting multimodality and posthumanism in relation to the Thebuwa case study, in which I was a participant-researcher working with teacher, Robert Maungedzo. I begin by outlining three ideas in the frameworks of multimodality (Kress 1997, 2000, 2005) and its corollary in literacy education, a pedagogy of multiliteracies (New London Group 1996), which gave conceptual support to the Thebuwa experiment. These were:

i.   the emphasis on *meaning-making* in semiosis rather than on the *use* of an existing system, which we considered to be a challenge to the prevailing ethos of hegemonic domination and prescription, inherited from apartheid education;

ii. the focus on *production* rather than critique (Kress 1995, 2000), which was linked to a conception of all learners as potentially creative; and

iii. the principle of semiotic multiplicity, which was aligned with a view of diversity and difference at the basis of meaning-making and with social justice.

The social semiotic view of sign-making informed my pedagogic and research agendas at the time. It is captured in Kress's simple but startling clear formulation of what is required for a theory of semiosis (the making of meaning through signs):

> An adequate theory of semiosis will be founded upon the "interested action" of socially located, culturally and historically formed individuals, as the remakers, the transformers, and the re-shapers of the representational resources available to them.
>
> Kress 2000:155

The Kressian conceptualisation of learners as agentive meaning-makers who engage in semiosis through reshaping resources challenged the prevailing view of learners as empty vessels in many English Additional Language classrooms; it made the representation of meaning, and learning itself, an active, transformative process, in which all learners could engage creatively. Representation was not the sedentary, static process that Deleuze and Guattari (2013/1987) impute to representational thought. Furthermore, the use of alternative modes of representation to language was appealing, since language itself had been such a fraught issue in schooling, the imposition of Afrikaans as a language of learning being one of the triggers of the Soweto student uprising of 1976. Since my implementation of multimodality was both a political and a pedagogic move, I was not hamstrung by what has recently been argued to be an inaccurate and partial view of meaning-making in the frameworks of multimodality and multiliteracies by Leander and Boldt (2012).

Moving towards a diffractive analysis

The opportunity to diffract the previous multimodal analysis (Newfield and Maungedzo 2006; Newfield 2009, 2013, 2015) through a posthumanist one is therefore provocative and welcome, providing the possibilities for an enriched understanding of the data in relation to socially just pedagogies for South Africa at the present time. But, first, some remarks on bringing the two waves of multimodality and posthumanism together. It may seem that they are not amenable to being diffracted, being waves at opposite ends of the ocean. For example, a key difference is the place of the *human*. Multimodal social semiotics is a human-centred theory, especially in its educational applications where students and teachers are the key participants (Kress 2000, 2005) and where agency is located in the individual who has it or gains it in the act of sign-making. However, posthumanism is an anti-anthropocentric philosophy, which critiques the humanist view of people as the universe's agentive beings; agency in posthumanism is rather enfolded in the entangled intra-actions of matter, place, time, human and non-human animals and machines.

What will a diffractive reading of the Thebuwa case study bring? How will it return a 'done and dusted' case study back to life? What differences will the diffractive reading highlight and what synergies will emerge? What will be brought into view that may have been occluded? And, finally, how might the diffractive reading deepen our understandings of what might constitute a pedagogy for social justice in higher education in South Africa at the present time? These are large and difficult questions, towards which this chapter can only gesture.

Thebuwa and the wave of multimodality

Although situated at school level, Thebuwa has been used extensively in higher education, particularly teacher education, as a case study in the possibilities for meaning-making and democratic practice offered by multimodal pedagogies. The *Thebuwa* project – a project employing a multimodal approach to the teaching of poetry – was undertaken by a young black, male teacher, Robert Maungedzo, and myself, a white, female university lecturer – as a response to the problems he was having in the teaching of literature. What follows is my own outline of the project fifteen years later, shaped mainly by previous multimodal analyses.

The Thebuwa case study is set in an under-resourced English Additional Language (EAL) classroom in a Soweto secondary school in 2002, during the first decade of South Africa's democracy, when the education of the majority of black children was still in the pedagogic grip of Bantu Education, an inferior system for black children during apartheid. The case study concerns the transformation of teacher Robert Maungedzo's Grade 10 classroom from a place of lethargy and resistance to one of excitement and creativity. His students did not see the value of schooling and the level of truancy was high: 'Why should we come to school when the educated are walking the streets and the criminals are cruising around in posh cars?' Furthermore, they were reluctant to speak, read and write in English – the target language – as seen in student explanations: 'English suffocates my soul' and 'All this talk is strangling me'. Nor did they see the value of literature: 'Just tell us the characters and we'll write it down.' Even though poetry was considered difficult and had been dropped from the school's curriculum seven years before, Robert decided to substitute poetry for the novel, one reason being that poems could be photocopied and thus alleviate the lack of texts in his classroom. 'Out of desperation', Robert would try out a multimodal pedagogic approach – to which he had been introduced in his studies at the University of the Witwatersrand – to poetry. He read out a couple of poems he found in the only anthology in the 'book room' (the school had no library) and asked the students to respond to the poems in any form they wished – through writing, drawing or the making of an object. The students returned a few days later with careful drawings showing their interpretation of the poem and with narratives that re-interpreted it – some of them three pages long. One student made a sculpture from the putty her father had used to fix a broken window. Encouraged by the positive response, Robert carried on. His next move was to delink poetry from print and from the language of English by showing his students that poetry was an indigenous South African cultural practice which existed in their own languages in oral forms. He asked them to present to the class their family or clan praise poem – an African poetic form which praises the unique qualities of family or clan and captures its lineage – in the vernacular. If not familiar to the student, consultation with parents, grandparents or elders in the community would be expected. The praise poem occasion was a great success; the students enjoyed using their own languages and watching one another's performances.

At this time Robert was going to an educational conference in Beijing to present a paper on his teaching difficulties, so he asked the students if they would like to send a message to people at the conference. The students grabbed this opportunity and began zealous discussions. What form should the message take? A drawing, a book, a model, or what? They decided upon a cloth, a sort of wall hanging, because – so they said – this could be folded up in their teacher's suitcase. These students were from poor backgrounds; many of them had never left Soweto, some had never even been to Johannesburg, which was only 20 kilometres away; most did not know what a conference was and could hardly believe that their teacher was going to China! However, the idea of communicating with the outside world spurred them on. The cloth that they made – a complexly textured, multilingual and multimodal ensemble – became their way of saying hello to the world. It served as an identity object to show the world who they were and where they came from. They named it Thebuwa ('to speak'), a coinage from words in the three most spoken languages in the class, 'thetha' (isiXhosa), 'bulabula' (Xitsonga) and 'buwa' (Sepedi), because they said they had moved from silence to speech. They sent the cloth with this message:

> We made this cloth with love for the people of the world. We hope to hear from other children of the world. We have stitched our nation and we are trying to build bridges with other people. We speak through our ambassador, Thebuwa.

The scale of the cloth is large; it is 3.0 metres x 2.2 metres in size. It consists of twenty-two smaller cloths or panels made by individuals or small groups out of scraps of material and old, recycled maize bags which have been stitched

Figure 12.1 Thebuwa Cloth.

together. On each panel is a coloured and embroidered map of the reconfigured, post-apartheid South African map with its nine new regions; a praise poem in the vernacular, a few with translations; and a colour photograph of the maker of the panel, taken by a class member. Re-used envelopes containing English poems composed by the students are pinned around the large central panel. Here is an extract from one of them:

The Humble Soweto
Our township is a resurrection
We are doing our correction
It will soon be a perfection
That will go along with a mission
We all have a bright vision
They think Soweto is guilty
But it's more like a city . . .
Hamba, Soweto my love
Hamba, Sthandwa
Mama of all the dark children

Themba Kula (Newfield and Maungedzo 2005: 47)

In the coming months, the students became 'hooked' on poetry. They insisted on having a live poetry performance of their own poems at the start of every English lesson. Attendance in class improved dramatically. They organised a performance event of song, dance and poetry to celebrate the Thebuwa project and to hear about the conference in Beijing.

The delegates' response to the cloth was enthusiastic and Robert's class embarked on a year-long exchange project with a school in Dandenong, Australia, sending poems, pictures, letters and stories to one another, through an arrangement with a teacher who had attended Robert's presentation. At the end of the year, the pass rate in English improved dramatically. Many students continued writing poems in English during the next grade. Eventually, we had so many poems that we published them in an anthology (Newfield and Maungedzo 2005), and had book launches in Soweto and at the University of the Witwatersrand. The project had exceeded our wildest expectations. Students responded with comments like 'I think this was the most precious thing I have ever done in my life', 'I inhaled my understanding deeper', and referring to the question of whether their work should be graded or not, a number said 'No, because there is no number that can say how good it was'. The poetry project continued informally across three years and beyond. For a number of years, I set the anthology for study in my second-year university module on South African youth poetry and in courses for English teachers, and I invited the Thebuwa students to talk to the university students about their work. A month ago -- fourteen years after the Thebuwa project – one of the students phoned me to say that the project had changed his life and that he wished to work with me again.

As a participant-researcher, I was inspired by the project, and sought to explain it through multimodal social semiotics and its focus on the modal choices made by agentive 'meaning-makers', drawing on African cultural studies to explore the use of local semiotic resources as well as learning theory to show the kinds of learning that had occurred. I concluded that the shift in mode had played a highly significant pedagogic role; it had provoked semiosis. Although the expanded semiotic space of the classroom (Stein 2008; Newfield and Maungedzo 2006) had caused consternation, perplexity and a sense of discomfort at first, it had actually opened up unimagined possibilities. Through the concept of 'the transmodal moment' (Newfield 2009, 2014) I analysed the passage from one mode to the next (print to oral to visual to multimodal) as an in-between, liminal moment (Turner 1982) which brought both losses and opportunities. My method was to look at the texts as 'punctuations' or 'points of fixing' in a 'semiotic chain' (Kress 2003; Stein 2003, 2008; MODE 2012). I looked at each of the different punctuations – the initial canonical poem; the student drawings and narratives; and at the details of the Thebuwa Cloth itself, this panelled, polyglot, multimodal assemblage of praise poems, embroidered maps, emblems and contemporary English poems. I described the modes, materiality, genre and site of display of each text in order to derive its meanings, taking into account the affordances, constraints and provenance of each mode. I found that each mode had been used to communicate a different aspect of the students' multi-layered identity: the maps their national identity; the praise poems their family and clan identities; and the English poems their identities as contemporary township teenagers during the first decade of liberation. I attributed the choice of a cloth to cultural factors, linking it with African cloth-making traditions such as the Minceka and Weya cloths of southern Africa, with which the students were familiar. Returning years later to my analysis, I felt that some element had eluded me, as I mentioned in a chapter in the Routledge Handbook of Literacy Studies (Newfield 2015, p. 277).

Thebuwa and the wave of posthumanism

In decentring the role of human beings, posthumanism creates a new conceptual imaginary. But, as African philosopher Achille Mbembe points out, there is frequently a gap between the power of new conceptual imaginaries and their implementations and practices (Mbembe 2017). To compound the gap in this case is the fact that the Thebuwa project is a complex and entangled 'assemblage' (Deleuze and Guattari 2013/1987) which is difficult to investigate. Barad says that 'entanglements are highly specific configurations' and that it is 'very hard work building apparatuses to study them, in part because they change with each intra-action' (2007, p. 74). I had felt this many years ago and had decided to focus on texts – concrete and bounded entities – as manageable units of analysis. A posthumanist reading would move beyond such a focus and would appreciate the Thebuwa project as more than text, as a dynamic assemblage propelled by, and constituted by, multiple and intertwining entanglements. What follows is a modest attempt to use a few posthumanist concepts to shed new light on the Thebuwa assemblage, and in order to illuminate the project of social justice in South African higher education in its classroom manifestations.

The posthumanist concept of *entanglement* is founded upon the *constitutive intra-action* (Barad 2007) of entities, rather than simply their contextual connection. These concepts, derived from quantum physics, challenge the ontological inseparability of seemingly individual particles (Barad, p. 385) and form the basis of Barad's premise of the 'world's ongoing intra-activity' (Barad, p. 352). The concept helps to articulate the deep and inseparable intertwinings of the Thebuwa project – the way in which it is constituted by the intra-actions of time, place, matter, people, journeys, histories, circumstances, semiotic material and modes, affect and intensities. Agency is enfolded in all of these, as opposed to being something that the students and the teacher came to 'have'. For example, to ask a pedagogic question, how did the praise poem occasion (the day on which they performed their praise poems) come to be? The concept of intra-action foregrounds a number of agentive encounters: the intra-action between the students' negative attitudes to English and the multimodal pedagogic framework; the intra-actions between indigenous South African practices of orality, such as praising at weddings, births and funerals; the emphasis on diversity in writings on literacy education at the time; the multilingual make-up of the Grade 10 cohort; and the intra-actions between students and elders in the community when researching their praise poems. These, as well as the students' use of their own languages and their watching of one another's performances in the vernacular, produced the success of the praise poem lesson. The concept of intra-action means that each component in the assemblage is re-formed or transformed in and through each one of the abovementioned intra-actions – students, teacher, researcher, the praise poems themselves, and more. None is exactly the same as before. Marks of the intra-actions are made on their bodies. So the concept *of intra-active entanglement* shines a different light on the 'secret' of the Cloth and its ongoing trajectories. It foregrounds the intra-activity of the participating people, things, histories, cultures, languages, curricula and pedagogies, student aspirations and dreams: the entities co-constitute one another in the particularities of each intra-action. This is an important new understanding, or, at least, a useful formulation. Furthermore, as Barad (2010) argues, intra-active entanglements imply responsibility to and for the other, since there is no dividing line between self and other, past and present, here and now. One is responsible to and indebted to the other, who is bound to and threaded through the self (Barad 2010). The intra-active entanglements of Thebuwa gave rise to a sense of responsibility in the classroom – by students to their communal project as well as to their personal and social histories and futures.

A posthumanist lens also makes visible the infectious energy, the vitality – the *affective intensity* – of the Thebuwa project, an energy that propels it forward and injects itself into the different activities and events. Affect refers to energy, intensities and dynamism that are pre-conscious, subliminal, non-linguistic, rather than to particular emotions felt by individuals (Deleuze and Guattari 2013/1987; Massumi 1995). Affect is frequently seen – following Spinoza and Deleuze and Guattari (2013/1987, p.xv) – as the capacity to affect and to be affected. Thebuwa affected others and yet was open to being affected by, to intra-acting with, other humans and non-humans. An affective, inter-subjective intensity augmented the students' capacity to act, by creating a 'state of suspense' (Massumi 1995, p. 86) in which the body prepared itself 'for action' (Shouse in Leys 2011, p. 442), thereby creating the conditions for learning as doing. Affect is not easy to demonstrate through traditional data, but it may be inferred from its effects – in this case, the ongoing Thebuwa trajectory which extended across three years and beyond, as well as the substantial and collaborative nature of its various texts and events, such as the year-long exchange project with the class of Australian students. Amongst these, the Cloth represents a point at which the project's dynamism found a powerful 'incarnation in matter' (Massumi 2013, p. xiii). Its intensity affected delegates at the Beijing conference in 2002, as well as – much later – members of a posthumanism and social justice pedagogical research project in South Africa, leading to the current diffractive endeavour.

While the multimodal analysis is based on interpreting the meaning of the student texts – seen as 'points of fixing' in a semiotic chain – in order to determine the pedagogic impact of the transmodal pedagogy, the diffractive approach shows Thebuwa as an agentive, intra-active process of *becoming*. Becoming is a process in which an object or being 'changes in nature as it expands its connections' (Semetsky 2011, p. 3; Deleuze and Gauttari 2013/1987). The Thebuwa process is one in which the elements or beings constituting the Thebuwa assemblage 'became-other', expanded their connections, broke out of their old habits and attitudes to poetry and brought the new into existence through multiple intra-actions propelled by affective intensities. These intra-actions involved, amongst others, conversations among students, teacher, elders inside and outside the classroom, as well as at a distance with an unknown global audience; spoken word performances by students of their own poems at the start of every English class; the intra-actions between traditional and contemporary cultural practices; and between an array of different materials used in the making of the Thebuwa artefact. Whereas the multimodal analysis emphasised the multi-layered identities of the students, a posthumanist reading demonstrates their becoming. They became 'other' through 'becoming-with one another' (Kruger 2016:80) in imaginative, uncharted ways. They became makers and poets. While the multimodal analysis emphasised transmodal doing and performing as an approach to learning, doing and performing in posthumanism are more than a pedagogic approach – they are 'acts which express the vital energy of *transformative becoming*' (Braidotti 2011, p. 25; 2013, pp. 166–67). For example, one student, Thando, at first wordless and unable to produce even one poem, became through the Thebuwa project 'madly in love with poetry' (Newfield and Maungedzo 2005, p. 2), produced over a hundred poems and had seven poems published in the *Thebuwa* anthology. Using an everyday Soweto means of transport as a metaphor for his experience with Thebuwa, teacher Robert said he had been on a train journey from desperation to empowerment. A posthumanist approach highlights the way the classroom became a space of jouissance, of 'potentia' (Braidotti 2013, pp. 136–38), of life's vital energy.

Deleuze and Guattari's concept of *rhizomatic thinking* (2013/1987) and Braidotti's concept of *nomadism* (2011, 2013) challenge and modify multimodality's delineation of the Thebuwa students' activities as a semiotic chain – to some extent a linear model. These concepts foreground and articulate the way in which the Thebuwa project grew and developed unpredictably, with sudden offshoots in different directions, without a central root or core, and how it 'zigzagged' across modes and meanings, developing in an unplanned, non-linear, metamorphosing trajectory – from the reading of canonical poems to the performance of praise poems, the embroidering of maps, the composition of poems in English, the making of the Cloth, the transnational exchange project, the publication of the anthology, the revivification of the data for further analysis, and so on. These were its unexpected offshoots; they broke away from beaten paths, dismantled and then reconstructed themselves in different forms. For me personally, these concepts – of the rhizome, of entanglement and intra-action, of affective intensities and becoming – all feed into my abovementioned concept of the transmodal moment in most helpful ways.

The overlapping of waves: social justice, human rights and posthumanist becoming

South African higher education at the present time is in crisis. Aside from the economic question of providing access to those previously excluded by the former regime, a decolonising project is underway, which poses curricular and pedagogic questions around relevance to place, time and indigeneity that are not easy to answer. What should be taught and researched? How should it be taught in order to prepare students for the society and world in which they live? What forms of knowledge, what forms of living, are appropriate to the present? What principles might be appropriate to socially just pedagogies in South Africa at the present time? How important are human rights, including the right to speak in your own languages and communicate through your own semiotic practices in education (Stein 2008); how important are different ways of perceiving reality (Hawkins 2011)? To what extent are socially just pedagogies specific to the particularities of each entangled situation of teaching and learning?

This chapter has shown how multimodality interpreted the meaning of the Thebuwa project by examining its differently modalised texts and signs in their social, cultural, historical and semiotic contexts. The multimodal reading placed human actors in the centre, and portrayed students as agentive and creative makers of meaning and culture, in keeping with democratic values of equality, diversity, inclusivity and participation. Representation and communication in different forms shaped by different cultures were portrayed as a human right in the face of the dominance of standard western forms. The posthumanist reading, however, based on a conceptual imaginary of connectivity, decentred the human and instead focused on relationality: on the intra-actions amongst, and zigzagging between, humans, materialities, histories, epistemologies, cultures, times and spaces, and on the affective intensities sensed and exchanged amongst all of these. Through these, thinking was performed and possibilities for becoming opened up.

Barad describes social justice in the following way:

> Intra-acting responsibly as part of the world means taking account of the entangled phenomena that are intrinsic to the world's vitality and being responsible to the possibilities that might help us flourish. Meeting each moment, being alive to the possibilities of becoming, is an ethical call, an invitation that is written into the very matter of all being and all becoming. We need to meet the universe halfway, to take responsibility for the role that we play.
>
> 2007, p. 396

I hope that the overlapping, the diffraction, of the waves of multimodality and posthumanism through the Thebuwa data raises issues, principles and practices – some of them in tension – that are pertinent to the difficult question of socially just pedagogies for higher education in South Africa at the present time. Teachers, scholars, researchers and students may wish to consider the usefulness of the following issues and practices for their particular situations: the role of semiosis in learning; the different forms of representation in teaching, learning and its assessment (which today would include the digital); 'meeting the universe halfway' in course content and method; the pedagogic assemblage as entanglement; different conceptualisations of thinking and learning; the role of affect in learning; the issue of becoming and the responsibilities we carry as teachers and researchers to the other, to history and to the future. The question of socially just pedagogy is an ethical, ontological and epistemological matter according to Barad (2007, p. 381). It has to do with being and knowing as well as 'responsibility and accountability for the entanglements "we" help enact and what kinds of commitments "we" are willing to take on, including commitments to "ourselves" and who "we" may become' (Barad 2007, p. 382). Responsibility in education entails an ongoing responsiveness to demands of the present and the future in relation to the past, and South Africa in relation to Africa and the world. The intention of this chapter has not been to create a blueprint or a roadmap for the complex and highly contested field of pedagogy in higher education. Rather, it has been to share a rich project and to diffractively read it through the two waves of multimodality and posthumanism. The diffraction has pointed to principles and practices that made a previously inert and alienating classroom a space of radical hospitality, which contributed to the world's vitality.

Acknowledgements

I pay ongoing tribute to the inspiring work of Robert Maungedzo and the Thebuwa students, and that of the late Pippa Stein, as well as to Vivienne Bozalek's unfailing commitment to pedagogy. I also thank the reviewers and editors for their helpful comments.

References

Andrew, D. (2014), 'An Aesthetic Language for Teaching and Learning: Multimodality and Contemporary Art Practice', in A. Archer and D. Newfield (eds), *Multimodal Approaches to Research and Pedagogy*, New York and London: Routledge, 191–194.

Archer, A. (2006), 'Academic Literacy Practices in Engineering: Opening Up Spaces', *English Studies in Africa*, 49(1): 189–206.

Archer, A. and D. Newfield (eds), (2014a), *Multimodal Approaches to Research and Pedagogy: Recognition, Resources and Access*, New York and London: Routledge.

Archer, A. and D. Newfield (2014b), 'Challenges and Opportunities of Multimodal Approaches to Education in South Africa', in A. Archer and D. Newfield (eds),

Multimodal Approaches to Research and Pedagogy, New York and London: Routledge, 1–16.

Barad, K. (2007), *Meeting the Universe Halfway: Quantum Physics and the Entanglement of Matter and Meaning* Durham and London: Duke University Press.

Barad, K. (2010), 'Quantum Entanglements and Hauntological Relations of Inheritance: Dis/Continuities, Spacetime Enfoldings, and Justice-To-Come', *Derrida Today* 3.2: 240–268.

Braidotti, R. (2011), *Nomadic Subjects: Embodiment and Sexual Difference in Contemporary Feminist Theory*, 2nd edn, New York: Columbia University Press.

Braidotti, R. (2013), *The Posthuman*, Cambridge: Polity Press.

Brenner, J. and D. Andrew (2006), 'Be An Artist in Words, That You May Be Strong, For the Tongue is a Sword!', *English Studies in Africa*, 49(1): 207–220.

Cope, B. and M. Kalantzis (eds), (2000), *Multiliteracies: Literacy Learning and the Design of Social Futures*, London and New York: Routledge.

Deleuze, G. and F. Guattari (2013/1987) *A Thousand Plateaus: Capitalism and Schizophrenia*, trans. B Massumi, London: Bloomsbury.

Dolphijn, R. and I, van der Tuin (2012), *New Materialism: Interviews and Cartographies*, Ann Arbor: Open Humanities Press.

Haraway, D. (1997), *Modest_Witness@Second_Millenium.FemaleMan©_Meets_OncoMouse*, New York: Routledge.

Harrop-Allin, S. (2014), '"The Pen Tells My Story": South African Children's Multimodal Storytelling as Artistic Practice', in A. Archer and D. Newfield (eds), *Multimodal Approaches to Research and Pedagogy*, 19–40, New York and London: Routledge.

Hawkins, M. (ed.), (2011), *Social Justice Language Teacher Education*, Bristol, Multilingual Matters.

Jewitt, C. (ed.), (2014), *The Routledge Handbook of Multimodal Analysis*, 2nd edn, London and New York: Routledge.

Kress, G. (1997), *Before Writing: Rethinking the Paths to Literacy*, London and New York: Routledge

Kress, G. (2000), 'Design and Transformation: New Theories of Meaning', in B. Cope and M. Kalantzis (eds), *Multiliteracies: Literacy Learning and the Design of Social Futures*, London and New York: Routledge, 153–161.

Kress, G (2005), *Writing the Future: English and the Making of a Culture of Innovation*, Sheffield: National Association for the Teaching of English (NATE).

Kress, G. (2010), *Multimodality: A Social Semiotic Approach to Contemporary Communication*, London and New York: Routledge.

Kruger, F. (2016), 'Posthumanism and Educational Research for Sustainable Futures', *Journal of Education*, 65:77–93.

Kuby, C. and R. Christ (2017), 'Productive Aporias and Inten(t/s)ionalities of Paradigming: Spacetimematterings in an Introductory Qualitative Research Course', *Qualitative Enquiry*, 1–12, doi: 10.1177/1077800416684870

Leander, K. and G. Boldt (2012), 'Rereading "A Pedagogy of Multiliteracies": Bodies, Texts and Emergence', *Journal of Literacy Research* XX(X): 1–25. doi: 10.1177/1086296X12468587

Leys, R. (2011), 'The Turn to Affect: A Critique', *Critical Enquiry* 37, (Spring): 434–472.

Massumi, B. (2013), 'Translator's Foreword: Pleasures of Philosophy', in Deleuze, G. and F. Guattari (2013/1987) *A Thousand Plateaus: Capitalism and Schizophrenia*, London: Bloomsbury.

Massumi, B. (1995), 'The Autonomy of Affect', *Cultural Critique* 31, Part II (Autumn): 83–109.

Mbembe, A. (2017), 'Future Knowledges', Paper presented for WISER, University of the Witwatersrand, 29 May.

MODE (2012), 'Glossary of Multimodal Terms, "Chain of Semiosis"'. Available online at: www.multimodalglossary.wordpress.com (accessed 31 March 2017).

New London Group (1996), 'A Pedagogy of Multiliteracies: Designing Social Futures', *Harvard Educational Review* 66(1): 60–92.

Newfield, D. (2009), 'Transmodal Semiosis in Classrooms: Case Studies from South Africa', Unpublished PhD thesis, Institute of Education, University of London. Available online at UCL research archives.

Newfield, D. (2011a), 'Multimodality, Social Justice and Becoming a "Really South African" Democracy: Case Studies from Language Classrooms', in M. Hawkins (ed.), *Social Justice Language Teacher Education*, Bristol: Multimodal Matters, 23–48.

Newfield, D. (2011b), 'Multimodality and Children's Participation in Classrooms: Instances of Research', *Perspectives in Education*, 29(1): 27–35.

Newfield, D. (2014), 'Transformation, Transduction and the Transmodal Moment', in C. Jewitt (ed.), *The Routledge Handbook of Multimodal Analysis*, 2nd edn, London and New York: Routledge, 100–113.

Newfield, D. (2015), 'The Semiotic Mobility of Literacy: Four Analytical Approaches', in J. Rowsell J and K. Pahl (eds), *The Routledge Handbook of Literacy Studies*, London and New York: Routledge, 267–281.

Newfield, D. and R. Maungedzo (eds), (2005), *Thebuwa: Poems from Ndofaya*, Johannesburg: Newfield Publishers.

Newfield, D. and R. Maungedzo (2006), 'Mobilising and Modalising Poetry in a Soweto Classroom', *English Studies in Africa* 49(1): 71–94.

Newfield, D. and P. Stein (2000), 'The Multiliteracies Project: South African Teachers Respond', in B. Cope and M. Kalantzis (eds), *Multiliteracies: Literacy Learning and the Design of Social Futures*, 292–310. London and New York: Routledge.

Semetsky, I. (2011), 'Becoming-Other: Developing the Ethics of Integration', *Policy Futures in Education*, 9(11): 138–144.

Simpson, Z. (2014), 'Resources, Representation and Regulation in Civil Engineering Drawing: An Autoethnographic Perspective', in A. Archer and D. Newfield (eds), *Multimodal Approaches to Research and Pedagogy*, New York and London: Routledge, 41–56.

Stein, P. (2003), 'The Olifantsvlei "Fresh Stories" Project: Multimodality, Creativity and Fixing in The Semiotic Chain', in C. Jewitt and G. Kress (eds), *Multimodal Literacy*, New York: Peter Lang, 123–138.

Stein, P. (2008), *Multimodal Pedagogies in Diverse Classrooms: Representation, Rights and Resources*, New York and London: Routledge.

Stein, P. and D. Newfield (2002), 'Agency, Creativity, Access and Activism: Literacy Education in Post-Apartheid South Africa', in M. Kalantzis, G. Varnava-Skoura and B. Cope B (eds), *Learning for the Future: New Worlds, New Literacies, New Learning, New People*, Australia: Commonground, 155–166.

Stein, P. and D. Newfield (2006), 'Multiliteracies and Multimodality in English in Education in Africa: Mapping the Terrain', in D. Newfield and P. Stein (eds), (2006), *English in Education in Africa*, Special Edition of *English Studies in Africa*, 49(1): 1–21.

Turner, V. (1982), *From Ritual to Theatre: The Human Seriousness of Play*, New York: PAJ Publications.

Index

Milton Keynes UK
Ingram Content Group UK Ltd.
UKHW022023120923
428550UK00004B/108